Transitions

Transitions

Four Rituals in Eight Cultures

Martha Nemes Fried
and
Morton H. Fried

W · W · Norton & Company · New York · London

From BABA OF KARO: A WOMAN MUSLIM HAUSA by Mary Smith.
Introduction and Notes by
M. G. Smith
Preface by
Darryll Forde. Copyright © 1977 by the Overseas Development Council.
Reprinted by permission of Holt, Rinehart and Winston.

From KALIHARI HUNTER-GATHERERS edited by Richard B. Lee and Irven
DeVore, Cambridge, Mass: Harvard University Press, copyright ©
1976 by the President and Fellows of Harvard College. Reprinted
by permission of the publishers.

Library of Congress Cataloging in Publication Data
Fried, Martha Nemes and Morton H. Fried
   Transitions.
   Includes index.
   1. Rites and ceremonies.   2.   Initiations (in
religion, folk-lore, etc.)   3.   Ethnology. I. Title.
GN473.F68   1980   301.2'1   79-24473
ISBN 0-393-01350-2

DESIGNED BY MARY A. BROWN

1 2 3 4 5 6 7 8 9 0

To Nancy and Steven

Contents

Acknowledgments 9

 O N E. The Ages of Our Kind 13

T W O. Birth 28

T H R E E. Puberty/Adolescence 58

F O U R. Marriage 93

F I V E. Death 145

S I X. Socialist Countries 175

S E V E N. Transitions in Transition 256

Notes 275

Bibliography 283

Index 299

Acknowledgments

OUR deepest gratitude goes to Richard B. Lee, Professor of Anthropology at the University of Toronto and eminent expert on the !Kung hunter-gatherers. There seemed to be no limit to his generosity in sharing with us his deep knowledge of the San, gained through several extended stays in the Kalahari desert. He gave us unpublished materials of his own, and suggested where unpublished papers written by other scholars could be obtained.

For information about the Muslim Hausa, we are greatly indebted to Dr. Charles Anwame Imokhai, A'isha Aliyu, Lois Umar, and a male informant who preferred to remain anonymous. Their willingness to spend a great deal of time giving us lively and colorful accounts of the crisis rites and the milieu in which they take place is deeply appreciated.

We thank Paul Slater of NYANA for assistance in locating persons to whom we might speak about life transitions in the Soviet Union. In particular, we are grateful to Yefim Zlotin for his careful participation in conversation about Russian rituals, including funerals. Dr. Wesley Fisher of Columbia University not only helped us to locate people whom we could interview about transitions and rituals in the USSR but encouraged us to consult the manuscript of his dissertation, which is the basis of his forthcoming book. He also supplied us with a number of leads to the Russian literature on the subject, and to tidbits in the *Current Digest of the Soviet Press.* We express our delight to the editors of that publication and to its contributors. We are impressed by the breadth of their criteria for selection of materials, and urge their continuation. We are also extremely appreciative of the materials put out by M. E. Sharpe, Inc., of White Plains, New York. They publish several journals of translations of carefully selected articles from Russian and Chinese periodicals indispensable to anyone interested in those countries.

Dr. Susan W. Williamson and Dr. Roy E. Brown were very helpful with information about gestation, parturition, and lactation.

A good reference librarian is worth her weight in gold; we were fortunate in being aided by Diane K. Goon of the Lehmann Library at the School of International Affairs, Columbia University, and Susan Pasquariella of the Center for Population and Family Health, Columbia University.

We have been fortunate to enjoy the editorial assistance of Ed Barber, of the W. W. Norton Company, who couples criticism with wit. Thanks also to Mike Harner and Elliott Skinner.

Our son repeatedly reminded us that writing the chapter about adolescence would be a cinch, as we had a live specimen on the premises. Our daughter gave us invaluable help with proofreading and informed comments on the manuscript as it was progressing.

Finally, we thank the scores of individuals whose works have informed us in large theoretical ways or have provided precise nuggets of information at crucial junctures. At least as much as any culture it studies, the field of cultural anthropology is a collective social enterprise in which the individual workers are constantly interdependent. We hope, in this spirit, that this work will provide for its readers the same kind of resource we so gratefully acknowledge.

Transitions

CHAPTER ONE

The Ages of
Our Kind

"AND one man in his time plays many parts," writes Shakespeare, in *As You Like It.* He goes on to enumerate: First, "the infant, mewling and puking in the nurse's arms," followed by "the whining schoolboy," who will turn into "the lover, sighing like furnace," becoming a soldier, "bearded like the pard." Then comes the justice, "in fair round belly with good capon lined." The sixth age is one of shrunk shank, and a voice "turning again to childish treble." It all ends in second childhood, slipping into oblivion "sans teeth, sans eyes, sans taste, sans everything."

The idea that life falls into a fixed number of distinctive periods—infancy, childhood, adolescence, young and old adulthood, senescence, and finally death—is far from obvious. Ethologists who have made observations on many animals in natural habitats found that although the life cycle shows fairly conspicuous differences in the behavior of the newly born, the young, and the adults, nothing remotely resembling a ritual marking transition from one life status to another has ever been seen among nonhuman beings. On the other hand, no reliable observer has ever described a human society that did not have some ceremonial ways of marking such transitions. Of course, the passages they celebrate and especially those they emphasize may differ from the ones most familiar to us.

The divisions of our lives that seem so commonplace and obvious to us today are the product of historical development. Our more recent ancestors, perhaps even of the seventeenth or eighteenth centuries, might find them a little strange. As we will see in a later chapter, childhood was not always regarded as it is now, as a time requiring special psychological understanding. Instead, all children, from the smallest to the biggest, were regarded as little men and women. What is more, since long before the ancient Greeks, the life cycle had been cut up in many different ways. At times the cultures that ultimately produced ours have favored a conception of "seven ages," but at times the preference was for as many as twelve, or as few as three.

Today our own society is not quite homogeneous in its regard for the divisions of a life span. There is, however, a predominant view that roughly coincides with the one chosen for this book: infancy, adolescence, maturity, and senescence. But what to do with childhood beyond the infant stage? What about middle age? Quite evidently it is possible to divide the life span in many different ways, not only when comparing cultures, but even within one complex society. What we *can* say is that every known human society, simple or complex, whatever its economic or political structure, provides for ritually divided phases of life.

No one knows how long ago human beings began to mark transitions with rituals. Our kind, the species *Homo sapiens,* which includes all living people, has been in existence for over a hundred thousand years, according to current scientific opinion. Earlier, our forebears were probably members of the species *Homo erectus.* Close to one hundred members of that extinct species have been found in different parts of the world—in Indonesia and China, in eastern and northern Africa, and in western Europe. Were these ancestors of ours human? Most anthropologists say yes, because of their anatomical resemblance to us, and, more importantly, because *Homo erectus* fossils are often found in association with evidence of cultural activity. That is, bones of those extinct people are found close by stone tools or the remains of fire. Some of the fossil bones of *Homo erectus,* particularly of individuals who reached relatively mature ages in their own lifetimes, show pathological medical conditions, such as major bone tumors, that must have been painful and disabling. Yet they continued to live for many years with such crippling diseases, which implies that they were supported and cared for by the social groups to which they belonged.

About four hundred thousand years ago, one population of *Homo erectus* type, sometimes called "Sinanthropus," lived at a place call Chouk'outien (Zhoukodien), in northeastern China. They are known to have made stone tools and to have lived in limestone caves, where they used fires for cooking and keeping warm, although the climate there was milder than it is now. They also broke open the skulls of their own dead, apparently in order to get at the brains. The simplest explanation of this custom is ordinary cannibalism. Another possible explanation is of greater interest to us, because it could be evidence of the earliest marking of a transition. Ethnographers describe a very special form of cannibalism among certain peoples in the world—the Fore people of New Guinea, for example—in which some part of a dead person is ritually eaten by close relatives in order to keep him "alive" in the survivors. The practice is known as endocannibalism. If the Sinanthropus man cracked open the skulls of his deceased relatives for this purpose, it would provide the earliest indication yet available to suggest the existence of rituals marking the transition from life to death.

In terms of the actual evidence of archeology, a long time elapsed between the skull breaking of *Homo erectus* and the next set of data suggesting the use of transition markers in human society. We must also journey from China to northern Iraq, where in a cave at a place called Shanidar the archeologist Ralph Solecki found a number of skeletons of people who lived forty to fifty thousand years ago. The skeletons are of a variety of our own species, *Homo sapiens,* but show regular differences from modern people, especially in the heaviness of bones and the massivity of particular structures, such as the bony ridge of the skull over the eye sockets. These features apply to the variety known as Neandertal. Among these remains are some that were deliberately buried after death, which of itself is a cultural activity showing concern for transition. The interpretation of such a find in terms of the marking of life change is reinforced by Solecki's analysis of the soil in the grave, which showed unusually high concentrations of the pollen of wild flowers. The conclusion is inescapable. Some Neandertal people, tens of thousands of years ago, laid their dead to rest, symbolizing the rite of passage by covering the bodies with flowers.

The term "rite of passage" was originated by an ethnologist and specialist in the study of folklore, Arnold van Gennep (1873–1957), whose most widely read book, *Les Rites de Passage,* appeared in 1909. Van Gennep, like many scholars of his time, was deeply interested in comparative religion, and wished to assemble the widely diverging and seemingly chaotic data on the multitudinous religious systems of the world, especially those of simple and peasant societies, into a systematic unity. In the course of his investigations van Gennep also recognized that rituals existed with regard to many phenomena that cannot be regarded as life transitions; for example, rites associated with healing an illness, or celebrating a successful hunt or battle, or marking a harvest. Nonetheless, van Gennep argued the special importance of those he named rites of passage. He believed that such rites, studied and analyzed in the larger setting of the cultures to which they pertain, could illuminate our knowledge of these cultures and provide understanding of more general processes of cultural evolution.

He developed a scheme of three categories, distinguishing rites of separation, incorporation, and transition. He noted, however, that "these three subcategories are not developed to the same extent by all peoples or in every ceremonial pattern." For van Gennep, the typical rites of separation were those marking death; rites of incorporation were those associated with marriage; those of transition appeared in connection with pregnancy, engagement (leading to marriage), and initiations of various kinds.

We cannot regard van Gennep's categories as more than historically interesting examples of the analysis of ritual. Their utility is limited. For one thing, it is all too obvious that his categories spill over into each other. Is not a funeral rite also a transition rite? If it separates the deceased from the living, it is also likely to "incorporate" that person with the ancestors who went before. Accordingly, we acknowledge a debt to Arnold van Gennep for his pioneer efforts, but choose to disregard some of his contributions and to proceed more descriptively, emphasizing periods of transition in the life cycle in a number of distinctively different cultures.

We concentrate upon four critical transitions—birth, puberty, marriage, and death. While the focus of interest is upon the ritual involved in these transitions, it would be a sterile exercise to deal with them in a vacuum, separating them from the longer periods of the individual biography to which they mark entrances and exits. You will thus find more extensive accounts of the lives of the peoples we have selected, thereby framing the transitions in larger contexts.

The cultures have been chosen to provide for different kinds of diversity. They are drawn from a variety of environments, ranging from the tropics to the Alaskan panhandle, not far from the Arctic Circle. Our cultures display a great range of technologies. One of them, the nomadic !Kung*use metal tools only when they receive them as gifts or by barter. Their ordinary tool chest is less complex than would have been known to many peoples of the Upper Paleolithic period, described by archeologists as including a broad range of carefully chipped stone tools, plus bone and wooden ones. Our selection of cultures also represents a range of social and political organizational forms, from the small mobile camping group with limited and generally powerless leadership to Taiwan, one of the most industrialized states in Asia.

Another variable separates our choice of societies into three categories. This is our own personal experience of these cultures. We have lived and done fieldwork in China and Taiwan. We have visited and worked personally with informants from Tlingit, Hausa, and the Soviet Union. We have relied entirely upon the work of other ethnographers and writers in dealing with !Kung, Tikopia, and Cuba.

A major characteristic of culture is its spongelike facility to

---

*The language of the !Kung is in the linguistic family known as San, the word "San" being derived from the Hottentot morpheme that referred to the entire population formerly known as "Bushman." Since the term Bushman is now widely regarded as pejorative, the San designation is preferred. The San languages characteristically include a range of sounds not usually found in wide use elsewhere. These are the "clicks" produced by quickly taking the tongue away from different points of the mouth, thus interrupting the air stream and producing a distinctive sound. English uses one or two clicks, but the words produced are not included in our dictionaries. One of them is the exclamation usually written "tsk-tsk". The "tsk" sound in San orthography is represented by the symbol / while the sound itself is produced by drawing the tongue away from the front teeth. The other click that may be heard in our own culture cannot be represented in our script, but in the orthography of the San languages is written //. This click is produced by pulling the tongue away from the side teeth and is a sound we may make to start or speed up a horse. The San languages include two other click sounds. One, represented by $\neq$, is made by drawing the tongue away from the alveolar ridge, breaking the air stream. The final click sound is that which appears in the name of the !Kung, the ! click being produced by snapping the tongue away from the point directly between the alveolar ridge and the palate.

take in material from the outside, the "outside" comprising any recognizably different social and cultural contiguous aggregation. A "pure" culture is a contradiction in terms, except to the degree that any two distinct cultures have been physically separated for very long periods of time. Even then we cannot be entirely sure that intermediate cultures did not act as transmission devices between them, or that casual wanderers did not bring some cultural traits from one to the other. Still, to attempt to minimize this kind of "noise," we have selected our examples from widely separated regions.

The !Kung and the Muslim Hausa share a continent, but are separated by more than three thousand miles. If members of either population ever met, it was not recorded, nor are there any signs, archaeological or ethnographic, of contact between them. The !Kung are one of several groups speaking quite distinctive languages. As long as they have been known, and back into the archaeologically defined past thousands of years old, they have inhabited great arid and semiarid tracts of the Kalahari desert and adjacent regions of South and Southwest Africa. They probably once spread over a much wider area than they inhabit today, having lost substantial portions of their terrain to more complexly organized cultures, especially to farming peoples, who spilled into their region over a period of several thousand years, a process which has speeded up in recent centuries and still continues at an ever increasing pace. Particularly in recent years, this process has been marked by an accelerating tendency for !Kung and other San peoples to desert the nomadic hunting and gathering life in favor of a settled existence. This usually entails a shift from the sometimes risky dependence on natural supplies of water and food to a more regular diet based on wage labor for a settled farmer, whether African or European. The advantages of such a shift are a somewhat higher standard of living and an increased population of San people. The disabilities lie in their separation from the old culture and the loss of many of its values, including the loss of freedom and independence from constant contact with ever increasing numbers of aliens—a loss that now places the !Kung in a position of inequality with strangers and with each other.

To the extent that the !Kung retain their old ways, they depend for their food mainly upon the vegetables, tubers, roots, and nuts that the women collect almost daily. These are the staff of nomadic

!Kung life, to which are added small animals taken by men and women and, occasionally, by children, during the course of daily activities. The foods the nomadic !Kung prize most highly are the meats of different animals taken by the men on their hunts— giraffe, wildebeest, antelope, kudu, gemsbok; these are among the principal animals found in their range. There were many more kinds of animals a few decades ago, but some species are now but rarely seen in this area. Elephants and rhinoceros are no longer found here; the once abundant zebras are few. This alarming decline of animals, not a lack of appeal of the hunting life, is perhaps the most important cause of the shift to new life styles.

Separated from the !Kung by more than three thousand miles of varying landforms are the Hausa peoples of present day Nigeria, the largest single country in Africa. It is also a country in the throes of economic development, now being recognized as a critical producer of petroleum and an active member of the OPEC bloc. Nigeria is an amalgam of many peoples, historically distinct in language as well as culture. Though now sufficiently placid to have recently held national elections, Nigeria was not long ago the scene of civil war, as one of its largest and most richly endowed sections attempted to establish itself as the independent state of Biafra. The effort failed, and the Ibo—the ethnic population mainly responsible for the attempt—are more or less reintegrated into the nation. Hundreds of miles to the northwest of those earlier troubles lies the part of Nigeria that is inhabited by the Hausa.

The language spoken by the Hausa is one in the great Afro-Asiatic stock, a stock that is still occasionally referred to as Hamitic. Hausa itself is within that Afro-Asiatic substock known as the Chad, after the region that surrounds that great lake. It is interesting, therefore, that the Hausa traditions speak of their coming from the region about Lake Chad, although most of them now live in northern Nigeria and immediately adjacent countries. Within Northern Nigeria, according to official sources, there are about 11.5 million Hausa, the greatest part being followers of Islam, hence usually referred to as the Muslim Hausa. Smaller numbers of Hausa are Christian (Catholic and other denominations), while the smallest part of all is composed of the Pagan Hausa, who have shrugged off proselytization. We will be concerned with the Muslim Hausa.

Although Nigeria has petroleum, it is still a rather poor country with a small but expanding industrial sector. The Hausa, who live intermingled with their former conquerors and rulers, the pastoral Fulani, occupy much of the countryside and are found in most of the cities of Nigeria, especially in the north, where they play an important role in commerce and politics. Western education on the British model is widespread in Nigeria and important in the Hausa-dominated areas. In recent years, more and more Hausa students have come to the United States for advanced education; they can be found on most major university campuses.

Almost on the other side of the globe are the Tlingit, a population of Native Americans living along the southern Alaskan coast. Thanks to the Japanese current the winters are less severe than might be imagined for such a northerly location, but the area is rugged. Yakutat, where Martha spent a brief period of research, is almost adjacent to Glacier National Park. Traditionally, the Tlingit lived by fishing and gathering, and not by cultivating the soil. Today, fishing remains the main occupation for Tlingit men, with lumbering second, and the women hold government jobs or other year-round positions. Tlingit settlements are small, and shared with outsiders. Yakutat has about five hundred people of whom perhaps three hundred identify themselves as Tlingit; the remainder are people from the other forty-nine states. There are also some Eskimos, and even Hawaiians, giving the little place a remarkably cosmopolitan population. Though tiny, Yakutat cannot be considered remote, for there is daily plane service from Anchorage to Seattle. There is also frequent sea transport. Long before the arrival of Europeans, the Tlingit plied the coastal waters to the north and south, traveling impressive distances. Their traditional way of life is a variant of what is generally called Northwest Coast culture.

Far across the Pacific, deep in Melanesia, is one of the westernmost of the islands on which a Polynesian culture may be found. This is Tikopia. It is known mainly from the work of a lone anthropologist, Sir Raymond Firth, a native of New Zealand, who has returned to the island a number of times, most recently in 1979. He first saw Tikopia in 1928, from shipboard. What met his eyes was "a solitary peak, wild and stormy, upthrust in a waste of waters."

Even thirty years ago, Tikopia was so isolated that when Firth returned for a second visit, he found the Tikopians in desperate conditions. A typhoon had brought devastation, and food supplies were almost exhausted. Largely through his efforts, help was obtained, and many survived who might otherwise have perished. Then, as now, the people subsisted on the taro, breadfruit, coconuts, and bananas grown on the land, and on fish taken from the sea or from the central lagoon, mainly by nets. Even before that time, however, some of the men had gone elsewhere to work as plantation laborers on faraway islands, but had returned to resume traditional lives after accumulating goods that they used mainly for acquiring wives. During the 1950s, a number of Tikopians left their tiny island and established a new settlement in the Russell Islands, closer to the Solomons. Indeed, since 1978 the Solomon Islands have been an independent, self-governing country to which both Tikopia and the Russells belong.

Beyond the seas in a northwesterly direction lies the island of Taiwan. Its history, or, more accurately, its prehistory, is somewhat obscure. Before 1644, which marked the end of the Ming period on the Chinese mainland, hundreds of farmers and fishermen from the provinces of Fukien and Kwangtung began to settle the island, which they found already inhabited by people resembling the natives of the northern Philippine Islands both physically and culturally. In the second half of the present century, archaeologists, working on Taiwan, discovered that the ceramics made on Taiwan some two or three thousand years ago were similar to those associated with various horizons of the Chinese neolithic periods. Was an ancient "Chinese" culture on Taiwan displaced by a Malayo-Polynesian one? The question remains open.

Whatever the answer to that riddle, the Chinese population of Taiwan has grown since the advent of the Ch'ing Dynasty in the middle of the seventeenth century, while the remaining elements of the Malayo-Polynesian peoples and their cultures have been hemmed into the island's rugged central mountain regions, or scattered along the east coast or among the islands off that coast. The Chinese population is largely composed of speakers of Min-nan (Fukienese) languages, and Hakka. The Hakka people in Taiwan came mainly from northern Kwangtung. Our Taiwan research, begun in 1948 when we first visited the island and continued through many visits since, has been centered on the Minnan-speaking people.

For most of its history, Taiwan has been almost entirely agricultural, but since the Second World War it has had a rapidly growing industrial sector. The political events of the past thirty-five or more years forced remnants of the Chinese Nationalists to seek refuge in their detached province, and they and their descendants now comprise about ten percent of the population of about eighteen million.

These, then, are the primary cultures from which we have drawn the materials in this book. For contrast, we also include some details of transitions in three socialist countries. Neither of us has been in Cuba, but some of the information on that young socialist state is extremely interesting. We have, however, had the opportunity of traveling widely in both the Soviet Union and the People's Republic of China, albeit for restricted periods of time. In any case, the greatest portion of our materials concerning the Soviet Union and the People's Republic of China are derived from published sources, supplemented by interviews with expatriate Soviet citizens who left only recently, and some personal anecdotes of our own.

The contrasts provided by the five cultures previously enumerated and the three socialist countries enable us to see that the rituals of transition may be handled in sacred or secular fashion. It is not necessary to link solemn social rites to a conception of the godhead. The Chinese have known this for more than two thousand years. Confucius is quoted in the *Analects* as saying, "If you cannot serve humanity, how can you serve the spirits?" As will be seen, the rituals performed in Taiwan are full of religious symbolism and efficacy. Those carried on in the mainland have undergone a great deal of secularization but, at least in the countryside, are not yet devoid of sacred references.

Large segments of American society, of course, carry out transition rituals without a trace of sacred reference. The limiting case, however, is provided by the Soviet Union, which carries out such rituals on a mass scale while derogating and making difficult, if not impossible, the celebration of religious rites and ceremonies. Although Soviet dialectitians are not amused, the tendency of things to turn into their opposites shows every sign of continuing in the

USSR. This is manifested in at least two ways in transition rituals. On one side, a significant number of persons continue to hold religious beliefs that influence their choice of transition rituals; they include, among others, Old Believers, Baptists, Jews, Jehovah's Witnesses, and a great many Muslims and some Buddhists. This is not a notably dialectical twist, but a continuation of old traditions in new social and political surroundings. Much more ironic is that ritual, once outwardly the butt of official contempt, has staged the most remarkable comeback. Since the 1960s, the Soviet Union has openly encouraged an expanded set of rituals, including ceremonies celebrating each of the transitions discussed in this book. Ritual specialists are provided who are instructed in the techniques that have been developed for these occasions. These rituals are regarded as devoid of religious significance, yet what is the concept of the sacred? Emile Durkheim found it based upon the intensification of feelings of social identification. What was being celebrated was the group, its élan, its membership. In a sense, what the Soviet Union has come to is not unlike the view of the rite that is found in Confucianism, or in some forms of Buddhism or Hinduism, in which notions of godhead have become attenuated or have vanished.

The sum of the world's culture, made up of all the cultures that have ever existed, up to those of today, will never be known in full. The civilizations recalled for us by archaeology are often glimpsed only in their technological phases; their ideologies and their rituals cannot be reclaimed, even though some of their ritual objects have been discovered. Those we do know about, however, supply enough information to dazzle us by the range of possibilities they display. We see ceremonies drawn tightly into the compass of a small family group or a densely populated public setting. We see some rites carried out with little pomp and no specialized equipment save for the words pertaining to the occasion; others are marked by richly dressed processions, intricate performances, banquets that last for days.

As we ourselves feast on the diversity in the transition rites of the different peoples described in this book, we also raise certain additional questions. Are there fundamental aspects of these rituals common to all cultures, or are they shared by some but lacking in others? If we find universals, do they reveal deep, necessary processes of culture? For example, are there regular differences between rituals of transition celebrated in simple hunting societies, among simple farmers, or in complex industrial societies, or do humanness and general insecurity surmount details of cultural difference even as great as that between the tiny, small-scale culture and the massive, industrial one? Is there any relationship in the way a society provides for its living, the transitions it emphasizes, and the way it celebrates them? We hope to throw light on this key question after our review of the ceremonials is completed.

Many societies pay little ritual attention to the actual process by which the child is delivered. Usually, the ritual occurs well after the infant's birth. Not infrequently, the rituals are given in full for certain children and not at all for others, or a truncated version may be substituted. The decision may be made at the time, based on local conditions. The !Kung tailor the size of their celebrations to their current food supply, and that holds true for many peoples. But there is a limit to the time a ritual can be postponed, although some peoples do move beyond the appropriate time. Or the ritual may not be held for one person or another. Usually, however, a total cancellation is considered a bad omen, something to be avoided, and a celebration is somehow scraped together, if not by a great and memorable feast, at least by a small but proper dinner. Then, too, in many societies, such as Tlingit once was, only the oldest, the first child, will be honored, either at arrival or at any other life transition. Or it may be the youngest who is feted. Simple societies clearly provide equal attention for all, however, if food stocks permit. That is not the case in complex, ranked societies that bestow different amounts of prestige upon different individuals, or stratified, unequally dividing the access of its members to the resources that sustain life. In these, the administration of transition rituals tends to increase in importance and in associated consumption in proportion to the rank and wealth of the subject and the subject's family.

Once past birth, the dating of subsequent transitions is somewhat flexible, either because of variable natural circumstances, or because the cultures play with what is given. The most variable is the transition of death. Under premodern medical conditions, the death rate was high not only in childbirth, but at most ages. The coupling of death and age is not unique to medically sophisticated cultures, and while a child's or a young adult's death is certainly not unknown to us, it was far more familiar to our ancestors.

Moving back to puberty, we will see a considerable variation in the timing of rituals over a period of some ten years during which the onset of sexual functions is believed to begin. In many cultures the relationship between puberty and sexuality remains latent; the connection is not made and certainly not stressed. This tends to be the case with such complex societies as our own. We are likely to attach pubertal significance to a school graduation or a first automobile license rather than to the first signs of sexual capacity. It should not be concluded that the nonsexual references in ritual concepts are evidence of the social repression of sex. The standards of sexual conduct for adolescents and young adults have changed in the United States, yet the marking of adolescent and young adult transitions is no more sexually symbolized than it was decades ago in a much more sexually repressive time.

Of the four transitions discussed in this book, marriage, in our own society, has seemed the most likely to become an endangered species of ritual. It is not that marriage was threatened by divorce, for after all, the divorce rate is linked to the marriage rate. Rather, in the 1960s, it appeared that living together outside marriage, was spreading rapidly through our society. It could be noted among the young, but was also recommended for the old to ensure maximum social security benefits and minimum income tax. It spread to all classes and ages. Yet, even at its height, living together outside marriage accounted for only a minority of pairings. In recent years, statistics have shown the reversal of whatever trend was under way, and marriage is still increasing in popularity.

Obviously, although marriages tend to constellate at different ages in different cultures, they are often distributed throughout the life cycle. The discussion of marriage in this book, however, concentrates on first marriages, which take place in most of the societies discussed during the period from late childhood and early adolescence (the !Kung) to the early thirties (urban China).

As has long been noted, marriage often unites a particular woman and man for the purpose of providing linkage and recurring exchanges between two kin groups. The functional truth of that adage is not absolute, but depends on the kind of organization involved. In any case, it reaches peaks in different kinds of society. We will see that it is not a very important factor with the !Kung, but is now of great significance in Tikopia, as it formerly was among the Tlingit. It has lingering significance in Muslim Hausa and among the Chinese in Taiwan. However, it is under attack in the People's Republic of China, where it is in decline in the cities but still holding in the countryside. In the Soviet Union it is almost a dead issue. The families of the parties to a marriage may never see each other, may have no obligations to each other, and may play little or no role in the affairs of the married couple, unless the housing shortage that characterizes every socialist country forces a newly married couple to take shelter with the parents of one of them. Such necessity does not entail relations with the other in-laws; in fact, it can quickly erode any existing cordiality.

Ceremonies marking marriage, especially a first marriage, are among the most colorful we will describe. Again, their range is great, dependent to some extent upon the supply of food and other materials. This may be a societal problem, as among the !Kung, or a problem of access and distribution, as in societies marked by class divisions. But the socialist countries provide a separate and interesting set of cases. Rebounding from earlier disdain for marriage ceremonies, most socialist countries now provide in their larger cities great Wedding Palaces, where brides and grooms, all decked out in finery, can be married in the presence of their families.

Displays associated with death are also mounting in the USSR, and only partly diminishing in China. Elsewhere, rituals of death provide the most variable models compared with other ceremonies. Some societies seem eager to get the thing over with, and they provide very simple funeral occasions. Others have built the treatment of the dead into an elaborate and expensive set of occasions. We see something of this wide range even within our restricted sample.

All of life is a risky business; transition rituals are a way of channeling anxiety. We accept the evidence that most human behavioral phenomena are rooted in the mode of production, in the social formation in which it occurs, in the availability of food, in the quality and extent of arable land, in the type and extent of industry, all adding up to the necessaries of human survival. After all this is considered, however, there remain modes of behavior that are only incompletely explained by this form of social analysis. We plan to explore these cultural mysteries in this book. We choose to do so through the close examination of crisis rites. The ordinary, everyday activities of human beings give us clues to the nature of a particular culture, but a crisis situation throws into sharp relief how people function, and it usually helps us to see why they function that way. Fears and desires that lie concealed under ordinary circumstances are clearly revealed at these special times.

You will notice that some of the ceremonies and rituals are explained in detail and others not at all. The reason is simply that some of the ethnographic materials available are merely descriptive, while others offer analysis and interpretation. In some cases we were able to speculate as to the meaning of a particular phenomenon, while in others the ethnographic data defied such analysis.

Not all aspects of any particular ritual can be explicated in simple, logical statements. For one thing, too much of the historical background may have been lost. For another, some cultural developments are either not completely rational, or do not operate in terms of our western, basically Aristotelian, concepts of logic. The very question of rationality, then, is a profound one for anthropologists, making simplistic statements or explanations difficult and sometimes impossible.

In a world that is growing smaller and more dangerous, a feeling for the range of cultural behavior is essential. By learning about the variety of cultures we become better able to see deeply into our own: we realize that our way is not necessarily the most "natural."

There is beauty and delight in difference, and through it we can experience a heightened awareness, a fresh way of looking at the familiar, and thus gain a deeper understanding of the world about us.

CHAPTER TWO

Birth

UNTIL she feels the first contraction of her uterus, a !Kung woman continues to perform her daily tasks and to participate in the social and recreational activities of the camp. She goes out into the veld to gather roots, plants, berries, melons, and nuts; she catches small game, fetches water, and gathers firewood. When she is in the village for the day she sits outside her tiny hut, which she has made of pole and thatch, and creates body ornaments out of the shells of ostrich eggs or softens her *kaross,* a cape made of the whole hide of one animal, which she wears tied at her waist. She usually sings while she is engaged in these activities, sometimes to the accompaniment of a simple string instrument, for the !Kung are very fond of singing and music.

!Kung men and women of the Kalahari desert in Africa have the most egalitarian relationship we know of anywhere in the world. Although women do most of the gathering and hut building, and men hunt for larger game, men and women are perfectly willing to perform almost any chore. They spend about the same amount of time at work and play, in camp or out in the veld. While spending the day gathering, women reconnoiter the area for tracks of large animals, and tell the men of their sightings when they return to camp. Men depend upon this intelligence and get up a hunting party on the basis of it.

Very often, men and women work side by side near the family

fire, the men sharpening *assegai* blades, mending other hunting equipment, and poisoning the tips of arrowheads for the next hunt. Both men and women keep an eye on the children and are equally affectionate with them.

Unlike most Western societies, where church and state accept sexual intercourse as consummation of the bond between a man and his wife, the !Kung do not consider a marriage consummated until the birth of a child. A newly married !Kung couple stay with the wife's parents until their first child is born, after which they may leave and make their abode elsewhere.

There are few special beliefs concerning gestation and parturition among the !Kung. According to some accounts, the pregnant woman is not supposed to eat certain plant foods and must avoid consuming the reproductive organs of animals, lest the birth be attended by complications.

!Kung women take great pride in self-sufficiency in parturition. They have a keen sense of competence and independence. As soon as a woman's contractions become strong and close together, she goes out in the veld. She collects some soft grass, which she piles into a mound. During the second stage of labor, when she is pushing the fetus through the birth canal, she crouches over this soft mound to assure a safe landing for her infant. For her first delivery she is assisted by her mother and other older women who support her back and massage it. If her delivery is uncomplicated, she will have her subsequent children entirely alone. If her labor begins at night, she will not even bother to wake her sleeping husband, but quietly slip out of the hut and go out into the veld, to return in the morning, glowing with pride, with the new infant.

No man may be present during parturition. An exception is made in case of a difficult delivery, when the husband is fetched to aid his wife. Using his walking stick, he draws a line in the sand in front of his wife, and keeps drawing the line as he walks back to the village, saying: "Come out, come out, come to the village, everyone is waiting for you." We do not know the origin of this custom, but can readily understand its efficacy in some cases. An abnormal delivery is exhausting and ridden with tension. Tension leads to pain, and the delivery is slowed down. The emotional support of her husband's participation may help relax a woman's muscles, and, instead of fighting the urge to bear down, her labor resumes and delivery is expedited. She draws strength from his concern.

As soon as the mother has given birth, she wipes the baby with the grass of the veld. She cuts the umbilical cord with a stick and places the baby in her *kaross*. She then sets about eliminating all traces of the delivery, gathering together the stained grass, the placenta, and the bloody sand, and covering them all with stones, loose soil, and branches. She marks this spot with a tuft of grass that sticks up as a warning, for it is believed that if a man stepped on it, he would endanger his potency as a hunter and a sexual partner.

If there is sufficient food on hand at the time of the birth, the parents may give a feast, followed by a dance. If not (and the !Kung know hunger well), the ceremonies are indefinitely postponed, and may never occur. In any event, the child is named shortly after birth, usually in the following manner: if it is a first son, he is named for his father's father; if a first daughter, for her father's mother. Subsequent children are named for the mother's parents and relatives. There is no special ceremony to mark this occasion.

A !Kung woman and her baby have almost constant skin contact. The naked babies are carried on their mothers' bare backs, and nursed whenever hungry. !Kung women, whose diet is lacking in milk and grains, continue to nurse their babies for three or even four years. An infant's sucking produces a change in the mother's hormone balance, causing a secretion of the prolactin that suppresses ovulation. This condition, combined with demand feeding and a limited diet, produces natural birth control, enabling !Kung women to space their children three or four years apart. If a woman does get pregnant before her child is off the breast and walking—a rare occurrence—she buries the newborn alive, as she is not able to nurse and carry two babies at the same time. The !Kung consider a birth as live only after the baby has been named —usually three days after it is born. At night, the baby sleeps in its mother's arms and, during the day, if the mother is not carrying or holding the baby, her husband holds it, and hugs and kisses it often. Everybody loves babies, and they get held, kissed, and dandled constantly. When the baby begins to crawl, it climbs all over its parents and other adults who are attending to their chores in camp. No one ever gets irritated or impatient with a baby. Great care is taken to remove all sharp or otherwise dangerous implements from the infant's reach. !Kung babies enjoy total freedom of movement. As babies become toddlers they try to get involved in the games and dances of older children and adults, often bumping against their legs. They are never rejected, resented, or shooed away.

One of the markers of the baby's growth is the first ritual haircut. This requires the presence of relatives, both on the father's and the mother's side. The !ku n!a, the person for whom the child is named, is expected to present the child with a fine gift on this occasion. Often this gift is of metal, which is rare among the !Kung and obtained through barter with Bantu neighbors.

!Kung children of both sexes and all ages play together. Their villages are very small, both in population and area, limiting the choice of playmates. Such heterogeneous groupings account for the lack of competition among !Kung children in their games. They skip, using rope made by women from the leaf fibers of the sansevieria (*!hwi*) plant for hut building; they play "ball" games, sometimes using the seed of a palm fruit called *!hani,* and have a variety of other games, but no scores are ever kept. The members of the band recognize that some children seem quicker and more talented than others, but the emphasis, for both children and adults, is on the sheer enjoyment of the activity. !Kung of all ages are very adroit at imitating the gestures, postures, and sounds of animals, and also at mimicking each other. This provides a form of theater for the entertainment of the band. The person who is imitated does not feel any loss of face, and joins in the general hilarity at the mime's skill.

Unlike our own and many other societies, the !Kung have a minimum amount of sexual identification with particular tasks. This condition of relative equality and overlapping that marks adult !Kung society is clearly based in the arrangements of childhood. !Kung girls grow into women who have a very high degree of self-esteem.

A child who behaves badly is not physically punished by older persons, but simply gathered up and removed to another area, where its attention is diverted. Indeed, although violence is not unknown, children grow up witnessing a minimal amount of it among their elders, and in later life they too tend to resolve their conflicts peacefully.

The social organization of the !Kung is marked by the absence of authority. Several nuclear families, consisting of husband and wife (or wives) and children, usually related to each other, form a band. Such a band may have anywhere from twenty-five to sixty members, and over the years will lose some people and gain others. After depleting the resources of one place the band will have to move to a new area. When a new campsite is found that has satisfactory water and food supply, the women set about building huts in a circle, each nuclear family having one to itself. The open side of each hut faces the center of the village, hence physical privacy is virtually unknown to the !Kung. They are in full view of each other all the time, even at night, each nuclear family unit sleeping by its own fire. Only by going individually into the veld can they be alone. Even here there is no secrecy, for they are experts at tracking, and the footprint of each member of the band is known to all the others. Everyone's movements are obvious to all. As a consequence, it is impossible to take something used by another without being found out.

The survival of the band depends on the cooperation of each member, and antisocial behavior on the part of any individual can endanger the existence of others. A full and conscious knowledge of this interdependence acts as a powerful brake on inflamed tempers. If members of one family get too angry with another family to continue peaceful coexistence, the whole family simply detaches itself from the band and joins another one. However, before things get to that pass, other techniques are usually used to relieve tension. The !Kung articulate their feelings very freely, and share their possessions. An individual member of the band may obtain an object—a fancy pocketknife, perhaps—by barter from the outside, but he will not keep it long to himself. Bye and bye he will yield to social pressure and give it to another member of the band, who in turn will use it for a while and then pass it on to someone else, until the knife will have been used by everyone in the band.

Knowledge of the !Kung hunter-gatherers is essential to our understanding of more complex societies, for theirs is perhaps the simplest human social organization known to us in empirical detail.

Unlike the nomadic !Kung, whose birthing customs are simple and uniform, the Muslim Hausa of Nigeria, living about three thousand miles north of the Kalahari desert, engage in a variety of practices that depend on personal wealth and location in the Hausa territory.

After she misses two periods the rural Hausa woman begins to suspect that she is pregnant. She may vomit and feel flushed; she loses her appetite for certain foods. Her third period missed, she becomes certain that she is expecting a child. Hausa informants told us the important signs the woman and those around her observe. "She becomes beautiful. If she is not dark-skinned, her complexion gets even lighter than it was before." Her weight gain becomes obvious, as does the increasing size of her breasts. She develops a preference for certain foods. "When a woman feels life, she usually does not tolerate the smell of perfume. She becomes lazy and moves more slowly. She feels lazy all the time."

If there is a clinic in the village, the expectant mother goes to see the midwife after she has missed four periods. The midwife asks her the date of her last period, or simply how many periods she has missed, then examines her by palpating her body. She is told to come to the clinic once a month for a checkup, and is given vitamins, iron, and tonics to be taken regularly during her period of gestation. The midwife also advises her on proper diet— oranges, bananas, spinach, okra, rice, and yams. Meat is very expensive in Nigeria, but if the pregnant woman can afford it, she is encouraged to eat it twice a day. She is told to eat liver, kidney, and fish.

Even though she feels tired and languid, she continues to keep herself clean, and works at her usual occupations. As Muslim law allows her husband to have as many as four wives, spending two nights in rotation with each, the Hausa woman has time to engage in pursuits apart from marriage and motherhood. She prepares *marmare,* snack foods, for sale at the local market, makes thread, and weaves rough cotton blankets for home use and local sale. She raises goats and poultry, some kept for home cooking, the rest sold at market. She also trades in medicines, vegetable oils, and cigarettes. The proceeds of her industry are hers to keep.

When her husband is not visiting her, she spends her evenings spinning cotton and receiving her *kawaye,* female bond-friends.

If she has older children, she expects them to help out with chores. If she is not able to cook, her husband has to hire someone to prepare food, unless he has a co-wife who will take over the responsibility for cooking.

When the woman is seven months pregnant, she rests more and works less. If she engages in small trade, she stops going to the market, but if she is an only wife having her first child, she continues to perform domestic chores until the day of delivery. She stops calling on friends and relatives, and depends on visits from them for companionship.

Rural women are not given a due date in advance. When they are nine months pregnant, the midwife cautions them that the baby may arrive any day. As soon as her pregnancy becomes obvious, a woman expecting her first child in a village without a clinic is asked by her mother or mother-in-law when she had her last period. Older women, experienced at having and delivering babies, can estimate a fairly reliable due date.

When labor begins, the woman feels discomfort enough to want to lie down. Her mother-in-law suspects that contractions have begun when she does not see her daughter-in-law emerge from her hut in the morning. She goes to her, knocks on her door, and asks her if anything is wrong. The response is indirect—her daughter-in-law tells her she is not feeling well and is lying down. If the older woman is certain that labor is in progress, she either takes her to the clinic, if there is one in the village, or sends one of the children in the compound to go fetch the *ugawzoma,* the midwife. She also sends someone to the compound of her daughter-in-law's kin to convey the news. Aunts, grandmothers, sisters, and sisters-in-law come to the woman in labor. When word reaches the husband that his wife is about to give birth, he either stays confined in his own room or goes to the compound of a friend.

During the first stage of labor the woman lies on the floor on a *katifa,* a cotton mattress, or a *tabarma,* a woven mat. The midwife never leaves her side during the birth process, but the mother-in-law or a co-wife or other female kin stay only if they choose to keep her company. They converse, and if the laboring woman feels like participating in the small talk between contractions, she does. If not, she lies quietly—Hausa women do not cry out during parturition, according to our informants.

During the second stage of labor, when the woman is pushing the baby down the birth canal, she gets on her hands and knees. The midwife takes a clean skirt from the mother's wardrobe, and, holding it in position, she catches the baby as it slides out. The midwife cuts the cord, then washes the baby thoroughly and wraps it in a clean blanket. She washes the afterbirth and places it in a crockery bowl that is subsequently buried in the ground back of the hut. She places the baby in a cradle near the mother, who averts her gaze and refuses to touch it if it is her first child. This is a very old custom, still practiced in rural areas. The old-fashioned mother does not call her firstborn by name. She calls her son *yaro* (boy), and her daughter *yariya* (girl).

When the baby is born, the husband's mother or a co-wife or a female relative goes to the husband to notify him. This is a happy moment for him—he may even hold the baby but he will not kiss it. The Muslim Hausa do not kiss babies. Theirs is not a demonstrative culture. In the case of the birth of a child, there are special reasons for restraint. It is customary to give the first child to relatives for adoption, and sometimes even the second and third. The infant mortality rate in Nigeria is one of the highest in the world, about forty percent, and it is wiser not to get emotionally attached to an infant one has to give up or may lose.

The new mother is fed highly spiced gruel, and she begins her ritual of bathing twice a day with near-boiling water, a practice she continues for forty days. During the first three days, before the baby is nursed, it is given either cow's milk purchased from the pastoral Fulani,*or a prepared formula. The midwife washes the mother's breasts and massages them to encourage the flow of milk. As soon as the milk starts to come in, the mother nurses her baby, placed beside her on the *gadonkasa,* a raised platform of clay, but she moves as far from the infant as she can after nursing.

*Today's six million Fulani are descendants of a pastoral people who were the former rulers of an empire covering much of what is now Northern Nigeria, plus parts of adjacent countries. Formerly speakers of Fulfulde, a language in the Niger-Congo family, many have since learned to speak Hausa as a first language. (Hausa belongs to a totally distinct family—Chadic of the Afro-Asiatic stock.) The Fulani Empire peaked at the beginning of the nineteenth century. The population is predominantly Muslim and has become increasingly urbanized and influenced by the Hausa in this century.

The husband's parents purchase and prepare rich and delicious foods spiced with ginger, black pepper, cinnamon, cloves, and dried red hot peppers, and everyone in the compound enjoys a feast. The new mother is given hot, spicy foods to eat in great abundance, and a fire is made in the hollow part of the *gadonkasa* that forms her bed to prevent her from catching a cold. A great deal of wood is used to cook food, to boil water, and to keep the fire going under the mother's bed—wood the husband purchased in preparation for the arrival of the baby.

The major ritual takes place on the seventh day, which is the *suna,* the naming day of the child. On the preceding day the baby's father buys a ram, and sends a large amount of kola nuts, a mild stimulant produced by the Yoruba,*to his wife's close kin. The new father's mother takes a piece of cloth to her daughter-in-law on the naming day. The new mother's parents bring rice, millet, guinea corn, maize, palm oil, peanut oil, pepper, and okra. They also bring clothing for their daughter and their grandchild.

On the morning of the naming ceremony, the husband has the compound swept clean, and spreads mats for his guests to sit on. A *malam,* a man learned in religious matters, slaughters the ram the father purchased, saying a short prayer during which he utters the child's name. It is the father who has chosen the name, in consultation with his elder brother or parents. If the baby is a boy, the name chosen is that of a prophet or other religious figure in the Koran. If a girl, she is named after a woman who is famous in religious history. Children are given additional names, such as that of the day on which they were born, that representing the season of the year, or that denoting the order of birth in the family.

The *malam* invites the guests to join in prayers to the prophet, and professional praise-singers announce the prayers to those present. The *malam* prays aloud in Arabic and Hausa, blesses the child, announces the name for all to hear, and expresses the hope that

*The Yoruba, with a population of about seven million, are another people overlapping with the Hausa in Northern Nigeria, but their main concentration lies somewhat to the west. Linguistically, they belong to the Niger-Congo family, hence speak a language related to that of the non-Hausa-speaking Fulani. The Yoruba have inhabited their present land for more than a thousand years. Farmers and traders, they have been involved through history in a variety of states, often headed by Yoruba rulers.

the child will live a long and useful life within the Islamic faith. Other members of the gathering offer prayers, and while they do so, professional butchers are busy skinning and cutting up the slaughtered animal.

The midwife brings out the baby tied to her back. The *wanzami* (barber), at the request of the father, cuts out the baby's *belu* (uvula, the pendent fleshy lobe in the middle of the soft palate), shaves its head, and, by making fine cuts, puts the family marks on its face. If the baby is a girl, a tiny bit is clipped off her clitoris by the *wanzami,* inside the compound, as the mother's aunt or grandmother holds the baby. The mother is never present at this genital operation.

The new father makes payments to the *malam* and the *wanzami,* and to the women, the relatives, and the neighbors who have performed all the household chores during the week of the new mother's confinement to bed.

The new mother's closest female kin and bond-friends gather in her hut eating kola nuts, staining their teeth, powdering their faces, and rubbing their arms and legs with oil and henna. They all dress themselves in their finest garments. The young mother also dresses in her finery, and her friends stain her arms and legs with henna and dress her hair.

There is no sleep for anyone in or near the compound, for the drummers perform all night, as a continuing part of the celebration.

On the morning after the naming ceremony, the mother goes to the compound of her own kin, accompanied by the midwife, who carries the baby tied to her back. The mother nurses her baby freely in her girlhood home, and need not avert her eyes as she did when she was with her husband's kin. The midwife ties the infant on the grandmother's back and returns to her own home, her work completed.

A woman who has had her first child may remain with her mother for six months. After the forty days of ritual bathing is over, the new mother puts on her finest garment and best ornaments, the baby is dressed, and one of the younger girls in the compound ties him on her back and takes him to all his relatives to show him. Everyone holds the child, plays with him, and sings to him.

After forty days of washing twice a day, the mother washes only in the morning for five months. She is given presents by her relatives, and returns to her husband's compound, accompanied by drummers and praise-singers, who are given money for their services.

A child is nursed until the age of two. The nursing mother must refrain from sexual congress with her husband during this period lest she become pregnant, for the Muslim Hausa believe that a pregnant woman's milk can harm a baby seriously, even fatally.

The child, weaned from the breast at the age of two, is then adopted by one of his grandmothers, or by an aunt, either the mother's or the father's sister, or by some barren female relative.

This event is a major trauma in the child's life. Mary Smith has recorded the words of a Hausa woman, Baba of Karo, describing this situation:

"Two years after the child's birth, one of the child's grandmothers, usually his father's mother who often lives in the same compound, comes at dawn and knocks on the mother's hut door; she goes in and picks up the child and takes him or her off to her own hut. The child's mother runs off to her own mother's home. In the morning the child bursts out crying, he cries bitterly. Then his grandfather, the father of his father, writes a text on his board and washes off the ink and gives the child the ink of the text to drink, then the womenfolk make gruel and he drinks it. He keeps running to his mother's hut, but he doesn't see her there and he bursts out crying. After three or four days he forgets about the breast. His grandmother has him in her hut and she looks after him. . . . When her child sees her [the mother] she pushes him away and says 'Go on, run off to your own hut!', his grandmother picks him up and comforts him, then he comes back to his mother, and the grandmother carries him off to her own hut. . . . Some children put up with it and stay in their grandmother's hut, some don't and come back to their mother's hut and stay there. Sometimes a child is adopted into another compound, a father's sister or a mother's sister, or one of the grandparents, adopt him. The child's own parents give him to her and she carries him on her back. The kinsfolk of the child's father usually take the first child, and the kinsfolk of the mother take the second. Sometimes the third child is also adopted, but the rest usually stay in their mother's hut."

When the above passage was read to Hausa women, one of them responded, "When the mother tells her child to go back to his own hut she is saying it for the other people in the compound to hear it. Inside, she feels grief and loss. Her heart is bleeding. No mother wants to give up a child. But she cannot ever show this grief in public. She may only cry when she is alone in her room."

Most women who live in big cities like Daura, Katsina, Kano, Sokoto, or Zaria, give birth in a hospital. The procedures followed are quite similar to ours. When the woman suspects that she is pregnant, she visits an obstetrician at the hospital, either as a clinic patient or a private patient. She is examined, and if she asks, she is given a due date. She visits the doctor on a regular basis all during her pregnancy and takes whatever vitamin and iron supplements are given her. She is advised about proper diet, and follows it to the best of her financial ability. When her contractions begin, her husband takes her to the hospital, and then either returns home or goes to work. He visits the hospital a few hours later to find out if his wife is still in labor or, better, if she has given birth.

The age and educational level of the new mother is a crucial factor in the way she deals with motherhood. A more mature and better educated woman, even though criticized by her elders and subject to their anger, can follow her own inclinations and ignore the old ways. She touches and handles her child immediately, and calls it by its proper name. However, there still are university-educated women who have their first child after the age of twenty, but who still choose to follow the old customs.

All Muslim Hausa women do not nurse their babies for two years, nor do they abstain from sex for a prolonged period of time. Some women breast-feed their babies for as long as a year or eighteen months; others start supplementary feedings of formula and thin gruel when the baby is only a few months old. The decision to stop nursing rests with the husband—if he can afford to purchase the imported formula, he asks his wife to wean the baby. Some women nurse for the full two years but their number is shrinking, and the trend to nurse for only three months or not at all is growing.

The Hausa custom of releasing so many of their children, particularly those born early to a marriage, to others through adoption has been the subject of much speculation. Why do they engage in this practice?

While Chapter Four deals with marriage in detail, it is essential to point out here that Hausa marriages are very brittle. Women are married off at an early age, thirteen or fourteen at most, to men chosen for them by their parents. Having entered a relationship without any voice in the decision, and dominated by a husband they do not love, they frequently divorce after the first child is weaned. A woman cannot take her child with her, so she returns alone to stay with her mother for a period of three months, remaining celibate until the divorce is considered final and she is free to remarry. One of the important obligations of kinship among the Hausa is to give children for adoption to relatives who have no offspring of their own. An unmistakable pattern emerges, that of providing the child with a stable home where care and affection are given during those years in the mother's life when she is still young and attractive to men, and is able to change marriage partners with ease. If she can find someone she truly loves, or is able to secure a position as a head wife, or has passed her youth, the marriage she then contracts is the one she will stay in, and at that point she keeps her children. Having reached her "advanced years," she lavishes attention and affection on them. The Hausa treasure their last child, the happiness and comfort of their "old age," the one they treat as a playmate.

The Muslim Hausa face an interesting predicament concerning abortion. Muslim law allows abortion as a method of birth control within the first sixteen weeks of pregnancy because, according to the Koran and the Sayings of Muhammad, the Prophet of Islam, a four-month-old fetus ". . . does not come within the definition of human life. In case of abortion within 16 weeks, mutual consent of husband and wife is necessary." If the mother's life is threatened, no permission is needed at all. The government of Nigeria has very strict laws against abortion. It may only be performed if a doctor certifies that the mother's life is in danger. This conflict of state and religious law is not unique to Nigeria, which embraces some two hundred fifty ethnic and language groups, but can also be seen in other complex societies.

Although nowhere is the transition from fetus to person clear-cut, it was particularly obscure among the Tlingit of Alaska in the past. The Yakutat Tlingit believed that each newborn child possessed the spirit of a departed relative. In the words of one Tlingit woman: "What you dream when you sick with the child, his spirit come to you. . . . Sometimes they find markings on them [the baby], and then you know it is the same spirit."

The woman who was about to become a mother took no chances. She ensured reincarnation by taking the hand of the corpse of someone who had been especially dear to her and, holding it to her breast, wishing with all her might that her unborn child would inherit the spirit of the beloved. After the burial she circled the grave eight times, then drew a line from the grave about seven feet long, squatted at the end of it, and urinated, appealing to the dead spirit to return.

Although the Tlingit realized that pregnancy was the result of intercourse, they did not have a sharp definition for the beginning of the life cycle because of their belief in reincarnation.

No matter how poor a family or how many children they already had, the birth of a new baby, whether it was a boy or a girl, was greeted with great rejoicing. Children were very much desired, and twins were especially valued by parents, grandparents, and other loving relatives. A great deal of affection and attention was lavished on children.

When a woman believed that she was pregnant, she consulted a midwife, who ascertained the position of the fetus by palpating her body. Through this external examination the midwife predicted the date of birth.

The expectant mother continued cooking, preparing the hides of animals killed by the men, and making baskets. She may have harbored a number of beliefs about prenatal influences on her child. If she was frightened by a bear, she expected her child to be ill-tempered; if a mouse ran over her feet, she feared the child might be born with the features of a rodent. Although there was anxiety about such occurrences there were no rituals to avoid them or prevent their consequences.

A few days before delivery the midwife attempted to maneuver the fetus into the right position by massage and pressure. She then wound a tight sash or belt around the mother's body to hold the fetus in the desired position.

There was a permanent birth house in the village to which every woman went for parturition. Built of wood, with thick walls, it contained a large fireplace where steam was produced by pouring water over hot rocks. The house had a birthing pit about twelve inches deep, filled with soft moss almost to the top. When a woman was delivering a baby, the moss was covered with a soft cloth onto which the baby could easily fall as it was born.

The woman in labor squatted over this pit and was supported and helped by the midwife and two female assistants. When she had a contraction, she was instructed to "swallow her breath down." When the contraction was over, she lay back and rested on the knees of the midwife.

When the baby was born, the umbilical cord was cut and tied, and delivery of the afterbirth was hastened by pulling on the remainder of the cord still attached to it. When it was all over, the tired mother lay down, prevented from catching a chill by the warm rocks. The placenta was burned without any ceremony.

If the baby did not cry out at birth, it was turned upside down and slapped on the back. It was then bathed in warm water, wrapped in clean cloths and blankets, and placed in a large basket.

While traditionally no man could be present during parturition, a shaman, acting as intermediary between human beings and supernatural forces, could be paid to use his powers at a distance to facilitate an easy delivery.

The new mother was given herbal tea and other warm liquids to ensure a good supply of milk. Midwives liked to keep the new mother in bed for two weeks.

An infant was put to the breast whenever hungry. In addition to mother's milk, an older baby got a variety of foods that had been prechewed by its mother, or by whoever happened to be tending the child—a grandmother, an aunt, or an older sister.

Directly after birth the infant was given the names of the deceased relative whose spirit had previously been selected by the mother. The prerogative of choosing the name belonged to the closest female relative of the departed. The Tlingit were very fond of nicknames, and each child received one, either the nickname of the person whose "real name" he had been given or one that described a particular characteristic of the child.

The Tlingit believed that certain magical practices facilitated the infant's growth into the kind of adult the society considered ideal. To make sure a boy grew up to be a brave hunter, his umbilical cord was placed in the hiding place of an animal. The tendon from the hind leg of a wolf was attached to his ankle to make him a fast runner. His hammock was made out of the hide of a wolf. The mother of a baby girl incorporated her umbilical cord into something she was sewing, or wove it into a basket to make sure her daughter would acquire the essential feminine skills of sewing and weaving.

Babies received a great deal of affection, being held and fondled by their mothers, fathers, grandparents, aunts, and siblings. The Tlingit were very casual about toilet training and showed equal permissiveness about meals. Children were neither punished nor ridiculed for wetting their beds, and they were fed whenever they were hungry. This attitude applies even in present days until they are old enough to attend school, when their lives become more structured. Children are showered with gifts of clothing, ornaments, toys, and special foods. Modern Tlingit are described by contemporary observers as so generous in giving their children sweets, or money to buy candy in the village stores, that an unusually large number of children suffer from toothache and tooth decay. This sometimes results in young Tlingit having to wear dentures.

A Tlingit child delighted in being sung to by parents and grandparents and, in turn, entertained them by dancing to the tunes. Yet, not all was pleasure. When children got noisy or quarreled, mothers threatened and scolded, but they did not mete out physical punishment unless the father was present. By the time the fathers got home, the pranks were forgotten or, at most, the children's feet were tied together for a while, or they were made to stay in a dark corner for a short time. The Tlingit believed that fathers were generally more indulgent than mothers with daughters, and mothers more patient with sons. Adult Tlingit males still speak of their mothers with great affection, while adult females are fonder of their fathers than of their mothers.

There was chronic anxiety about the safety of small children. Boys and girls were cautioned about the dangers of animals in the forest and the possibility of drowning. Some fathers created an enclosure for safe play by building a fence.

Before a baby could walk it was carried by the mother on her back in a blanket drawn over her shoulders and fastened around her waist with a belt. Sometimes the father carried the baby in a similar fashion. Babies were not carried about in the house.

Children were weaned when the next baby was born to the mother. The weaned child expressed dismay at the rejection and grew quite angry, fussing a great deal. The Tlingit accomplished rapid weaning by rubbing a powder prepared from wild heliotrope on the mother's nipples. The powder had so terrible a taste that the child gave up the breast quickly.

All of this has changed. The birthing house is a dim memory now—women in their thirties cannot remember ever having seen one. Several weeks before delivery almost all Tlingit women are flown to Anchorage or Juneau to stay with relatives or friends until their contractions begin and it is time to go to the hospital. The Health Center in Yakutat provides prenatal care, gives the expectant mother a due date, and reserves a place for her in a hospital. Once in a great while a woman has a baby at home, usually because the baby is premature or because the mother miscalculated and lingered too long in Yakutat. She is usually aided by older women or by the head of the Health Center, a certified Physician's Assistant who is trained in midwifery. Breast-feeding is out and bottles are in, much to the chagrin of the Sister who regularly visits the Catholic community in Yakutat. This nun, who is a social worker, pointed out that at the time of the interview, in July 1978, only one woman in Yakutat was nursing her baby, and was considered strange by other women for it.

However, children suffer no neglect, even if parents are unable to take care of them. A grandmother or an aunt will immediately take over the responsibility, and will rear the child with great love, tender care, and infinite patience.

Pregnancy is quite common before marriage among the Tikopia who live north of the New Hebrides Islands in the Western Pacific Ocean. However, unlike the Tlingit, the Tikopia frown upon illegitimacy. When an unmarried woman finds herself with child, her brothers force her to reveal her lover's name, and they confront him verbally. If he shows resistance to marriage, they escalate their tactics and threaten him with bodily harm. Things are usually kept in hand, as the man who allegedly sired the child ultimately yields to pressure and agrees to the marriage.

Having a child is considered a perfectly normal activity, and no embarrassment attaches to gestation. Children are aware of women's having "big stomachs" when they are carrying a child, and will point to any child with a bloated belly (a common effect of their starchy diet), saying that he or she looks like a pregnant woman. Tikopia children, like the !Kung, understand from an early age that pregnancy is the result of sexual intercourse. Such knowledge is regarded as routine; there is no concern when it is displayed by a very small child.

Nobody fusses over a pregnant woman. She receives no special treatment, but carries on her usual work. She can be seen bathing in the ocean early in the morning, working side by side with her husband in the orchards, wading in water up to her waist to catch fish with a net, cooking the major meal of the day in the late afternoon, and resting in the shade of a casuarina tree plaiting pandanus mats at sunset.

The anthropologist to whom we are indebted for the bulk of our information about Tikopia is Raymond Firth. He notes that the people of Tikopia have few special beliefs concerning pregnancy, but among those they do hold is a set that resembles a mild form of a pregnancy- and birth-associated institution known mainly from South America's tropical forest region. No suggestion is made of historical connection between the South American custom of couvade and the Tikopian belief that a father-to-be experiences a general decline of working efficiency, skill, and luck. In Tikopia it is thought that men whose wives are pregnant will catch fewer fish or harvest a smaller crop. There is an association of the husband's vital power, his personal *mana,* and the wife's condition, which involves a profane state of bodily function, implying, as it does, distortion of the body and an inevitable sequence of birth and blood, with ever present danger of death to mother or child. This is related to the beliefs in taboo, a variable scale of avoidances extended to places, persons, things, and activities. The net effect of the system is to encourage the man whose wife is pregnant to take it easy. Tikopia does not go as far in its beliefs as, say, the Amazonian Wittoto, who have a full couvade: the Wittoto husband experiences the equivalent of morning sickness and, as his wife's pregnancy develops, becomes less and less active until, at last, he takes to his hammock to rest and groan until the child is delivered.

A Tikopia woman expecting her first child goes to her parents' house when she is a few weeks or days from delivery. Turmeric, a spice of reddish hue extracted from the plant of the same name, is smeared on her head and over the upper part of her body. As this ritual is performed, a special incantation is addressed to the unborn child:

> *"Your earth will be cleansed away*
> *Continue to dwell, listen,*
> *And then descend."*

Directly after this ceremony, which is called *furunga kere,* the "cleaning of the caul," the pregnant woman's kin present food and valuables to her husband's kin. The next day the husband's family reciprocates by giving presents to the wife's family.

When new life comes into being, the Tikopia say *"fafine ne fanau nanafi,"* "a woman gave birth yesterday," which contrasts sharply with our usage of "a child was born." The Tikopia saying clearly establishes that the woman is not a lump of flesh to which something happened, but an active creator of life. The labor and successful birthing are her glory.

In the face of repeated experiences to the contrary, the Tikopia say that boys and girls are born at different times of the twenty-four-hour day, depending on the position of the moon. One phase is called *potangata,* when boys are born, and the other *pofafine,* when girls are born. When the reverse happens, as it often does, nobody is upset by it, but neither do they explain the deviation, or drop the folk belief.

When the expectant mother begins to have uterine contractions, a small ceremony is performed to facilitate delivery. The woman's whole family gathers, and one of the older men, or a chief, gently rubs her belly with oil. Then he intones a prayer:

> *"Male ancestor,*
> *Stand firm to make strong*
> *And give power to my hand.*
> *Be turned the face of the little child*
> *Down below.*
> *Erect the twice-breaking wave*
> *And send it down below.*
> *You come down on to your property*

Which has been spread out
By your house of father's sisters and your house of grandparents
That they may nurse you."

This is an appeal to a special ancestor that the child may come down the birth canal in the normal position and that delivery may be made easy by the flooding of the amniotic fluid. The child is exhorted to land on the cloth spread out to receive it. The word "property" in this instance refers to the gifts that have been brought to the house for the occasion of the birth. This is still being done. Although the Tikopia have all been converted to Christianity and have been taught Christian prayers, the appeal of old ritual has not died.

In contrast to every other culture described in this book, Tikopia provides an active role in the delivery for males. The parturient's brothers support her by sitting behind her and pressing their feet against her buttocks. She leans back while her brothers push against her with their feet and press their hands on her shoulders. A woman helper sits in front of her holding a soft piece of bark cloth for receiving the child. As soon as the head of the baby appears the woman supports it with the cloth. She is called "the woman of the catching," *te fafine o te siki.* As the child is born other female assistants come and pull down the placenta. The cord is cut, and the woman's vulva is anointed with turmeric. She is then given a great deal of hot water to drink, in the belief that this will hasten the postpartum discharge.

The cord of a firstborn son is cut with a sliver of bamboo, *parakofe,* attached to a club. This is said to enhance his skills and strength. The afterbirth of male children is buried at once. The procedure is somewhat more complicated with female children. The placenta is carefully examined, and those particles in it that are considered objectionable, because they might bring harm to her for the rest of her life, are taken out and buried separately, some distance from the rest of the afterbirth. The placenta is always buried in a shady place.

The father of the child, particularly after the first and second born, is very proud and happy, and immediately sets about the task of preparing vast amounts of food and drink for the postnatal ceremonies. All the women of the new mother's and father's families assemble, bringing gifts and food prepared in their own homes. If the infant is the first child born to a woman, its head will be rubbed with turmeric as a sign of special status.

In a week or so, when the umbilical cord has dropped, the women in the family gather in the new baby's house for a feast, after which food and a piece of bark cloth are given to each guest to take home.

When a first child is about a month old, it is taken for a week's visit to the home of the mother's eldest brother. The invitation to visit is in the form of an exchange of food. The brother sends his sister a basket of good things to eat, thereby inviting the newly born baby for a visit. The baby is taken to his house along with a basket of food. In the same manner, the child is invited to stay with a number of different relatives, and is always accompanied by its parents. These visits can go on until the baby can crawl or even walk.

The Tikopia are very casual about the naming of their children and do not attach any ceremonial importance to it. In fact, at intervals, a child may be given different names by its parents as it grows up, and relatives may also offer suggestions.

There used to be a special ceremony, called *pea*, held only for the firstborn daughters of Tikopian chiefs or men of high rank. According to Firth's calculations, this ceremony was held about once in seven or eight years, and neither Firth nor his research associate, James Spillius, ever witnessed one. The ceremony is known only through the description given to Firth by a male informant.

Pea is said to be the most important ceremony that could be held for a female child, and had to take place while she was still nursing and before she could walk. The decision to hold the ceremony was made by the girl's father. He was called *tau anga*, "the holder of the feast." It often developed into a group enterprise, however, as the fathers of other baby daughters were invited to join or volunteered to participate. Their role was to assist the principal holder of the feast by contributing food from their own and their relatives' gardens and orchards. Firth points out that few men had resources capable of supplying the very large amounts of food required, which limited participation in this event. The feast was called *te anga o nga maroro,* "the feast of the robust," or *te anga o nga mafi,* "the feast of the industrious."

Contributions of food were taken to the house of the principal man on the first day, when the oven was heated and the food prepared. When the food was ready to eat, baskets were filled on behalf of each female infant being honored. One went to the *pea*, others to the house of each honored child's principal maternal uncle, along with the baby, who was adorned with beads and bracelets made of shells. Other gifts, such as sinnet cord and bark cloth were also sent. At the uncle's house, the child's ornaments were removed and replaced by new ones. The gifts were reciprocated with items of equal value, and the basket of food was exchanged for another. The child was then carried back to her father's house. This part of the ceremony was called the *tama pa tonu*, "the definitely acknowledged child." The social rank of the child was established for life. Special foods were cooked and eaten every day. The kava ceremony* was presided over by the daughter of the Ariki Kafika, the chief of the most eminent lineage, and through her intercession the children for whom this rite was performed received the protection of the Female Deity.

A major social activity of this ceremony was dancing. The women danced alone for four days while the men prepared the food. Each child to be honored was taken to the dance and smeared with turmeric. Men and women partook of the feast at separate times of the day. The dance was taboo for married women; only young girls or widows could participate.

The men went fishing on the evening of the fourth day; on the evening of the fifth day, they adorned themselves with flowers and danced. The women could not join actively in this dance but merely watched.

On the sixth day, each participating father fed a group of young people in his house; they then spent the day working in his orchard, returning to his house in the evening for another meal. Each was given a basket of food to take home. The *pea* ended when the site of the dance was changed from one village to another.

Another ceremony for the first female child, held less frequently and considered less important, was called *fangainga*, the "feeding." The first time a girl was given fish to eat, when she was

*A kava ceremony is a religious ritual requiring the preparation of a libation made of the root of the same name. Unlike people in other Polynesian societies, the Tikopians do not drink the brew, but make offerings of it to their ancestors and spirits.

two or three years old, a feast hosted by her father was offered. Taken to the house of her mother's brother, the child ate the fish as the assemblage of her mother's kin exchanged ornaments, other valuables, and food.

When their first son was about two, men of high rank held a ceremony called the *taumaro*. This was similar to the *pea* in the way it was initiated and organized, but it only lasted two days, and the foods collected were raw, the main food being taro. Only those relatives who participated in the rites at the time of the child's birth were invited to this ritual. The mother's brothers attended with their wives. Each woman came with gifts—a pandanus mat and some bark cloth, one piece dyed with turmeric—for the women in the baby's house, and each woman received food in return. Similarly, the men exchanged gifts. This ritual established the high rank of the firstborn son for the rest of his life.

Firth points out that Tikopian fathers are very devoted to their children, and take their turn caring for them with pride. Although primary responsibility for child care rests with the mother and the female relatives, fathers do their share with affection.

In the spring of 1956, a small group of men left Tikopia at the joint invitation of what was then the British Solomon Islands Protectorate and of Levers Pacific Plantations to establish the Tikopian colony of Nukufero in the Russell Islands. The British government was concerned that the tiny island of Tikopia could not support its increased population, for it was on the verge of physical and social disintegration following a hurricane in 1952 that caused the threat of famine. Another factor that motivated the Levers and the British officials was a long-standing, chronic shortage of labor in the Protectorate. Although similar previous efforts had failed, the Eastern District commissioner visited Tikopia and waged a vigorous, persuasive campaign to assure the successful colonization of Nukufero.

Over the years, more and more workers with their families were recruited by Levers. Anthropologist Eric H. Larson arrived in Nukufero in June 1964, and except for a two-month stay on the island of Tikopia, he spent a year there. When he left, in July 1965, 160 Tikopian colonists were in residence.

Larson points out that the elaborate rituals accompanying the birth of a first child were never practiced in the Russell Islands, primarily because most Tikopian women in the colony go to hospitals in larger places, such as Yandina and Honiara, to give birth. When they return, their child is baptized in church, with members of the family in attendance. The child frequently receives a Christian name. The only part of the native ceremony that has survived is the preparation of a small oven by the new parents. The food cooked in this oven is given to the priest in gratitude for bestowing the sacrament.

By 1964 the government had established a small clinic on Tikopia, with a resident medical assistant. Although women called for help if they were having a prolonged and difficult delivery, the practice of most of the old elaborate rituals continued. All Tikopians were converted to Christianity by that time, and they ceased having the *pea,* since it required praying to a pagan god. Since 1978 Tikopia has been part of a new state called the Solomon Islands. A former British colony, it has become politically independent.

Just as the !Kung do not take a marriage seriously until the birth of the first child, so a Chinese woman is not fully accepted into her husband's family until she has produced offspring. When she presents her husband with a son, her position in the household is greatly enhanced. While in imperial China a woman was not supposed to meet her husband until the day of the wedding, in Taiwan today it is not unusual for a bride to be pregnant when her union with the father of her child is made legal. There are societies in which a man will not marry a woman unless she is visibly pregnant, fearing a barren woman like a plague.

The desire for sons has always been paramount in Chinese culture, and female infanticide, by drowning or suffocation, was common practice until quite recently. While male children are still preferred, girls receive nearly as much affection, care, and treatment as boys.

The Chinese woman's desire for children is great. She prays to many gods for help in becoming pregnant, but the most popular divinity for this purpose is the Buddhist goddess Kuan-yin. When a woman finds herself with child, she expresses her gratitude for divine intervention by offering rich foods to the gods in their temples.

There has been rapid industrial growth and urban develop-

ment in Taiwan in the past ten years. Western medicine is practiced in most hospitals, but it has not eclipsed traditional Chinese
medicine, which continues to flourish. Most women living in and
around Taipei and the great urban centers go to hospitals for
parturition, and are frequently attended by a male obstetrician.
This directly violates an old Chinese taboo against men's presence
at delivery. Although the city dwellers have been subject to western influence, they continue to observe many of the traditional
customs by which their country cousins still live. A rural family
may own a variety of electrical appliances, but babies are still
delivered the same way they were fifteen years ago.

When a woman is in her fourth month of pregnancy, she
begins to take special herbs. She continues this practice through
her confinement until the onset of labor.

It is believed, particularly in rural areas, that *Tai Shen,* the god
of the pregnant womb, enters the expectant mother's room and
lurks there during her entire period of gestation and labor. He is
greatly feared, and care is taken not to disturb him. The bedroom
may not be swept or cleaned, for, once aroused, *Tai Shen* may harm
the baby or cause a spontaneous abortion. A woman knows that
Tai Shen has been offended if she experiences a sharp pain in her
abdomen. A part-time religious practitioner, a *tang-ki,* or shaman,
is then called in to pacify the god.

The Taiwanese have a host of beliefs about the dangers of
pregnancy, and a woman must observe a number of restrictions.
She may not tie strings in her bedroom, for it will adversely affect
her baby's fingers, nor may she use scissors, for that may harm his
ears. She may not use a needle in her room, for to do so may harm
the baby's eyes, nor may she go anywhere near a funeral cortege,
as that might cause her to miscarry. She is barred from attending
weddings, as either she or the newlywed couple might suffer
harm. If she violates these taboos, a shaman may be called upon
to counteract her inadvertent offenses.

Women continue to perform their regular tasks right up to the
onset of labor. They fetch water and wood, do the family's laun-
dry, market and cook, and, if they have a child who still cannot
walk, they carry the baby on their backs in a special sling that ties
around their waist and shoulders. Folk wisdom has it that hard
work and strenuous walking will facilitate delivery; in this in-

stance, folk wisdom coincides with the advice currently given by obstetricians. During the first three months of gestation, some women experience morning sickness, and when the nausea passes, they crave strange foods, sometimes out of season, much like their American sisters.

Most rural women have their babies in the home of their husband's parents, lying on their backs in bed, with the assistance of a local midwife and a few older women. When a country woman is going to a hospital for delivery, a religious specialist may be asked to come to her room at home to find the object in which *Tai Shen* is hiding. Once this object, which could be a mirror, a chair, or a picture, is located, it is taken to the hospital with her.

Some ethnographers report that a woman is not supposed to cry loudly during parturition, although no mention is made of specific sanctions applied to women who do. Since in our experience Chinese households tend to be noisy, we wonder how anyone would notice a few cries during the last contractions, or the grunts that accompany the bearing down as the baby is pushed through the birth canal.

The newly born baby delivered at home is wiped with sesame oil, and a cloth that has been soaked in salt water is used to clean its mouth. The lips are then dabbed with sugar water, and the infant is wrapped in a cloth and put next to the mother, whose breasts are massaged to encourage the flow of milk. The baby is given water boiled with sugar, until the mother is ready to nurse.

Shortly after the birth the maternal grandparents are notified, and sent a gift of rice, wine, and chicken. They, in turn, send gifts, such as personal items for the mother and chickens, wine, and noodles. If it is a first child, and if they can afford it, the mother's parents send a year's supply of clothing and some gold jewelry.

When the baby is three days old, the midwife returns to bathe it. On that same day food offerings are made to *Chng Bu,* the Bed Mother, who is asked to protect the child and to help in rearing it.

After giving birth the mother has one month for complete rest. She must observe a set of strictures faithfully and do what traditional Chinese medicine prescribes. The thirty-day period is called *tso yueh,* to "do the month," and its observation can be traced back to the tenth century. The medical formulations on which it is based are at least four thousand years old, and they may have neolithic roots.

For the thirty days of *tso yueh* after delivering a child, a woman is not allowed to wash her body or her hair. She may not wash dishes or clothes. She must avoid even fleeting contact with cold water. It is believed that if she breaks this rule, wind will enter her body through her joints and apertures and cause her permanent damage, such as chronic asthma, arthritis, or rheumatism.

She must not be caught in a draft or wind, and it is considered safest for her to stay lying on her back in bed, with all the windows of her room closed. If she catches cold during this period, she will have aches and pains for the rest of her life.

She must not consume any raw or cold food. "Cold" describes not merely the temperature of the food but its nature—the Chinese consider turnips, Chinese cabbage, bamboo shoots, leafy green vegetables, and most fruits as cold foods. Some of these foods grow in watery places, others in the damp earth. Ducks and fish are equally anathema, because they swim in water. The food the woman eats may not be salted.

Her room is considered "dirty" for thirty days, because the postpartum discharge has blood, which is polluted, in it. For this reason, anyone who enters her room may not go to weddings, enter temples, or view fire-walking, lest they offend the gods and bring great harm to themselves or to those they come in contact with.

Both reading and weeping are to be avoided, for they will weaken her eyes for the rest of her life.

For her health and welfare she must eat one whole chicken a day, cooked in sesame oil and rice wine. All three ingredients are considered "hot," and therefore essential for her future well-being. Hot foods are considered good for her; the Chinese view parturition as an illness from which one must recover by consuming foods that will "create fire," and thereby restore health.

The new mother must abstain from sexual intercourse, for it would bring misfortune to her husband. He is advised not to enter her room for the same reason. She is not, however, isolated, for one of the prescriptions of *tso yueh* is that the new mother must have a companion. The person who stays with her and takes care of her is her mother-in-law, in most cases, or sometimes her mother, if she lives nearby.

All the restrictions and prescriptions fall into the category of preventive medicine. The Chinese medical view is that during an illness a person's vital forces are in a state of imbalance, and health is regained by the restoration of balance.

There is a striking similarity between the postpartum care of Chinese and Muslim Hausa women. The latter also must be kept warm, consume hot foods, abstain from sexual intercourse, and be taken care of for a prolonged period of time. This is not a coincidence. The Chinese conception of disease and its causation is among the most ancient medical traditions in the world, and it was incorporated into Islamic medical practices through a variety of historical intermediaries.

At the end of *tso yueh* a major ceremony is performed, called *man yueh*. The baby's head is rubbed with oil, and his head and eyebrows are shaved. He is dressed in his fine new clothes, which are traditionally red, and he is taken out so the neighbors may see him. A lunch party is provided by all four grandparents to celebrate the occasion, and during the ceremony everyone is told the child's name, which, among the most traditionally oriented, has been chosen after consulting with the temple elders.

After *man yueh* the new mother's room is thoroughly cleaned. She is then free to leave her house and resume her normal life.

Husband and wife usually resume sexual intercourse at this time, which gives the local wags an opportunity for joking and teasing. In the old days, when infant mortality was very high in China and knowledge of effective methods of birth control nonexistent, women kept bearing children until their menopause. Now that the standard of living is higher and infant mortality extremely low, married couples are vigorously urged not to have more than three children. Although it was long resisted by Chiang Kai-shek, Taiwan now has one of the most effective birth-control programs in the world, and no village is too remote for the public health nurse to visit to educate women in a variety of means for preventing conception. Spacing children and limiting their number enables families to give them better care and educational opportunities denied them in the past. Taiwan is one of the few countries where the dissemination of this advice is official policy.

Infants are nursed on demand, and sleep with their mothers. During the day the mother carries her baby tied in a sling on her back while she goes about her chores, although there is always some other female relative—a mother-in-law, a sister-in-law, or an older child—who can be called upon to hold the baby and carry it. Most Chinese fathers are very affectionate with their children and love to dandle them, but few take active care of them. Children are nursed for about two years; in some cases, much longer. We have seen preschoolers run up to their mothers who obligingly loosened their clothing and nursed them.

Babies are diapered at night, but during the day they wear clothes that are open around the genitals. When a baby is about six months old, every so often his mother picks him up and holds him over a drainage ditch with his legs apart. She makes a hissing sound, like running water. The baby quickly learns to respond to this stimulus and to the approval he gets when he has performed successfully. However, there is no pressure and no punishment meted out even to older children who have enuresis; their liquid intake is just reduced in the evening. Bowel training is equally casual, with the result that most children are toilet trained by the age of two.

Toddlers play together, very often at games imitative of adult activity, such as cooking or card playing, but they are separated much of the day from the older children, who are attending school.

Babies start receiving rice gruel at about the age of three months, and by the time they are two years old they eat all table foods, although they may still use spoons rather than chopsticks.

The Taiwanese woman, unlike her American counterpart who has purchased her independence at the price of isolation, is rarely alone. She is surrounded by family, friends, and neighbors who, while knowing every detail of her life and sometimes giving unsolicited advice, provide a support system and a sense of security unknown to most American women. It should not be thought, however, that most women in Taiwan live in the bosom of a large, extended family. By far the greatest portion of the population is contained in small domestic units of the nuclear, or stem, variety. These are usually limited to one reproductive couple per generation, in contrast to joint families, which have several married couples in residence of each generation. Even at present, many women living with their own small families in the large cities are not far from mothers, sisters, mothers-in-law, and some relatives. Less than half a century ago, residence among relatives was even more common. Indeed, Taiwan was settled largely within a system in which lineages were very important social, economic, and political instruments. Migrants often came to Taiwan in clusters whose foundation was the existence of patrilineal ties. The most common bond was fraternity, and a set of uterine brothers often provided the nucleus for a village community. This brought to Taiwan a pattern well known on the mainland. Even today, a glance at a detailed Chinese map, particularly of a southeastern province, reveals a high frequency of place names such as "Yang family village" or "Li village," testimony to the exclusive occupation of those places, or at least their domination, by people of a single surname.

To the Chinese, one major reason for migrating in tight kin groupings was the necessity for actual pioneer defense against hostile natives. Although the Chinese have been expanding into their own southwest for several thousand years, they have continually run into resistance from non-Chinese inhabitants, much like the experience of European colonists who came to America and migrated to the west. Where Americans, pushing into areas inhabited by Native Americans, reacted by emphasizing individualism and personal independence, the Chinese reacted to the pressures and tensions of frontier life by increasing dependence on large kin groups—joint families, lineages, and clans.

CHAPTER THREE

Puberty/Adolescence

IN our world, where crisis is ever at a boil, every period of life provides a special set of hazards. The time of birth and infancy is regarded in Western cultures as the least roiled, despite struggle over abortion and the probably related problem of a seemingly mounting incidence of child abuse. When we turn in later chapters to the transitions marked by marriage, and then to senescence and death, we will again encounter crisis. None of these, however, seems a time as perilous as adolescence. Why? Perhaps because adolescence is a time of tension between pleasure on the one hand and of high turmoil and danger on the other. In fact, although many societies provide special rituals or other markers of transition into and out of a more or less clearly marked period of youth, a distinct period of adolescence is not marked in all cultures. Our view of adolescence is not universal.

In common with other sexually reproducing organisms, mammals in particular, we come quite gradually to the maturation of our reproductive capacities. We are born with the basic equipment. Females have their lifetime supply of eggs present at birth, although males will not begin to synthesize sperm for many years. Neither males nor females are capable of reproductive activities for a period that may exceed fifteen years, during which the sexual organs continue to develop and critical physiological processes, including the successive triggering of such vital chemical processes as the secretion of hormones, begin.

A world sample of cultures displays great variation in the treatment of adolescence, ranging from those in which such a period of life is not recognized to those in which it is a focus of anxiety. Our own limited set of cultural exemplars will show something of this range.

Although adolescence receives no particular recognition in some cultures, awareness of puberty is difficult to escape. Yet the two terms are sometimes confused, especially in our own culture. If the definition of words could be legislated, we might pass a law designating puberty as the physiological onset of reproductive capability and adolescence as the period of psychological and social development preceding adulthood. Unfortunately, usage is not so easily controlled, but finds consensus over or around obstacles. Our own culture tends to consider puberty and adolescence synonymous, and ignores the significant differences between them. Confusion arises from the fact that the boundaries of adolescence are as indeterminate as those of puberty. One may reasonably expect that a social and psychological status such as adolescence will vary from individual to individual and from culture to culture, but one does not expect physiochemically based phenomena to show comparable variation. Nonetheless, the beginning of puberty does vary, in part because human beings are greatly affected by such cultural factors as diet, stress, and cultural expectations. In the United States, menarche, the beginning of female puberty, usually occurs around the age of twelve. (The age of first ejaculation of sperm for boys in the United States, is reported to be fourteen, on the average.) There is, however, great individual variation. Some girls have their first menstruation as early as ten, and some not until the late teens. Moreover, menarche is sometimes followed by so-called adolescent sterility, a temporary period of amenorrhea, or cessation of menstruation, for a period of a few months or even years.

The Hausa age of menarche is similar to the contemporary average in the United States. The same applied to menarche in classical Rome, judging by the legal age of puberty in that society. In brief, then, the onset of menarche and the subsequent possibility of pregnancy varies to such an extent as to provide only the roughest guide to socially set ages of adolescence.

Like puberty, the word adolescence is derived from a Latin root. It originates from *adolescens,* a form of the verb *adolescere,* to grow up or mature. The past participle of that Latin verb is *adultus,* "grown up." Thus the adolescent is linked to adulthood linguistically as well as developmentally, at least in some cultures, although, it must be said again, quite a few distinguish neither puberty nor adolescence as a formal period of the life cycle.

In fact, where both adolescence and puberty are concerned, the Greeks did not have a word for it. In Aristotle's time, the Greeks referred merely to three gross periods of life—childhood, youth, and old age. Lest one leap to the conclusion that their youth was equivalent to our adolescence, one must consider that "youth" could extend into a person's forties. The Romans had specific words for both adolescence and puberty, but sometimes they also confused the two. For the Romans puberty lasted, ideally, from age eight to twelve for girls, and from eight to fourteen for boys. This period of *pubertas* was followed by adolescence, but there is some confusion about its duration. Most sources date it from age fourteen (twelve in girls) to twenty-five; others suggest it could begin as early as eight and run on into the forties.

Censorius, a Roman writer of the third century A.D., has left a volume, *Liber de Die Natale* [The natal day], which has a chapter devoted to a historical assessment of diverse schemes for dividing the life cycle. One such analysis provided no fewer than twelve stages, three stages unfolding between the years fourteen to seventeen—from fourteen to fifteen was prepubertal, from fifteen to sixteen, puberty proper, and seventeen was postpubertal.

Like us, the Romans failed to achieve congruence between age and legal expectations of conduct at these stages. In general, they recognized in law only one break in the life cycle, that between minor and adult. However, the precise legal point at which the minor became adult varied with the function involved. For many purposes a boy became a legal adult at fourteen; for other purposes, such as the freeing of slaves, the age of discretion could be twenty-five. Commentaries attached to the enactments of Justinian and other codes reveal the complexity of this problem of legal age of maturity in Roman civilization.

Although anticipated in the code of the Etruscans, the stock view of the "seven ages of man" is usually associated with the

Byzantine Empire. In it, infancy lasted from birth to age seven, childhood from eight to fourteen, adolescence from fifteen to twenty-one, according to one system, but to twenty-eight in another. There followed youth, which lasted from the end of adolescence until forty-five or even fifty. Clearly, the desire to forestall age is not solely a modern conceit. The hypothesis of seven ages of man as expressed about twelve hundred years ago set forth three hazily bounded, somewhat overlapping periods for those no longer young. First came senectitude, followed by old age, and, finally, for those who persisted in life, senility.

In succeeding centuries the concept of the divisions of life fluctuated throughout the regions once comprising the Roman Empire or under its control. The tenacity of Latin in much of the area, particularly in association with Catholicism, kept the notion of adolescence philologically alive, sometimes only because the Latin word was difficult to render in the regional European languages of the time. Philippe Ariès, a historian, has contributed a lively account of the vicissitudes of the European recognition of childhood as a period in the lifespan with its own characteristic idiosyncracies and problems. Ariès calls to our attention a translator of Latin texts in the sixteenth century, who complained that where the Latin originals with which he was working used at least seven terms to cover the lifespan, his French provided only three, and adolescence was not one of them.

At the turn of the century, popular social philosophy in Europe and America was dominated by one vision of cultural evolution, that which took for granted the superiority of the technologically complex civilization and of the white man, or, more specifically, of the Anglo-Saxon male. Indeed, in many quarters, such an ideology is conserved today. Evolution in the socio-cultural realm no longer seems as straightforward as it did in the Victorian and Edwardian eras. There has been an enormous growth in the amount of material recorded by professional ethnographers who learned the languages of the people whose culture they were studying, hence were equipped to penetrate their belief systems as earlier writers could not. Incredibly, some earlier commentators on alien cultures had spoken to the "natives" in broken English, or through untutored interpreters, or had not spoken to them at all but had only presumed to interpret the fine points of their culture with unconscious, or sometimes overt, contempt for the local people.

As sophisticated accounts accumulated, sweeping and simplistic assumptions about the universality of adolescence as a period of storm and stress, antiparental rebellion, and sexual problems, fell away. Indeed, even the five cultures which provide the main focus for this book show the extent to which our culture's view of adolescence is inappropriate as a cross-cultural model. Consider the Tikopians.

A boy first gets to do a man's work in Tikopia when he participates in a *mataki ramanga,* a "torch [fishing] expedition." He does no more than paddle as one of the crew, but the event is of sufficient importance to warrant a celebration. The day after the young boy has gone fishing with the men, his cheeks, neck, and chest are rubbed with turmeric, whose use was noted in conjunction with rituals of birth and infancy. Relatives of various kinds and degrees of closeness congregate on his behalf, providing a behavioral announcement that a major event in the boy's life is taking place.

Tikopian society is dominated by patrilineally organized kin groups, but the mother's relatives are important, as is often the case in patrilineal societies. It is therefore not surprising that the boy is sent on the occasion of his first fishing expedition to visit the house of his mother's brother. There he is again anointed with turmeric and given a ceremonial present known as *maro,* often consisting of a bundle of bark cloth, a mat, other things, and a basket of food. Meanwhile, at home, his parents have fired the rock ovens and spend the day preparing food in lavish quantities. The boy arrives at home and displays the gifts he has received. His parents reciprocate by dispatching gifts of equal value. Care is taken to supply gifts of food and bark cloth to all who participated in the first torch-fishing party, who are not considered to be close family members. Some girls also participate in the ceremony, but the ethnography does not make clear how regular such participation may be. There is some hint that it is limited to girls of rank, such as the daughters of chiefs. If so, it is interesting, because Tikopian culture seems relatively neglectful of female puberty ritual.

If the fishing ritual comes first, it is by no means the most important transition marker for a young male. That honor is reserved for the ceremony centered on the superincision of his penis.

Because great quantities of food have to be accumulated and prepared, sometimes in several ovens, and because many things of value have to be assembled for distribution as gifts for this occasion, the ceremony is often performed for a group rather than for an individual. A number of boys of similar age—a cohort, as it were—are assembled to undergo the ordeal. Their parents, by combining efforts, enhance the occasion. Throughout their lives, the boys who undergo a common superincision ritual perceive it as a bond among them, and say, "We had our ovens fired together."

In recent times the ritual of superincision has usually taken from three to five days, but in the past it could take as many as eight, especially if the son of a chief of high rank was involved. Long in advance of the event, relatives are notified of its coming. Actually, they are probably well aware of it, since the festivities provide a major source of pleasure and excitement. Large supplies of food, pandanus matting, and bark cloth are stored up, and gifts made to be distributed, marking the occasion. The initiate responds to invitations to call at the houses of relatives living in other villages. Each visit begins with the ceremonial anointing of the lad with turmeric, now mixed with coconut oil. The mixture produces a dramatic appearance. The boy seems drenched in blood and the Tikopia themselves think of this as an augury of the bloody injury the boy will suffer in his passage to adulthood. Cleansed, he dons a new waistcloth, made for him by women who are closely related to the men slated to take a prominent part in the impending ritual. To further honor and show affection for the boy, they rehearse songs, some old and others newly composed for this occasion. The practice assures them that the performances will not go awry at the ritual itself.

Individually and in groups, the relatives collect taro, yams, green coconuts, breadfruit, and bananas, heaping it all outside the house of the initiate's father. The day before the ceremony, the menu is completed when men go fishing with nets from boats, while the women work their scoops, wading through the shallows at low tide.

Whatever nature's mood, the next day begins somberly. Sunrise may be bright and clear, but the sounds of weeping and moaning fill the village, a foreboding of the pain to be visited on the boys who come symbolically to manhood that day. No sooner does one group of relatives tire of making the mourning sounds than another group takes up the task with fresh vigor, keeping the air awash in a constant dirge of grief. Faces are bathed in tears and blood as the relatives tear at cheeks and foreheads with fingernails or knives. Others seated nearby present a placid contrast as they await their turn to wail, meanwhile quietly chewing betel and plaiting sinnet cord.

During this preparatory phase of the ritual, the initiate is repeatedly anointed with turmeric, and his waistcloth is changed again and again. As he waits for the operation, the boy hears dirges, such as this:

> I would be busy then with the voyage
> I would leap aboard to be borne aloft,
> For my namesake is carried on the journey.
>
> Fetch then to the sea your canoe
> Fetch with it the paddle while I sit
> To weep wildly at the trail of foam
>
> I weep for my necklet
> Who has leapt aboard the vessel
> But us two the mutual sight
> On that day alone.

As interpreted by the Tikopia, this song is directed to the boy who is identified as the "necklet." Do we also see here a cry of anguish of the aging man who sings the song? It could be a celebration of *that* man's youth, the time before he married and settled down, when life was exciting for him. In any case, it reminds us that times of transition are times of coming and going not merely for the initiate, but for everyone participating in the ritual. At weddings, in our own culture, for whom are the tears shed?

There are other songs. Some of them are addressed to the boy's father, praising his generosity:

> Friend! borne over the land, friend!
> The father of the Tikopia

Your wealth of goods has been distributed to Ravenga
It has entered into Namo on the lake-shore

It is scattered around, friend, and stands in the west
Till it strikes the lowlands of Faea

We shall go and eat of your meals from the vessel
The praiseworthy man, how we gather around him.

As the boy is clad in fresh waistcloths, the women who change him place the cloths they have removed around their necks; around his neck, they place string upon string of beads. The father leads a chorus of relatives in yet other songs of mourning, and sorrowfully presses noses with each boy in the ritual party who is awaiting initiation. Now the mother's brother of each initiate suddenly seizes him and carries him bodily to a place where coconut leaves have been strewn on the ground. Here the operation is to take place. A crowd assembles as the tension mounts. Each boy is supported by a man who places his arms around him. These are the *tangata me,* "the men on whom the boys sleep." They will cover the boys' eyes at the moment of the incision.

The man who takes the role of surgeon at the superincision is invariably an uncle of the initiate, specifically, the boy's mother's brother (*tuatina*). It is true that the term *tuatina* refers to a whole category of relatives, rather than a single, specific individual, but the ethnographer makes clear that individuals find very precise differences within categories, and the young man has as his supporter a *tuatina* in whose house he is a familiar guest. Although this uncle is probably around the age of the boy's parents, he is treated in a totally different way. Where the boy must maintain formality and respect with his parents, he has a joking relationship with his mother's brother, and when he is in his *tuatina*'s house, he is relaxed and easy. Possibly because of this close emotional tie, the *tuatina* who is about to superincise his nephew's penis is quite nervous. To keep his hands from trembling, he rests his elbows on his knees as he sits in a crouching position. The foreskin of the initiate is drawn tightly forward and just before the cut is made the *tuatina* says *"Fakatoa! iramutu!* (Be strong! nephew!)." Now the cut is made lengthwise on the front portion of the foreskin two inches in length from the tip of the penis. The tool is a razor; of old it was the shell of a bivalve, and many strokes were required to complete the operation, rendering the process so excruciatingly painful that it was only performed on much older boys. The young man's *tuatina* took him to a secluded spot in the forest, far out of earshot, to save him the humiliation of having others hear his terrible screams.

Even now, with a sharp razor, a bungler may have to cut more than once, to the dismay of all. After the cut the foreskin is parted and folded back on each side. Fresh bark cloth is applied as a bandage. Most initiates are rigid with terror—some react with an involuntary retraction of the penis. When that happens, the *tuatina* grasps the organ and forcibly extends it for the cutting.

Before the superincision, the boy must observe a taboo for some time, avoiding certain foods considered "gristly"—these include snails and clams. The lad whose superincision proceeds smoothly with one neat cut is said to be one who has "listening ears," that is, who is obedient to the taboos. If the hand that performs the superincision wavers and the job is botched, it is not blamed on the practioner but on his subject. It is obvious to all present that the boy has been refractory and has not properly observed the taboo.

After the bandage has been secured, the boy rises and drops his waistcloth, which is again replaced with a fresh one. His bead necklaces and ornaments are carefully taken by his mother's brother. They return to the boy's house, where mourning songs break out anew, describing the wounds just inflicted. Yet again his waistcloth is exchanged for a new one, this time perhaps one of calico. The new garment is put upon him by his *masikitanga,* his father's sisters. They are his aunts, but are of a different degree from his mother's sisters, who are considered "mothers" in this kinship system, although there are verbal adjustments to distinguish them from the woman who actually gave him birth.

As he enters the house, the boy presses noses with his father and then repeats this affectionate greeting with each relative in the room. This is followed by a lavish exchange of gifts and an elaborate meal.

After eating, the boy is taken alone into the forest or down to the sea by the uncle who performed the superincision. He is taught how to care for his wounded penis. Juice extracted from the leaves of a local plant called *kamika* is dropped into the cut to speed the healing, which will take about a month. During this period the boy avoids activity; soreness and discomfort are expected. When the healing is completed, the initiate is considered an adult. He has entered Tikopian society and may participate fully in all adult activities.

According to Firth, there is an initiation ritual for girls, called *rau fafine,* but it is rarely performed. He never saw such an initiation; in any case, none is described in any part of the large corpus of work he has devoted to Tikopian culture. Nor is any mention of *rau fafine,* much less a description of it, to be found in the work of any other ethnographer. Firth does tell us, however, that no form of genital mutilation is performed on Tikopian women. He described the clitoridectomy practiced in other cultures to some men in Tikopia only to find that they strongly opposed its practice. Male informants told him that long ago a genital operation was performed on two women; both died, and it was then decided never to repeat the practice. Firth does not accept this story but treats it as a myth. He was also told that *rau fafine* was a simple version of feasting and gift exchange.

The Tikopians in Nukufero in the Russell Islands held some greatly modified superincision ceremonies for their youths in 1958 and found the limited ceremonies so unfulfilling that they decided to forego them in the future. Instead, they decided that over a period of time funds might be accumulated to take the boys back to Tikopia for a proper ceremony.

In 1964, Eric Larson, who was studying the Tikopians in Nukufero, journeyed to Tikopia, where he observed two ceremonies of superincision. Firth had already noted the tendency to shorten the ceremonies from as many as eight days to as few as four. What Larson saw was further reduced to two days, but that was the only important change. Unaltered were the construction of rock ovens, the extensive feasting and gift exchange, and the ceremonies, including the incessant dirge singing.

Submission to an operation on the genitals may or may not have a profound effect upon an infant, but when it occurs at a later age, it is unlikely ever to be forgotten. We have had the opportunity of talking to a Muslim Hausa who graphically recalls his circumcision at age seven, more than twenty years earlier. What follows is his account as recorded, with the anthropologist's questions and conversational comments deleted:

"There were four of us, although there could have been anywhere from three to seven. They put us into one room early in the morning, telling us that we were to be taken somewhere, perhaps a visit to another place. We could not get out of the room, it was locked. We waited about an hour, then they took us out, and the barber-surgeon was already there with his straight razor. We then realized what was to happen and we got sick. We threw up. Some of the boys lost control of bladder and bowel. They cried. Our older brothers, uncles and fathers held us. They stood us over a hole that had been dug by our fathers or uncles, held our legs apart. One held each of us in his arms and put his hands over our eyes and others held our hands. They held us very firmly. The barber grabbed my penis, pulled the foreskin forward and with one quick move he cut it off. I screamed. The blood ran into the hole and the foreskin fell into it. They covered it all up. Corn stalk—the thin one—was cut into the shape of a triangle. After they put a local medicine, it's like a paste, on the wound, they put the corn stalk pouch on my penis and tied it around my waist to keep it from contact with my legs and testicles. It was during December, when the air is cold and dry. They want to avoid the hot moist air. We were taken to a room where we had to lie on our backs without any clothes on. A fire was kept burning all night to keep us from catching cold.

"They fed us very well to make us forget the pain. We got good breakfast, lots of hot chicken stew, prepared with hot spices, cold chicken soup with hot spices. The only food we could not have before circumcision and for a while after was lemon. They believe that it could make a man impotent, to have lemon at that time. Grown men eat lemon, limes, oranges.

"It took about a week to heal. Relatives came with gifts, of food, mostly, and some brought toys made of inside of cornstalk. We used them as flutes. We even made cars of corn. When I was healed, I was given a new *bante* (loin cloth), but before I could put the *bante* on I was thoroughly bathed, my head was completely shaved. Then I put on my *bante* and shorts and a shirt on top. Before circumcision, when you are still a small child, you can run around naked or with just a loin cloth, but after, you have to dress properly, with outer garments.

"While we were kept in a room, separated from others, the barber came every day to check on us, to make sure we were healing. There was no concept of sterilization. It's the same now, but I never heard of a case of infection.

"The barber was paid immediately after the circumcision and given a hot meal and a whole roast chicken. Sometimes, if a man is wealthy, he will take care of all the expenses for all the boys. We were all kin. Most of the time, only boys who are related are circumcised together, but sometimes a boy who is not related can participate.

"*Waina,* cakes made of millet or wheat, and *kosai,* cakes made of black-eyed peas paste, were given to the poor, even any passers-by, in gratitude for the healing.

"After that everything changed. I was given some responsibilities, more and more as I grew older. By the time I was ten, I stopped playing with toys."

Other changes follow the circumcision. As the boy grows, he begins to receive invitations to naming ceremonies and weddings, and he is expected to take a gift. Small children tag along with their parents, or just run in and out of these functions in packs in play or out of curiosity, but they have no responsibilities. Although the newly circumcised Hausa boy is clearly on the way to manhood, residual qualities of childhood are still apparent in his daily life. It is only gradually that he will emerge into full adulthood.

What, then, is the meaning of such rituals as the superincision of the Tikopia or the circumcision of the Muslim Hausa?*The problem nags anthropologists, because it raises in a particularly difficult form the question of the relationship between culture and biology. In another view, what comes into question is the relationship between the world of ordinary, daily life and the world of the ritual and sacred. While not entirely rejecting psychological explanations of ritual behavior, we prefer to deal with such behavior in economic and social contexts. Rather than seek universal human meanings in such institutions, we prefer more limited statements that provide for change as the economies and social arrangements

*In a brilliant, as yet unpublished paper on rituals of circumcision in Morocco, anthropologist Vincent Crapanzano reviews the history of theorizing about such rituals among psychologists and behavioral scientists. The theories are "Thick as autumnal leaves that strew the brooks in Vallambrosa," to use the lines from Milton's *Paradise Lost.* That simile was originally employed by M. F. Ashley-Montagu; others have been harsher. Crapanzano quotes Felix Bryk as complaining in the 1930s that "the explanations for circumcision 'furnish a splendid example of the versatility of human extravagant imagination, and are, at the same time, a document of the ambivalent validity of causistic argumentation.' "

of peoples undergo alteration. We will return to this problem and the controversies it has sparked in the final chapter.

As for change, its effects are already apparent among the Hausa. To begin with, a superordinate identity is being forged as Nigeria becomes a leading state in African and world affairs. The Biafran war of 1968 was a watershed in Nigerian history. The defeat of Ibo secessionism, like the defeat of the Confederacy in the American Civil War, meant that the primary unit in political struggle in Nigeria would be the class and not the ethnic component. Along with such political changes have come economic ones, some associated with the end of British colonial rule, others with the increasing industrialization that goes with Nigeria's role as a major exporter of oil. Associated with such changes are shifts in the relationships between the generations. Although the old people of every generation in every culture have probably grumbled that things are not as they were in the old days, there is little question that modern Nigeria presents the Muslim Hausa with sets of intense adaptive pressures never before felt by them.

Even a generation ago sons almost never questioned their fathers' authority. Father commanded and the son obeyed, often even after the son had married. The pattern broke only with the death of the old man. In such a regime, with options limited, adolescence tended to be tranquil, with conflict at a minimum. Now that the social and political distance between generations is increasing, the father's authority is eroding, and the young man is likely to be independent in his thoughts and actions. A major source of change is financial opportunity. Sons may now escape the immediate economic domination of the father. But because the world economy, in conjunction with local conditions, sometimes causes a lessening of such opportunities, fathers have not lost all their power or authority, particularly in the countryside. Kinship is still strong as an organizing principle in Hausa society, but in the long run it will probably weaken.

Physical mobility for young men should not be considered a total novelty among the Muslim Hausa. For a long time, the Muslim Hausa have known the institution of the itinerant *malam,* or teacher, of traditional Islamic culture. Especially on the heels of disaster, such as a drought or other inhibitor of the food supply, poor boys past the age of seven who have already been circum-

cised, will join the *malam* and follow him to a city where they
expect to receive their food and some education. What actually
happens to most of them is quite different. Some remain with
wealthy families encountered along the way. Originally entering
the family as a servant, some are well treated and may even be
brought up as members of the family. In the happiest cases, their
benefactors may provide the bride price and even the capital to set
them up in small trade when they are old enough to marry. Others
fall on hard times. Many end as cooks in restaurants or as food
peddlers; they are often transvestites and homosexuals. But some
of the boys who follow the *malams* ultimately return to their villages and resume ordinary lives.

Muslim Hausa informants tell us that males begin to display
sexual interest at fifteen. The problem is to find access to a woman.
Muslim Hausa society links sex and marriage quite rigidly and
while it provides for prostitution, in the not distant past fathers
tended to regard young men's use of prostitutes as immoral even
dangerous, and took measures to prevent it. A young man who
was caught disobeying his father in such a matter received harsh
punishment. Today Muslim Hausa are more lenient in this regard.

Although both boys and girls attend the same schools, education is not mandatory, and some children stay home until they
marry. For many Muslim Hausa the world thus remains strongly
sex-segregated. Indeed, this tends to be the case in the general run
of social life. Men have male friends, women have female friends
—the lines are rarely crossed. Segregation by sex is so rigid in the
Hausa territory that in preparing for the 1979 elections, the
Nigerian government attempted, at considerable expense, to provide separate polls for men and women. One exception to this
separation of the sexes exists—young men feel free to have a
joking relationship with women past menopause, for they are not
regarded as potential sexual partners.

There is tremendous concern about keeping a girl a virgin
before marriage. Not only shame and family disgrace but tragedy
can result if she has any sexual experience prior to marriage. When
a girl has her first menstrual period, around the age of twelve or
thirteen, she is unprepared for it and very frightened. A Hausa
woman told us: "She cries when she sees the blood coming from
her vagina, feels cramps in her abdomen, and pain in her breasts.

She is afraid to tell her mother, and runs to the home of a friend, or confides in one of her aunts or her grandmother about this scary thing that is happening to her." If she has older sisters or friends who are already menstruating, they tell her what to expect. When she starts flowing, the person in whom she confides tells her that she can now get pregnant and must stay away from boys. Her mother usually finds out about her daughter's menarche from a third person. The girls who do not attend school but stay at home to help their mothers with domestic chores and small trade are most likely to tell them directly and least likely to have any advance knowledge about menstruation. Rather than celebrate the event, as the !Kung do, the Hausa mother keeps it a secret. It is her responsibility to keep her daughter under constant surveillance. The strain on the mother assures that she will make every effort to get her daughter married off into another compound before the onset of menarche. It is customary for a girl not attending school to marry between twelve and fourteen, the marriage having been arranged by the two sets of parents and their representatives.

For those who do go to school, modern physiological explanations of menstruation, as well as other aspects of sexual biology, are taught in the third year of secondary school. By this time some information about menstruation has long since been passed on by older classmates to most of the girls.

When a schoolgirl begins to menstruate, she has had some preparation, however informal. Now she may seek out the woman who acts as counselor and welfare worker for the girls in her school. Or the girl may be more comfortable if she goes to stay at the home of a classmate for a little while. Ultimately, however, she will have to tell her aunts, if not her mother, that she has begun to menstruate, and they reassure her that this happens to every woman. All girls are warned that if they become pregnant before marriage they will end as prostitutes and outcasts, a terrifying prospect. No matter whom a girl goes to when she begins to flow, she will be given soft pieces of flannel, folded over twice, to be pinned to a strip of soft cloth, tied about her waist—a sanitary napkin. Each girl is given at least three and sometimes six of these reusable napkins. She puts on a fresh napkin each morning and removes it in the afternoon, puts on a fresh one, and washes the soiled one. The number of napkins she is given is determined by the amount of her flow. Some can afford to purchase disposable napkins imported from England, the United States, or other western countries, and Nigeria is now producing disposable napkins that are much cheaper than imported ones, and used by more and more women. When a disposable napkin has been used, it is discarded in the latrine. Women who live in big cities—in modern apartments or houses with flush toilets—wrap the soiled napkin in a piece of paper and throw it in the dustbin. It is then taken away with the rest of the garbage.

When a Muslim Hausa woman was asked what would happen if a girl got pregnant before marriage, her swift reply was "Her parents would kill her!" Upon further questioning it turned out that the answer was hyperbolic; no examples could be given in which such a drastic measure was taken. Instead, there are two practical ways of handling the potentially disastrous situation. The first is to arrange for a quick marriage before anyone finds out that the girl is pregnant. If a mother cannot work this out, she sends her daughter off to relatives in another town, where she can give birth and leave the baby in a relative's care, returning home with her reputation intact. Later, she can enter into a marriage her parents consider appropriate.

Taboos for the menstruating woman are the same from her first to her last period. When menstruating, she may not touch the Koran, pray, or fast during Ramadan. If she is married, she may not have sexual relations with her husband. After her period is over she must bathe thoroughly, wash her hair, cut her nails, create a new coiffure, and put on clean clothes.

The onset of menarche is not considered a transition from childhood to womanhood, neither is marriage before the onset of menarche. Only after the menstruating girl has consummated her marriage is she considered a woman.

As children get older they establish friendships with their peers that are strengthened by the constant exchange of gifts. Boys will select out of the group one special coeval who will be a bond-friend for life. This friend is by his side during every crisis, provides moral support when needed, is privy to confidences, and is the only nonrelated male who may enter his compound freely. The special Hausa term for this kind of friend is *babban aboki*. These friendships are reciprocal.

Because women move away from their homes each time they marry, they must form a new bond-friendship in every place they live, exchanging gifts and money, confidences and comforts. The bond-friendships of women are more formal and brittle than those of men, and require the exchange of gifts of money at each ceremonial, whether wedding, birth, or naming rituals. This leads the anthropologist M. G. Smith to the observation that "despite their marginal position in the cash sector of the economy, women provide the main outlay on kinship ceremonies and consequently control them."

With circumcision for males and strict adherence to chastity for females, the Hausa make the transition from child to adult a time of anxiety. In contrast, the !Kung hunter-gatherers of the Kalahari desert do not inflict genital mutilation or psychic trauma on their children as they move from carefree childhood to adulthood. They do not force any particular mode of conduct on their offspring, but simply tell them what they consider desirable behavior. The growing child develops control from within, in harmony with the knowledge that life in the bush is precarious, and provocative behavior is destructive not only to self but to the entire group.

As children grow up they play games imitative of adult activities, including sexual play. Both boys and girls stop sleeping by the family fire by the age of twelve. Boys and girls alike usually build their own fires in the camp, but girls may spend their nights with a grandmother or a widow. As the size of a camp is very small, consisting in some instances of as few as eight families, both boys and girls remain in close proximity to their parents.

The first ceremony for boys, called *choma,* is similar in some aspects to the initiation ceremonies of an adjacent Bantu-speaking people. The men and boys go to a place well out of earshot of the camp and dance for several days and nights. When the dancing is over, each boy has a vertical line incised in the middle of his forehead, and has his hair cut in a special *choma* way. Participation in this ceremony is purely voluntary, and no social pressure is placed on a boy to engage in it.

The next marker in the growth of a boy from childhood to adulthood is essential—he cannot take a wife until he has successfully killed a large animal such as a great antelope, a giraffe, or a buffalo. From the age of about twelve, a boy begins to prepare for this crucial feat by accompanying his father on hunts. As he gets older, he spends many of his evenings around the campfire listening to stories of the chase told by older men. He has spent years practicing on smaller animals with a bow and unpoisoned arrow, and has sharpened his ability to track animals by following their spoor. The nomadic !Kung man's principal occupation is hunting, and he spends years in preparation, learning from his elders, before his first big kill.

The Rite of the First Kill takes place twice in the life of each man: when he kills his first big male animal and when he kills his first big female animal. Vertical cuts are made in his chest, back, and arms, and a charred medicinal herb mixed with the fat of the animal he killed is rubbed into the cuts, producing permanent welts. Here is the way a !Kung explained scarification: "I cut his chest and put in medicine to lift up his heart and make him *want* to seek meat; I put (it) in his arm and wrist to make his arm soft *(swa)* and his aim correct; in his back to make sure that the game won't run away; in his brow so that he may see things quickly."

The occasion is also marked by the gift of a spear to the hunter by the person for whom he is named. Most boys make the necessary kills between the ages of fifteen and eighteen, and are then eligible to marry. Some men do not achieve these kills until later in life, and some may never qualify at all, but that is indeed rare.

In the strict physical sense !Kung girls mature later than most American girls. Their breasts begin to develop when they are thirteen and the onset of menarche is not usually until the age of fifteen or later, by which time they have likely been married and divorced more than once.

When a girl menstruates for the first time, she is carried by an old woman to an isolated, specially built shelter. The old woman stays with her, for there is a taboo on her feet touching the ground when she urinates or defecates, and she is carried on the woman's back and held when such functions are performed. The girl's head must also be covered at all times. This is done lest she encounter a man, for she must not gaze at men at this time or be seen by them. There is also a major belief among the !Kung that the sun represents death and should not shine upon her head when she is in this vulnerable condition. (There is a similar belief associated with marriage ritual.) !Kung concept of menstruation is not unlike that of the Tlingit, half a world away. They both fear menstrual blood as a source of pollution. The presence of this belief among the !Kung should dispel the overly simplistic idea frequently heard nowadays in our own society that equates a belief in menstrual pollution with the low status of women. As we have attempted to show, among the !Kung, female status is virtually on a par with that of their male counterparts.

While a girl is still sequestered in the special menstruation shelter, women and old men dance and sing the First Menstruation music. The Eland Dance, deriving its name from the twigs the male participants attach to their heads to suggest the horns of the animal, is fraught with sexual symbolism. Only the women who are present and two old men who have a joking relationship with the menstruating girl can participate in it.*

When the menstrual flow has stopped, a design is painted on the girl's face with red powder. She is washed and rubbed with fat and *tsi* nut oil. At this point, the girl may leave her shelter and resume her former activities, with one exception: the first time she drinks water or eats plant foods, the final part of the First Menstruation ceremony must take place. An older woman (it can be her mother) scrapes a root called *sha sha* into the water hole, then, taking the girl's hands, she chews *sha sha,* and, together, they cook plant foods in the fire. The older woman blows on the girl's hands and on the food she is about to consume before she can eat it. This is believed to prevent the girl's having an upset stomach.

Once the ceremonial is completed, the young woman need not ever again go into isolation when she menstruates, but there are still certain taboos she must observe during each period. She may not touch any implement that has to do with hunting, for to do

---

*Joking relationship—any social relationship, usually one between persons of different sex who are related by kinship, which emphasizes casual behavior. The most interesting joking relationships provide for extensive sexual interaction, sometimes including intercourse, but often merely suggesting it or permitting the parties to talk about sexual relations. The opposite of a joking relationship is avoidance. In avoidance, persons related in certain kinship ways must never come into face to face interaction and certainly are never to be alone together. Conversation between them is frowned upon, and they refer to each other rarely and only indirectly.

so would rob the hunter of his efficacy. She must abstain from sex with her husband, lest it render him lazy and rob him of the desire to go hunting.

Contrasted with the rough equality of the sexes among the !Kung, by the time a Chinese girl has reached puberty, she has accepted her inferior status, although in some cases with expressed bitterness. Until fairly recently, the stigma of this lowly status was shown by the infamous bound feet, "lotus feet," that were known in China from before the turn of the twelfth century. Almost certainly originating at the highest level of society, perhaps in the imperial court, the custom was widespread, although not universal. The Hakka, for instance, a linguistically distinct Chinese population, never accepted the custom; their women were known to other Chinese as strong and independent, undertaking work and occupations unknown to women elsewhere in China. Numerically, the Hakka are the second largest part of the Chinese population of Taiwan, where, through the years, they have displayed the same deviant approach to women's status. In any event, footbinding is completely gone now, and has been for decades, although one still sees some elderly ladies, and even an occasional woman of late middle age, hobbling around on "golden lotuses," or showing the still-visible signs of feet that were originally bound but released from their bandages before being permanently maimed.

Women in Taiwan continue to occupy secondary status, although for a time there seemed to be a change brewing. However, according to one study, the efforts of the generation now well into middle age have largely been repudiated by its daughters. This is not unlike the process of the woman's changing status in the People's Republic of China, where assertions of a higher female status level are somewhat exaggerated.

The picture is not simple. Though traces of earlier patterns remain in Taiwan (for example, in the role that prostitution plays in providing economic opportunities for women), the remarkable alteration of the economy of Taiwan has had a profound effect on the status of women. From imperial times through the Japanese colonial period and into the years following "retrocession"—the return of sovereignty over Taiwan to the Nationalist government of China—there were few career opportunities for women, most of whom were confined to domestic work and to specific farm chores, such as weeding, helping with the harvest, and feeding the pigs. School teaching, which Americans have long regarded as a field open to women and dominated by them in the lower grades, was almost entirely given over to men in pre-World-War-II Taiwan. Even the role of shop girl was limited mainly to the small family store.

In the past quarter century, things have changed almost beyond recognition. From an almost wholly rural operation Taiwan has switched to industry, and women comprise a significant part of its labor force. At the beginning of the 1970s, the number of women workers in Taiwan was estimated at about half a million (the total population of the island was about 15 million), and within that population of employed females some twenty percent were between the ages of fifteen and nineteen and another seventeen percent between twenty and twenty-four.

Though it may seem paradoxical, more young women appear to be ambivalent about work than do their parents. The parents, of course, are happy for the extra income, for daughters send home a goodly portion of their wages. Parents worry, however, about their daughters' living away from home, particularly those from fifteen to twenty, and, where possible, they insist that the girls get jobs close by. Given the distribution of industrial plants in Taiwan, this is sometimes impossible, although, in the seventies, there has been some decentralization of industry. But there has also been an economic recession in Taiwan during this period, so one effect has cancelled the other. Homesickness is rampant among fresh, young factory workers, and some leave their employment only a few weeks after they start.

Lydia Kung, an anthropologist who made a study among young factory women in Taiwan in 1974-75, takes issue with the stereotype that the status of women in Taiwan has improved in proportion to their involvement in outside occupations. She readily admits improvement in certain areas, and some of great significance, such as in greater freedom to choose their husbands, and more responsibility in buying their own clothing and occupying their leisure time. Indeed, older women usually point to such gains among young women; on the other hand, "it is remarkable that older women are unable to furnish concrete instances of how daughters now exert greater authority or decision-making rights at home."

Still, that a change has occurred is manifest in the shift of attitude regarding female children. Where earlier generations found them burdensome, at best, girls are now welcomed at birth. As one older woman told Lydia Kung, "Nowadays girls are just as, if not even more useful than boys. My two daughters do good work in the factory while my son who has some education stays idle at home." Furthermore, the greater economic value of young women does not alter the fact that they will ultimately marry, leaving their brothers to observe the rituals of ancestor worship, and removing whatever earning power they had previously used to contribute to their parents' budget. Consequently, parents display increasing hostility to a daughter's early marriage.

Girls themselves see early factory work, work they do between the ages of fifteen and eighteen, as a bitter and oppressive burden. The little glamor factory work has for the country girl is soon dissipated. Even girls who have done poorly in school bemoan the obstacle to their continuing educational opportunities, and an unusual proportion of factory girls enroll in night classes. Not that education itself is an open sesame to better jobs, but it is perceived as leading to higher social status and to more desirable marital opportunities. While they are working in factories, the girls who live close enough go home at the end of each shift. Others may be able to go home every weekend, but many can do so only a few times a year, and they live in dormitories, their lives monotonous and confined, as described in an acid short story by Yang Ching-kun, one of Taiwan's most popular young writers. The story relates the tightly asexual routine of the dormitory. Even when a party or a dance is provided out of welfare funds extracted from the girls, it is usually a lonely occasion or one that provides an opportunity only for sexual hunting to men in middle management.

Not all young women enter the labor force. Quite a few, mainly of more affluent background, continue in school beyond the legal nine-year minimum. Since 1969, Taiwan has required its children to attend six years of elementary school and three additional years of junior middle school. Despite the law, some children, usually girls, certainly do not finish junior middle school even if they attend it at all. For one thing, there are fees, even in the public institutions. On the other hand, employers may pay the fees, and very large factories often maintain their own night schools, so working girls can manage to graduate from junior middle school, or even progress further. The regimen is considered a very bitter one, and young women speak critically about it. The Chinese term for "adolescence" is *ch'ing-ch'un*, "green spring," or "the spring of youth." It is supposed to be carefree, the happiest time of a girl's life, yet it contrasts miserably with the reality of boring work and little play.

Actually, Chinese childhood is dull by American standards, even for boys. The children dread school as they rarely do in the United States. Until recently, people in Taiwan scarcely questioned the relationship between degree of education and social and economic achievement. Only during the past few years, when the number of graduates at each educational level showed a marked rise, and the level of the international economy a sharp drop, has the number of university graduates who occupy jobs alarmingly inferior to the quality of their educations risen significantly.

This has increased the pressure of a child's school years, beginning with kindergarten. Parents seek out nursery schools that offer not merely play situations but a record of success in teaching four- and five-year-old children to read and write. The pressure continues in elementary school, as students jockey for position on the way to middle school. Although passing an entrance examination is no longer required now that junior middle school attendance is mandatory, there are different degrees of excellence among such schools, and a good record, as well as a good grade on a required examination, may be necessary before a student can enter an elite school. The pressure mounts as entrance to senior middle school approaches, and it reaches a frenzied peak in the nationally administered college entrance examinations.

In old China, a child's entrance into primary school was a very special event in his life. Girls were seldom involved, for even if they came from wealthy families they would only be given private tutoring. One of China's most popular romances is the story of Liang Shan-po and Chu Ying-t'ai, tragic young lovers of many centuries past, who meet at school. Since it was impossible at that time for a girl to attend such a school, Ying-t'ai, a young woman from a wealthy and powerful family, convinces her father by a ruse that she can survive school by dressing in boy's clothing and keeping her sex a secret. Ultimately her secret is discovered, but by that time, she and a poor male student, Liang Shan-po, have fallen deeply in love. The story climaxes in the boy's tormented death and that of the girl who loves him, who, rather than accept marriage to a man she hates, leaps into Liang's tomb. Their souls, represented by butterflies, flutter heavenward. The most popular movie ever shown in Taiwan was a musical, made in Hong Kong, based on this story. One old woman is said to have seen it more than a thousand times and college professors admitted to half a dozen viewings. The story is revealing of China. It shows not only the contrast in education between older imperial times and now, but also reflects a major theme in Chinese culture—the high premium placed on platonic love, a simultaneous flirtation with heavily implicit sexual themes, and the ultimate triumph of chastity. Although China long had a tradition of pornographic literature and art, such materials were under absolute ban, or were disseminated only under tight restriction. Modern writers, like the above-mentioned Yang, have shocked Taiwan in the 1970s with their treatment of sex, especially the dawning sexuality of adolescents.

The Chinese culture is so vast, and includes so many local and temporal variations, that it is difficult to generalize about it, especially on the level of regularities of individual personality. To some extent, the problem of generalization applies even to Taiwan; an outsider, invited to observe a conference of specialists on Taiwanese society, remarked that when participants who had worked in northern Taiwan got together with those who had done their research in the south, they "often registered surprise at what they learned." With the implications of these remarks as caveat, we offer three generalizations about Chinese childhood and adolescence. First, that the struggle of a woman for security in her marital home is often played out in a contest for the affections of her son. Second, that childhood and adolescence—and indeed, adulthood—are strongly marked by the rigors of schooling. Third, a concomitant of these conditions is a marked repression of sexual drive until an age that most Americans regard as remarkable.

Although exceptions are not uncommon, Chinese children are treated quite indulgently, at least, for several years. We remember, for example, a long train ride from Taipei to Tainan some years ago. A young couple with a pudgy little boy of about five were riding next to us in the crowded car. At first, the little boy was content to alternate between sitting on his mother's or father's lap and standing in the aisle. After a while, however, he began to make a scene, demanding that his father stand and permit him, the child, to sit undisturbed next to his mother. The father very meekly gave up his seat and stood the rest of the way, a matter of several hours. This little domestic scene seemed to be noted only by us. The other Chinese in the car took it as normal treatment of a child less than six years old. What happens after age six is a sharp break. Suddenly the warm lap of the father is replaced by his cold eye and sometimes hard hand. It is widely believed in China that children cannot be taught reason in the context of warm relationships. Fathers become cool and distant, providing mothers with an opportunity to monopolize the affections of their sons. In an interview many years ago, Edgar Snow got Mao Tse-tung to talk about his childhood. Mao likened his father to a harsh, ungiving, reactionary "Ruling Power." His mother and he, sometimes joined by their hired hand, constituted the "Opposition." "My mother," said Mao, "advocated a policy of indirect attack."

T'ang Mei-chun, former chairman of the Department of Anthropology at National Taiwan University, has noted that the position of the father is strongly buttressed by the law. Filial piety is not merely supported by religious belief and ritual. The police authority of the state is also involved. Margery Wolf, another close observer of the Taiwanese family and a particularly sharp commentator on relations within these families, has characterized the conflict and contradictions distinguishing paternal and maternal roles within commonly encountered arrangements. She points out that fathers in Taiwan want respect, which is demonstrated by obedience. Love and affection will be sacrificed to achieve this. The opposite stance is the mother's: she places love first, however much she also wishes to have her son's respect. As seen by Wolf, the mother's attitude is closely related to her dependent position in the patrilocal household that she joined after marriage, and in which she remains something of an outsider.

The sudden turnabout in a father's relations with his son at about age six cannot be related solely to the structure of Chinese education, because it existed in the past among classes that had only a most irregular access to schools. Still, there is an association between strict discipline and learning; a feeling that a reasoning individual is the product of careful control. In any event, the typical Chinese school, whether in Taiwan or the People's Republic, provides a picture of obedient behavior that exceeds anything described in America since the middle of the nineteenth century. Added to the rigor of classroom discipline is the terror instilled in students of failing the examinations for entrance into senior middle school and university. Particularly at grade levels immediately juxtaposed with entrance exams, there are the cram classes in *puhsipan,* "supplementary schools." With regular school, plus homework and supplementary classes, a Taiwanese schoolchild may work at lessons twelve hours a day.

The study regime is hard, and failure at the examinations is a cause of suicide among the young. On the other hand, success is very sweet, and each graduation and each entrance examination passed is a major accomplishment. The names of the successful candidates appear in special sections of the newspapers. In Taiwan, for days in advance, the same newspapers carry extensive advertisements for gifts proper to the occasion: watches, cameras, transistor radios, sporting goods, and gift certificates. Diplomas are put up in the same room as the ancestor tablets and the shrine of the tutelary god, if the family has one.

Although elementary school and college are coeducational, some of the best junior and senior middle schools are segregated by sex. In any case, nonacademic activities show strong sexual separation, usually well into college. Friendships tend to form between people and groups of the same sex, a pattern that will extend into adulthood. Women with male friends and men with women friends are rare, although instances are more common now than in the past. Dating in Taiwan and in the United States nevertheless have certain similarities. In Taiwan, it is common for girls and boys to pair off with little change through the years, culminating in marriage. But there are differences. Surprisingly, the young Chinese may be less supervised in such relationships than their American counterparts and less harassed about them. This may be attributable to the much sharper differentiation of teenage and adult worlds in Chinese society, and the consequent lack of communication between them. Couples manage not only to date but to engage in sexual relations. Although reliable statistics are not available, it is our impression that in a significant number of marriages the bride is already pregnant.

Despite the stereotype of the Chinese adolescent as conforming and socially responsible, there are at least two major forms of delinquency. One applies primarily to youths of more affluent background and higher class status. These are the so-called *t'aipao,* boys and girls from perhaps fifteen to eighteen years of age, often in senior middle school (although sometimes they are academic dropouts), who join peer gangs and make trouble. Quite a few of them do not become involved in criminal activities, but attract attention and reprobation for behavior based on a perception of American or other foreign youth culture as portrayed in films or television. The pattern has therefore gone through vicissitudes from beat through hippie to whatever is now current. At times, ducktail haircuts, leather jackets, and tight pants, or short skirts, have been the identifying symbols. About twenty years ago, *West Side Story* was banned from Taiwan's movie screens for fear it would inspire a rash of Taiwanese youth gang wars. Such censorship continues to this day. Even without such models, the activities of the *t'aipao,* sometimes reported in the newspapers, especially in the bountiful scandal sheets, continue to titillate a large audience. Boys and girls of affluent background are picked up for shoplifting, minor drug offenses, fighting, and other petty crimes. When long hair was in vogue, the police often took young men in merely for that, and gave them free haircuts before turning them loose again.

Other youthful offenders who are much more traditional are usually recruited from poor and working-class families. These are the *liumang,* the youthful lumpenproletariat who live by theft and extortion. Curiously, the youths who are *liumang* often are deeply involved in their communities, especially in the religious activities of the local temples. They provide the membership of drum and dragon societies, performing the lion and dragon dances at the New Year and other festivals. Among them may be found candidates for *tangki,* shamans and spirit mediums, who will walk through fire and help communicate with the gods.

Thus, the years between childhood and adulthood can be troubled in Taiwan (there is a Taipei "hotline" number that can be called by teenagers who feel that they are in difficulty and need help), but even so, differences are vast between their situation and that in the United States. The amount of violence encountered in the roughest urban areas of Taiwan provides not even a shadow of our own.

It is not so with the Tlingit. Unfortunately, the turbulence of adolescence so familiar in the United States has become a well-known part of life in modern Yakutat. Before we examine the present, however, let us look briefly at the way things were for the Tlingit about a hundred years ago.

In the previous chapter we described the magical acts performed to assure that a male infant grew up to be a brave and successful hunter. The process of hardening boys to enable them to cope with the harshness of the climate and the difficulty of obtaining food and waging warfare started around the age of six. It was the task of the mother's brother to toughen his nephews by forcing them to bathe naked in icy waters while he flogged their wet bodies with branches. It was believed that this practice not only made the boys into strong men, but kept them from getting sick, purified them in the spiritual sense, and endowed them with a virtue that would reward them with a rich adult life.

Boys were taken on their first hunting expedition and their first fishing trip by their maternal uncles, who instructed them in the art of tracking and capturing game, handling a canoe, making camp in the wilderness, and preparing food on the trail. When a boy bagged his first animal, the family celebrated his prowess as a hunter. His catch was consumed with great pleasure, but he could eat none of his first kill lest the dead animal's head bite him in the face.

Boys learned that fasting was part of the spiritual preparation for hunting. Food and drink made a man weak. The first meal of the day could be eaten only after the hunt. For this reason, a hunting expedition always started early in the dawn. Another belief, that sexual intercourse also deprived a man of his strength as a hunter, dictated abstinence from sex for some time before he went on a hunting party. Hunters were convinced that animals understood what people said, and they never named the specific time of a proposed expedition. If they spoke of their plans, the animals would go into hiding and leave the hunters to return empty-handed. After a hunt a prayer was offered to the spirit of the animal killed to avert its wrath. When a boy became skilled at hunting and fishing, he was considered to be a man and ready to marry.

Until the latter part of the nineteenth century, the Tlingit isolated a girl at her menarche either in the back part of the house or in a hut built for the purpose. It is said that this isolation could last at least a year, the girl being kept in darkness and supervised by her father's sister or her own mother or grandmother. The onset of menarche required a fast that lasted eight days. After the first four days the girl was allowed a small snack and a sip of water. Her self-control was tested after two days by offering her water, which was quickly spilled if she reached out to accept it. The Tlingit believed that drinking the water after only two days of isolation would wash away all her good luck. During the first eight days, her fingers were tied with string so that money would not run through them easily in her adult life. The habit of frugality was an important part of a girl's training. During the first eight days of fasting, no knife could be placed in her hands, as that would cut her life short. After eight days her hair was washed with blueberry juice, a ceremony accompanied by wishes for good luck, a good husband, and permanently black hair. (Another indication that our search for perpetual youth is not unique.) When the menstruating girl broke her fast, the family celebrated by sharing the preserved foods in the house with relatives, friends, and neighbors.

While still in isolation, the girl's grandmother would choose a hard round stone from the beach and would rub it on the girl's mouth eight times, thereby keeping her from becoming a gossip. After this ceremony the stone was buried, in the belief that it would bring the girl good luck.

While in seclusion the girl was kept busy sewing, plucking the feathers of swans, and learning the art of basket weaving. When taking nourishment, all fresh foods were taboo; she could eat only dried foods.

Pubescent girls had their own dishes, which were kept carefully separate from those of the rest of the household. Indeed, as they approached the age of twelve, their mothers began to feed them last, for fear they might have started bleeding and thereby polluting all the food and vessels in the house.

After a girl was released from seclusion, her clothes were burned because they were considered contaminated. The ashes were placed in an old tree stump to assure her a long life. She was given new clothes and jewelry by her mother, and she was tattooed. A hole was cut in her lower lip and a stone ornament, a labret, was inserted to enhance her beauty. Her head was covered by a hood that was kept in place until she was married. She was constantly under her mother's surveillance before marriage, and frequently a marriage was arranged while she was still in seclusion. The bride price was collected by her parents, and the marriage took place shortly after she emerged.

Girls received no specific information about sex but were constantly warned away from men. Illegitimacy in those days is said to have been a terrible disgrace to the family. If a girl did get pregnant, she tried to abort herself. If her efforts failed, she killed her baby as soon as it was born; it is recorded that otherwise her brothers would have killed her and her baby as well.

When Martha visited Yakutat in 1978, she found that the old customs had completely vanished. To begin with, a young girl who finds herself pregnant need have no fear about her own or the baby's welfare. The child is incorporated into the mother's family and taken care of with great affection. No stigma is attached to illegitimacy. We may go on with changes: boys are no longer exposed to hardening regimens and girls are not isolated in menstrual avoidance.

Although families are close and kinship ties strong, the Yakutat Tlingit are now plagued by many of the same difficulties faced elsewhere in the United States. Adolescent problems involve alcoholism, drug addiction, violent crime, and vandalism.

Two instances of vandalism and abuse of the old occurred at about the time of Martha's visit. The community Health Provider, a non-native person who is paid by the government, rented a car from a rich white man whom the Tlingit were constantly subjecting to harassment. Two weeks later, a group of teenagers took the car for a joyride and left it, upside down and totally destroyed, next to the town café. The incident was immediately reported to the Alaska State Police in Yakutat. The state troopers did not apprehend the suspects, although many people in Yakutat knew who they were. The youngsters got off without so much as a slap on the hand.

The second incident, however, is more threatening in its implications for Tlingit society. A very old Tlingit woman was observed at the Health Center, painfully making her way with a walker from her room to the area where senior citizens congregated each day. The old lady had been severely beaten by her grandson and grandnephew, who came to her house to get all the money she had. They left her with a broken hip and extensive bruises. An expression of deep terror was still visible on her face. She said that she was afraid to return to her home where she would again be alone and unprotected.

Confronted by a recitation of teenage delinquency, one Tlingit high-school student defended his peers, saying, "Everybody is down on teenagers. They criticize everything we do, but what kind of example are the adults setting for us? What is there for us to do? How can they expect us to be different from them?"

Indeed, most people in Yakutat seem to consider the acquisition of American material goods their main goal in life. The two books that can be found in every home in Yakutat are the Sears and J. C. Penney catalogs. A good deal of conversation revolves around who has what, how much it cost, how long it took to come up on the barge, and what the next item of purchase will be.

Some boys make it to college, many girls marry out to reside in other states, but Tlingit adolescence is fraught with uncertainty, anxiety, boredom, and depression, which lead some of them into undesirable and antisocial modes of behavior.

Apart from outdoor sports, hunting or fishing, there is little for teenagers to do in their free time. The town does not have a library or a recreation center that could offer a program of interesting activities. The isolation of Yakutat adds to the cabin fever of the young people, just as it affects the adults. As of 1978, the biggest and busiest place in Yakutat was a bar and cocktail lounge with pool tables and a jukebox, where adults not engaged in work spent a great deal of time. The single café in town also has a pool table, and many youngsters seeking each other's society congregate there for hamburgers and fries.

At least one major problem of the Tlingit can easily be traced in history. Commodore Jean Françoise de la Perouse, in charge of an expedition financed by Louis XVI, reached the Alaskan coast in 1786 and spent nearly the entire month of July at Lituya Bay. He engaged in brisk trade with the Tlingit and left detailed accounts of his experiences with them. In one part of his journal he struck an ominous note:

> "Their arts are well developed and their civilization has made great progress in this respect. . . . Their mode of life excludes all sense of order, and fear of or desire for revenge makes them constantly uneasy. . . . I will predict without fear, that these people will destroy themselves if . . . they should have the misfortune to learn the use of intoxicating liquor."

La Perouse's perception of disorder in Tlingit society was probably an ethnocentric reaction to modes of behavior and social organization remote from those of the Europe of his time, but he was shrewd in his discernment of tension and unease among the native population and farsighted in his prediction about the effects of alcohol, which was introduced to the Alaskan native population by Europeans subsequent to his visit.

By 1843, both the Russian and American governments outlawed the sale of liquor to Indians, who then acquired it from smugglers. It became the most valuable item of trade. The first Alaskan Indians to learn the process of distillation obtained it from American soldiers stationed in the region. The use of liquor and the knowledge of distillation spread from Sitka to Yakutat by 1877, and accounts of the great amounts consumed at potlatches have been recorded. In 1879 Aurel Krause found a still in almost every house in Klukwan, another village of the Tlingit not far from Yakutat.

Alcoholism is a major health problem in the United States, where it afflicts a cross section of the population, none more seriously than Native Americans. What made its effect particularly devastating within this population? Ever since hard liquor was introduced to them, the belief has spread among whites and been accepted by many Indians that Indians are incapable of tolerating alcohol, thus being considered biological alcoholics. Many people still cling to this belief, not a few Tlingit among them. But rates of alcoholism among Native Americans overlap with those of the non-Indian populations living around them. According to Carol Molinari, Director of the Center for Alcohol and Addiction Studies at the University of Alaska, "alcoholism is Alaska's primary health and social problem." She further states that the problem has increased with the work force brought in to build the trans-Alaska pipeline. By 1976 about eighteen thousand people were engaged in the construction work. "The climate, the endless winter darkness, and overcrowded living conditions in each housing area all contribute to a high level of drinking among pipeline workers."

Ever since the arrival of new settlers from the mainland, alcoholism has been a problem among traders, soldiers, construction workers, and canning industry employees, for much the same reasons Molinari describes above. The Indians have had a double burden to bear—all the troubles already mentioned, plus a special set of their own. Any of these problems could lead them to seek solace in readily available booze: depopulation, the destruction of their culture, demoralization because of the paternalistic treatment accorded them, and the usual mountain of broken promises.

By 1933 the Alaskan Indians were "in a deplorable state of economic poverty and social disintegration," according to George W. Rogers, a historian of that vast territory. Although it could be said that they had arrived at that unhappy state decades earlier, few would disagree that the complex of causes included the infamous General Allotment Act of 1887. Ironically, the act was the product of liberal reformers who desired to benefit the Indians of the United States. At its core, the legislation enabled individual Indians to acquire title to portions of what had previously been common property. From that step followed others that quickly led to loss of title and the separation of Indians from some of their choicest lands and resources. With these losses went others, tearing apart the remnants of the social and economic fabric of Indian communities. Rogers sums it up: "Finally, destruction of the aboriginal means of self government and self expression only meant that government officials took over the direction of the Indians' lives."

The Yakutat Tlingit do not conceal their hostility toward

whites, and they blame them for every ill they suffer. Their reasons are good. European contact brought a scourge of new diseases that killed Indians by the thousands. The Indian population of the neighboring province of British Columbia, where relatives of the Tlingit lived, was reduced by half by the end of the nineteenth century. Because of this drastic depopulation much of the aboriginal economy was destroyed. While the extractive industries of mining and lumbering were introduced, so too was unemployment, which emptied household purses and sapped personal integrity and self-esteem.

The onslaught on the Tlingit way of life was made on many fronts. Missionaries and, later, government teachers separated children from their parents in the name of education. Children were forbidden to speak Tlingit and were punished if they were overheard doing so. Corporal punishment was used for minor infractions as it still is today in Yakutat. As recently as 1978, several children said that female teachers punished them by making them stand silently in a corner, but they reported that male teachers whipped them with their belts.

Alcoholism is the greatest health problem in Yakutat, according to the staffs of the Yakutat Community Health Center and the Yakutat Alcoholism Program that provides information on alcohol abuse and referrals to state institutions outside Yakutat. Despite its prevalence, great stigma is attached to alcoholism. So heavy is the feeling of shame that in 1978 many people who needed help refused to seek it because the sign on the building identified it as an alcoholic clinic. That summer, plans were made to correct this situation by replacing the sign with one that said only "Yakutat Recreation Center."

There appears to us to be a close connection between the painful nature of transition from childhood to adulthood in Yakutat and alcoholism. Alcoholism is a disabling illness that permeates the community and leads adults to acts of violence that are witnessed by growing children. Several surveys and studies show that young people at high risk to alcohol addiction come with a family history of heavy drinking, and in some instances, alcoholism itself. Drunkenness exacerbates the Tlingits' sense of injury, understandable in the light of our knowledge of past acts of paternalism, cruelty, and exploitation. Their sense of having been wronged persists, and a desire for retaliation continues to be a guiding principle governing their relations with whites. Young people can-not but be deeply affected by the boiling rage of their elders.

There are no longer any clear markers to separate childhood from adulthood, and few prescribed forms of behavior significant to the building of community solidarity remain. Individuals still display occasional behavior patterns rooted in the old culture—a particular style of fighting and bragging by men and a striving for excellence in the traditional skills of cooking and sewing by women—but, in general, the society lacks the cohesion it once had.

One old custom is still practiced in an attenuated form. Boys who reside with a divorced or widowed mother get training and companionship from her brothers. These uncles teach them how to fish and hunt and, during the summer vacation, the boys work on their uncles' boats. Girls, although no longer isolated between childhood and marriage, still have very few options. They are expected to marry, and are prepared for adulthood by learning the arts of housekeeping and needlework.

In the Yakutat of 1978, women had not yet been reached by harbingers of the women's movement further south. And these capable, strong women still equate femininity with second-class status, as do so many of their sisters on the mainland.

CHAPTER FOUR

Marriage

THE old people gather around the fire in the evening, smoke, and tell stories of olden times. They are gifted raconteurs and entertain each other by recollecting tales of the mischief of the gods, treachery and revenge, love and foolishness. They speak of a time long, long ago when animals were people. Toddlers run in and out of the circle of their elders and young people hang around the edges of the assemblage, hoping to learn the old tales, sometimes summoning the courage to offer one story of their own. The !Kung prize verbal abilities, and storytelling is one of the chief forms of recreation.

Of the many stories recorded by Megan Biesele, one in particular incorporates many of the themes making up the warp and woof of the fabric of !Kung life.

A beautiful female python, "Married to the kori bustard is tricked by her younger sister the jackal into climbing a tree after $n{\neq}a$ fruits. The branch of the . . . tree hangs out over a well, and the python girl falls in. Gleefully, the jackal puts on the python's discarded clothing and ornaments and struts off to alienate the affections of the handsome kori bustard.

"Back in the village, the kori bustard comes home from hunting and misses his wife. The graceless jackal, trying to imitate the smooth, regal step of the python girl so as to fool her husband, comes bouncing and clanking before him.

"The kori bustard greets her as he is accustomed to greet his wife, by passing a wildebeest-tail whisk, dripping with fat, across her forehead. But the foolish jackal, unused to this courtesy exchanged between well-bred beings, becomes very excited: "Ooh! Fat is dripping! Fat is dripping!" She greedily licks the fat dripping onto her chops from her hairy forehead.

"Thus the kori bustard knows that he has been tricked, and he schemes to do away with the jackal. As he is arranging their sleeping place for the night, he sets up rows of poisoned arrowheads in the sand under the skins where she is to sleep. She lies down, is pricked by the arrowheads, and cries out in protest. But the kori bustard says to her, "This is the same place you've slept ever since we got married; why do you suddenly begin to complain?"

"So the jackal keeps quiet. By dawn she has died from the effects of the arrow poison. The kori bustard gets up and goes hunting, leaving her lying inside the house.

"When the sun is well up and the jackal has not emerged, the old grandmother begins to worry whether the kori bustard's wife is sick. She sends the youngest child to investigate. The child finds the jackal dead in bed, with a dried clump of $n{\neq}a$ seeds protruding from her anus.

" 'Grandmother!' calls the child, 'N${\neq}$a !ko-!ko !kau-!kau !kwi-!kwi zi tsi-zi tsi!' (a childish way of saying 'n${\neq}$a seeds have dried in older sister's asshole!')

" 'What? Did you say I should put a leather pubic apron on her?' calls the grandmother, who is a little hard of hearing.

" 'N${\neq}$a !ko-!ko !kau-!kau !kwi-!kwi zi tsi-zi tsi!' shouts the child a little bit louder.

" 'What? Did you say I should put a beaded pubic apron on her?'

"At last grandmother is forced to come see for herself. She sees the dried clumps of seeds stuck in the jackal's anus, and she breaks off a piece and eats it. Then she and her granddaughter roast and eat the body of the treacherous jackal.

"Meanwhile, the kori bustard goes to get his real wife out of the well. But the well beneath the $n{\neq}a$ tree is very deep, and the python is lying at the bottom. The kori bustard calls all the animals together to help him get her out. First the tortoise sticks in his leg to try to reach her, but it is far too short. Then the eland gives it a try, but his leg only goes halfway. All the other animals, the kudu, the gemsbok, all of them, try to reach her and fail. At last the giraffe is called. He puts his long leg in, down, down, down, all the way to the bottom.

" 'I can feel her . . . and I think she has given birth while she has been down there!' The giraffe slowly pulls up his leg with the python girl and all her children clinging to it.

"The kori bustard, overjoyed to see his wife again, has skin mats spread all the way from the well to the village. Then he walks proudly back to their house on the trail of mats with the rescued python girl. They sit happily on a skin there in the midst of their rejoicing relatives."

Although it can be identified as San in its details, this story falls within a great genre of African folklore, tales in which animals and humans interact as part of a single society. This particular story highlights some features of !Kung marital relations, their conscious and unconscious attitudes toward polygyny, including that form in which the co-wives are sisters. As we see here, that does not prevent them from being rivals, and the solution, atypically !Kung, is violent, but the denouement, typically !Kung, is happy, ending in maximum social solidarity. Along the way, we are fascinated by the transparent sexual symbolism—the well, the (too short) legs, the long leg that brings up the real wife and, to our surprise, a rich litter of newborn children. We can guess at the scatological humor of the dry $n \neq a$ fruit (representing perhaps the aborted children of the foolish and wicked jackal), but we cannot be sure of precise local meanings. Grandmother's concern with pubic aprons reminds us of the functions of the old woman attending the girl at menarche (see above, page 75), and the mention of the beaded pubic apron sets the stage for the triumphant return of the python girl with the fruits of her womb. It is this fertile aspect of the marriage of Python and Bustard that the whole community celebrates.

Myths aside, what are the realities of marriage in !Kung society? How does boy meet girl in the Kalahari desert? To begin with, we can properly speak of girls, because the age of women at first mating is often so young that they are not menstruating or ovulating. On the other hand, as we saw earlier, the male has to be an adult by !Kung standards, meaning that he has killed two large animals. He may be more than ten years older than his intended mate.

A newly eligible young man may ask his parents to arrange a marriage for him with a girl he fancies. It is not unusual, however, for a couple with a very young son to long anticipate the day he will be ready to enter into matrimony. When he is still a stripling, his parents may approach another couple who have recently had a girl baby, seeking a commitment for the marriage of that baby to their son when he has achieved adulthood. Indeed, such an arrangement can be made speculatively with the parents of a child yet unborn. If they have a girl, the boy's parents hope she will grow up to be a beautiful, well-mannered and sweet-tempered woman, careful about observing !Kung customs and particularly the taboos that surround menstruation, thereby insuring their son's happiness.

The girl's parents are equally solicitous of her future when it comes to the choice of a son-in-law. Greatest stress is placed upon demonstrated hunting ability, again confirming the importance of the hunting test for male adulthood. It is striking to note that this !Kung institution acts more importantly in behalf of the social group than in the service of individuals. In fact, the !Kung system of distributing food, big game in particular, is such that no dweller in a camp will go hungry if there is anything at all to eat. In the final analysis, what the !Kung "own" are not meat and other consumables but the right to their distribution.

There are few things that do not circulate automatically. For example, a man makes his own weapons, and though he may not be forced or embarrassed into doing so, he is generally encouraged to lend out every part of his kit. That he passes arrows of his own making to other hunters should recall that !Kung custom splits the right to first distribution of game between the maker of the first arrow to hit the animal and the hunter who shot it. On the other hand, hunters also have leather cloaks and pouches that are normally not placed in circulation. Similarly, the *kaross,* the sling in which women carry their babies, and the personal ornaments they make, mainly of ostrich shell, are not casually circulated. But even these possessions can be given as gifts. When they are, they are likely to remain with the recipient. They do not constitute wealth —certainly not in the sense of an accumulation of goods that can be exchanged for other things. Unless the !Kung become enmeshed in financial dealings outside their own culture, they do not know invidious economic distinctions, and are total strangers to economic exploitation.

Despite the ease and significance of meat distribution, there are reasons why parents want their daughters to marry skilled hunters. Apart from rights of meat distribution, the hunter whose poisoned arrow is the first to hit an animal receives its hide. This, in turn, is used to make the pubic coverings worn by men and women, as well as the woman's *kaross.* The parents also wish to be united with generous in-laws. Since the !Kung tradition emphasizes the sharing of goods, withholding those things that are expected to be given freely can be difficult. Yet there are differences of personality and behavior in even the smallest human societies. It is one thing to give warmly, cutting large portions and distributing them gracefully and with pleasure; it is quite another to provide minimal shares grudgingly and without style. The !Kung appreciate the former and despise the latter. They also hope, in making marriages, to bring together people who live in separate camping groups, thereby extending the range of relationships and providing wide networks of exchange that are extremely useful if drought or famine strikes an area. As explained by Henry Harpending, it is not unusual that a young !Kung male will travel a hundred miles to find a wife. In their nomadic lives, the bride and groom who are members of separate camping groups, have been traveling since birth. By the time they meet and marital arrangements are concluded, they will have come into some physical proximity.

After marriage the husband stays with his bride's camping group and hunts for them until his wife gives birth to their first child. As this is unlikely to take place for at least a year, he may not see his parents and the other members of his band for a long time. If food and water supplies continue to be good, he stays with his wife's family until two or three children of his have been born. Ultimately he and his wife detach themselves from the wife's camp and join another one as a nuclear family unit; this is usually not the one to which his own parents belong. The later pattern is defined as neolocality, residence in a new locality or with a new group. Independent dwelling frustrates the formation of extended kinship groups, such as clans or lineages and, indeed, no such groups are known to the !Kung.

Anthropologists discomfit their audiences by defining incest in relative terms: incest is not the act of mating or marrying a close relative, but the act of mating or marrying by relatives deemed too close for such intimacy *in a particular culture.* The difference is that in the latter view, incest is a culturally defined activity, not a biological one. There are certain pairings that seem to be universally avoided—the mating of mother and son being most widely condemned, and father with daughter the next. Even with respect to these relationships, however, all societies do not necessarily punish the violators, though people who break incest taboos are considered foolish, crazy, or wicked. Brother/sister matings are not universally avoided. What is more, in some societies the mating of a male with the daughter of his mother's brother is considered the most desirable marriage of all, while other societies consider it incestuous.

The !Kung take their incest taboos seriously. The idea of mating with or marrying a parent, a sibling, or one's own offspring is unthinkable. Anthropologist Lorna Marshall risked ridicule when she raised questions about incest. The !Kung she spoke to were indignant; some of their responses were: "Only dogs do that—not men." "It would be madness." "It would be dangerous, like going up to a lion."

Beyond the nuclear family, the !Kung taboo matings with aunts and uncles, nieces and nephews, and with the children of those considered as aunts and uncles—people we would call cousin. There is also an avoidance of mating with certain close relatives, such as parents-in-law, and with what we call steprelatives, such as stepmother, stepsister, and so on. Also taboo are relations with relatives of the mother's co-wife, if the father is a polygynist. According to Marshall's informants, a !Kung man prefers not to marry a woman whose name is the same as his mother's, but she reports that this rule is not infrequently breached, seemingly because the number of potential partners is not great and the number of favorite !Kung names is small. Although including cousin in the forbidden mating category, Marshall records two cases violating the rule. The men who gave her the information were not outraged by it—on the contrary, they suggested that marrying the daughter of a father's sister was not a bad thing and, in general, they displayed a most tolerant attitude.

Although the wedding ceremony is simple, it lasts two days. The mothers of the groom and the bride build a marriage hut for the new couple, and gather wood for their fire. The bride adorns herself with beads and, on her wedding day, she keeps her head covered, shielding it from the sun much as she did during menarche. When the sun has set, a fire is lit in front of the nuptial hut, kindled with brands from the fires of both bride's and groom's parents. As at menarche, the bride must not let her feet touch the ground, and she is carried by her female friends into the hut. The groom's friends escort him to the hut and they all sit outside around the fire. The boys and girls of the wedding party sing, play instruments, and dance. If food is available in the camp, they eat. This festivity is not attended by the parents of either bride or groom; they must remain in their own huts. The new husband and wife also remain aloof, the wife inside the hut, the groom outside among the merrymakers but not joining with them. Very late at night, when everyone has gone off to sleep, the husband joins his wife inside the hut, but the marriage is not consummated that first night. The next morning, when the sun is high, the female relatives of both bride and groom come to the nuptial hut and anoint the couple with oil and rub their bodies with red ocher.

A young husband is expected to be gentle with his wife and not force sexual relations on her. The absence of such relations is part of the ritual of the first night of marriage. It may continue for a relatively long period, not clearly specifiable, since there is so much individual variation. The girl for whom this is a first marriage is very young, perhaps only ten or twelve. If her new husband is rough with her, if he forces himself on her, she will immediately complain to her parents who are but a few yards away in the small encampment. They could break up the marriage, taking the girl back to their own hut. This would not only shame the man but would threaten his sex life even more than does the indefinite period he must wait for the bride, for there is a shortage of women in this society, and the husband who has lost his wife may have to wait years before obtaining another.

There are some implicit contradictions. The !Kung bride is not an inexperienced virgin, even at ten or twelve. Several !Kung women were extensively interviewed by Marjorie Shostak. Published fragments of biography of one of these women, about fifty years old, indicate the nature of children's sex play: "boys know how to do things with their genitals. They take little girls and push them down and have sex with them. Even if you are just playing, they do that." The same woman, who had turned down two suitors, described the beginning of her first marriage. Nothing happened on the wedding night, which follows the rule. How long her resistance continued is not stated. Shostak reproduces the woman's narrative: "We lived together and after a while [my husband] lay with me. Afterward, my insides hurt." How long "after a while" represents is not certain. But the sequel is also interesting. The narrator resented the pain of intercourse with an adult man and sought to avoid further episodes. Ultimately, her husband tired of this behavior and made clear his intentions. His young wife told him that if he attempted intercourse, she would submit, but with total passivity. The !Kung equate sexual relations and food; what she said was: "You are obviously looking for some 'food,' but I don't know if the 'food' I have is 'food' at all, because even if you have some, you won't be full." Her husband nevertheless had sex with her, and she ran away. Her older brother found her in the bush and, after telling her to grow up, he brought her back not to the husband's hut but to that of her parents. Her husband came and talked her into going back with him. She went, and the same scenario was replayed several times until she grew to love her husband and to enjoy having sex with him.

!Kung marriages are ended by death or divorce. !Kung society, until this decade, was relatively unencumbered with property; it has no problems concerning child custody; both spouses are primary producers of food, which is shared anyway, so that livelihood is never an individual problem. For all these reasons, divorce among the !Kung is a far simpler and less traumatic matter than for us. No stigma attaches to divorce and people are free to remarry immediately. Still, many !Kung marriages endure, particularly those entered into in more mature years, say, after age twenty. Divorce is a matter of permanent, socially recognized separation. It can be achieved by the wife's "running away" that one additional time when her family will no longer seek her out to urge her to return to her husband.

Actually, girls often marry two or three times before they settle down. The early marriages are usually sterile; by the time a young woman is ovulating and married to a compatible man, children start to come. Early marriages work well as an institution for the !Kung, unlike what we have seen of trial marriages in our own culture. By the time of maturity, women and men have been through several marriages and understand the give-and-take of married life.

If a woman's parents are still alive when her husband dies, she may return to their camp, but they probably are a great distance away, in a direction unknown to her. She may know of other relatives in the area and go to be with them until she remarries, if she is not too old. If there is no one she wants to join, she may remain in the camp where she lived with her husband. If her husband's brother is there, she will be something of his responsibility, although, as already noted, the !Kung system of food distribution and circulation of other objects means that she will not want unless everyone in the camp is wanting. Widowers, too, may seek out relatives, or stay where they are. If too old to hunt, they will be provided for within the means of the little community. Adults who have never married are rare in !Kung society. There is only one case in the literature—a man who never passed the essential test of the hunter. He is said to have had poor eyesight.

Plural marriage is allowed, although it rarely occurs. Men enjoy the prestige it confers but recognize its drawbacks. To satisfy one wife is difficult enough. What is more, although polygyny among the !Kung is frequently of the sororal type, in which one man marries two sisters, even they may quarrel. Regardless of their prior relationship or lack of it, co-wives address each other as sister and share the work of gathering food, fetching water, and taking care of their babies. They are expected to maintain a harmonious household. If they fail to do so, their neighbors ridicule them in speech and song.

Extramarital sex does not seem a problem among the !Kung. As we have seen, children play very realistically at intercourse from an early age. In the years of puberty and just beyond, men and women make marriages that may be quite brittle. Often childless, these marriages may easily shatter when one partner becomes sexually attracted to someone else. It is very easy to break off one marriage and enter another. On the other hand, there is virtually no privacy in the camp and not much more outside it. Individuals are observed in their comings and goings, if not directly, then by the marks and signs on the ground all !Kung read as we read print. They soon know if so-and-so has run into the bush with what's-his-name. As far as we know from the ethnography, such behavior is rare, and most marriages seem to be quite stable.

From !Kung to Tikopia is a journey not merely of thousands of miles, but from perhaps the simplest of subsistence regimes to one of considerably greater sophistication. There is a major difference in food production, a greater disparity between self-image and reality, between cultural ideals and the vulgar truths of daily existence. For example, according to Raymond Firth, Tikopians prize virginity in a girl at marriage. Yet, according to the ethnographic record, most Tikopian girls get married after they are pregnant. In any case, there is a double standard; unmarried males are expected to engage in sexual activity. If, as Tikopians told Firth, virgins are prized as brides and married women are taboo except to their husbands, where do these unmarried men obtain their lovers?

Enjoying extensive sexual freedom, unmarried Tikopian men regard marriage as confining. At one stroke, marriage ends or at least curtails pleasurable bachelor pursuits. For a woman, however, marriage is the entry to legitimate sexual intercourse, to gains in social status, and to certain freedoms and privileges, not the least of which is to be mistress in her own dwelling. In light of these differences in motivation, it is not surprising that Tikopian women in the past seem to have played a dangerous game with sex. The unmarried woman who became pregnant is described as having been in a desperate situation. If she failed to persuade her lover to marry her, she was likely to commit suicide by swimming out to sea beyond the point of return. This practice has apparently fallen off drastically since the Tikopians established the Russell Islands colony in 1956. With relatively easy access to other islands, the isolation of Tikopia and with it the hothouse social environment of the past has been broken. The suicide rate has dropped with the possibility of change of locale and greater contact with different people.

Paradoxically, while some women may have wasted themselves in vain efforts to attract a husband, many men obtained their brides not by conventional plighting of troth, but by abduction. *Takunga nofine,* "carrying off a wife," what anthropologists call marriage by capture, is also referred to as *tuku pouri,* "carrying off in the dark." The latter phrase is most appropriate, because it describes the secrecy that surrounds the event and its actual method.

Although Firth did not observe any marriages by capture, he is certain that they still occurred at the time of his first visit to the island; such marriages are said to have gone out of fashion only in 1956, owing in major part to the Christian church's condemnation of the practice. Until then, bride capture was caused by diverse situations. Sometimes a man became enamored of a woman and could not directly obtain her assent. He would then set out to abduct her. On other occasions, a man's family would wish him to settle down with a woman of industrious habits and agreeable manners; they would also be interested in making an alliance with another house of appropriate status. These goals could be accomplished by capturing a bride for their son. In such a case the surprise, at least in theory, would be as great for the groom as for the bride.

We speak about theory because it is not clear in the ethnographic material whether marriage by capture was in fact secret and conspiratorial or whether it was some kind of elaborate social charade in which the principals played their parts, never so well as when they seemed truly outraged and resistant.

The plot might begin when the young man learned of his parents' intention. This could trigger a mammoth tantrum, in which the youth would stomp and bang about the house, even beating on the roof. Much of this behavior had to be in pantomime; the young man could not utter his father's name except by breaking taboo, nor could he by rules of proper behavior openly discuss matters of an intimate nature within the bosom of the family. It was precisely to avoid such dreadful scenes that parents might conspire without a son's knowledge to obtain his bride by capture.

Abduction of a woman required the help of brothers and other male relatives on the father's side, and was practiced mostly by chiefly families, because they had the resources to endure the struggle that inevitably resulted. The men met in secrecy to plan the capture. It was considered proper to abduct the woman only from her father's house; it was a severe breach of etiquette to attempt to capture her while she was working in the field or walking on a path. The resentment of the woman's kin in such a case was so severe that the subsequent struggle might end in serious injury or even the death of members of the capturing party.

When the abductors entered the woman's house in the dead of night, they and her kin struggled for her. Men of her household held onto her physically, and she was yanked back and forth between the two groups. It was proper for some members of the ravishing party to divert the girl's relatives by inviting physical assault while the other members of their party took her to the groom's house. This was but the first step in a long series of acts of atonement and payment to follow.

No ethnographer ever participated in or observed a Tikopian marriage-by-capture. What we have are accounts by people who may not have participated themselves but who heard of the proceedings from others. Firth is of the opinion that much of the violent behavior associated with such marriages was of a ritual nature, yet he believes that the capture party arrived to the complete surprise of the bride's family. That is possible, of course, and to challenge an ethnographer of Firth's deep personal knowledge of the area is rash. Still, one cannot help but be skeptical. The island, after all, has a self-contained population, quite small (only twelve hundred when Firth was there in 1928, and still under two thousand when he returned in 1956), in an equally tiny area, about six square miles. The hatching of a conspiracy is not surprising, but to keep it secret under those conditions would be a considerable feat, unless, of course, a cultural fiction of secrecy, in which certain information spreads but is unacknowledged, is involved. It is also possible that not the intended capture but only its timing was the actual secret. The ritual response to the abducting party could be understood in this light, and bolstering the interpretation are the social and psychological aspects of marriage by capture. Usually it involved the taking of a girl of lower status by a chiefly family. On one hand, this was definitely a social step upward for the family of the abducted bride. On the other, to submit too easily might appear collusive, hence social climbing. The ritual struggle is a face-saving device and also an opportunity for the wife-getters of high status to abase themselves before the lower-status wife-givers—in the dark! In any event, to appear eager or even complacent about the marriage of a daughter was considered shameful.

However necessary it was for parents to attempt to keep plans of abduction of a bride from a recalcitrant son, it was advisable for a man to inform his parents if he intended to do the same thing. By informing them he could more easily win their acceptance and cooperation. Although the new couple usually built a house of their own, the groom had to bring his bride to his parents' house first. Once they received her, rubbed her head and breasts with turmeric, and placed a piece of orange bark cloth around her waist, she became his wife.

The morning after the bride was captured a presentation, *te malai,* which is the customary gift of atonement to an offended chief, was taken to the bride's house and presented to her father. This gift was usually a wooden bowl and a coil of sinnet cord to which a bonito hook might be added. On some occasions, a paddle was also given. The gift bearers expected an unpleasant reception. Usually a gauntlet was formed by the bride's relatives, with the father of the bride at the end. The groom's representatives would attempt to traverse the distance to the father-in-law while the two files of the bride's kinsmen rained blows on them, pulled their hair, and screamed insults at them. If they succeeded in reaching the father-in-law, he might extend his protection to them and call off their beatings and humiliations. On one occasion related to Firth, that did not happen. Instead, the leader of the groom's representatives managed to crawl to a senior relative of the bride, pressed his nose to the man's knee, and said, "I eat ten times your excrement . . . ," only to have his arm broken by a blow from a club. His attacker, however, was forced to suffer a similar injury in return.

On the same morning, after the atoning gift had been delivered, the "oven of joining" was prepared by the groom's family. This was the first celebration of the marriage and its formal announcement. Food made in that oven was consumed by the members of the household. The oven is called *umu fakapariki,* "the oven of the woman who will be embraced in the night," or "the oven of the husband who is going to his wife."

Firth was told by a male informant that if a bride was snatched from her family without previous knowledge on her part she was usually unwilling to receive her husband. When he approached her, she turned her back to him and faced the wall. His brothers stayed to keep her from running away. When night fell and the house was quiet they held her down, forced her on her back, grasped her legs and pulled them apart. If she screamed, one of his brothers put his hand over her mouth. They loosened her belt and skirt and the groom had intercourse with her. He was the only one to have relations with her, and the Tikopians would have considered it abhorrent for any other member of the party to do so. The informant said that the brothers were present merely to assist the groom, and also pointed out that the bride was not ashamed the next day, as the only witnesses were her husband's band of brothers. This lack of shame in a shame-filled culture may be viewed in a somewhat different light. Unless she was obviously pregnant or known to have been her husband's mistress, she was in an excellent position to use this display of resistance in front of his brothers as proof of her virginity. Another custom tends to support this contention. The morning after the marriage was consummated the wife of the groom's mother's brother took the bride's skirt and washed the blood stains out of it in the sea, then hung it up on a beam of the house for all to see. A woman who had not been touched by another man was considered a treasure by her husband, and he took great satisfaction in advertising his good fortune.

Occasionally, at the time of the oven of joining, the friends of the newly married couple danced and sang songs that teased them about their loss of freedom.

One song mocked the absence of married people from the dances they previously so much enjoyed. Another described the bride as wailing and stupid. Yet another song slandered the groom and jeered at the inability of a man to have intercourse directly after ejaculation. It was sung by women:

> "The desire of man
> Interferes, interferes with me
> The rat-trap sprung
> No longer stirs."

Feasting is one of the most important events after a marriage has taken place. Large amounts of food are prepared by the family of the groom for family enjoyment, as are baskets of food to be given as ceremonial gifts. Although marriage by capture is no longer practiced because of the population's conversion to Christianity, all other ceremonial aspects of marriage have been retained and continue to be practiced as before.

Preparing the wedding feast, men and women share the work. Women scrape taro and peel bananas, the men grate and chop the foods with tougher fibers. The first oven of the day is prepared for the workers. The second oven is for the preparation of food to be sent to the house of the bride. The third oven is made in the evening, after the gifts of mats from the bride's house have been received. The groom's family take the food from this oven to the house of the bride, in reciprocation for the mats. The food, *te monotanga,* from the oven at midday, is sent to the head of the bride's clan. *Te monotanga* is the expression used to refer to gifts of food to a chief. Such a gift—a basket of cooked food, coconuts, and sugar-cane—is not a daily occurrence, but marks special occasions, such as weddings.

The extensive and complex exchanges of food and gifts that accompany a marriage ceremony are similar to those of initiation and mourning. In no sense can the presentation of such gifts to the bride's family be construed as an act of purchase. A Tikopian woman is no more the property of her husband than he is hers. The food and gifts exchanged by their two families are of equal value. Distant relatives are not assured of receiving gifts. They are proud and delighted to be included in the distribution, but are apprised of a gift only by its arrival. Such a gift enhances one's standing in the community, bringing the recipient great pleasure.

Gifts from the bride's house are delivered by two women, one carrying the contribution of the bride's father's relatives and the other of her mother's. When they arrive, the scene is one of high drama. After the first woman has set down her burden, the bride embraces her, slips to her knees, and sobs. The woman hits her with her fist, then sinks down beside her, again embracing her, and wails. The scene is repeated by the second woman. The ritual is symbolic of separation, and is similar in meaning to a wedding ritual enacted in Taiwan, described below (page 127).

The initial exchange of gifts is followed by a series of subsidiary exchanges. Gradually the married pair slip into routine and settle into their new positions in the society.

The people themselves believe that a good Tikopian marriage is built on the solid foundation of mutual respect and cooperation. Men and women work together, in the orchards as well as around the ovens, and take care of each other in illness.

Polygyny was practiced prior to the total conversion to Christianity, but Firth observed that such unions were not as felicitous and enduring as monogamous marriages—the only form of marriage extant since 1956 in the colonies as well as in Tikopia. Although sexual exclusiveness is the ideal, Tikopians, wherever they are, maintain a double standard. The burden of remaining faithful falls much more heavily on women than on men. If a wife transgresses, she is likely to feel the physical wrath not only of her husband, but of her own brothers. A man has much greater freedom to roam, and no stigma is attached to his philandering. His wife, however, has ways to punish him that tend to discourage his pursuit of other women. If a man is very late returning to his house or has stayed out the whole night, his wife awaits him with a stick and gives him a good thrashing. She also pinches his flesh until the skin breaks. The efficacy of this retaliation is common knowledge in Tikopia and has been recorded by Firth. There are husbands whose desire for illicit relations is stronger than their fear of their wives. When a man commits adultery repeatedly, his wife, as a last resort, may take her children and return to her home. In his remorseful state the husband attempts to regain her by sending her a gift of food and a message pleading for her return. This seems to achieve the desired result: the couple's resuming an amicable relationship. Tikopian husbands and wives do not engage in public signs of affection; rather than sweet-talk or hand-holding in the presence of others, they consider actions the proof of the felicity of their marriage. Working as a team in economic production and the rearing of children are the two essential elements that keep a marriage content and firmly cemented. Other chores are performed by husband or wife according to ability and physical strength.

The Tikopian family lives at a slower pace than do most of ours. Work is lightened by playfulness, and after a stretch of labor under the hot sun, relaxation is sought by plunging into the sea or the lake, followed by loafing.

Tikopian husbands and wives avoid pronouncing each other's names. Instead, they call each other by the housename, with a prefix of *Pa* for the man and *Nau* for the woman. Although husband and wife respect each other, the egalitarianism found among the !Kung does not exist in their marriages. The man is, without question, the head of the household. The power of the woman lies in the threat of her leaving him and returning home.

From the time of settlement in Nukufero through 1965 there were no drastic differences between courting and marriage customs in Tikopia and the colony in the Russell Islands. Ideally, women are expected to be chaste at the time of marriage. Closer to reality, a more general standard requires that a woman before marriage have only one lover at a time. Men, by contrast, are expected to be promiscuous, providing village gossips with an endless topic of conversation.

A woman's patrilineal kinsmen have to give the suitor consent before the marriage can take place. The man who wishes to marry goes with a party of his male relatives to the woman's patrilineal kinsmen and kisses their knees. The woman's relatives feign surprise, then sadness, as they "reluctantly" give their consent. At that point the couple is considered to be married; the woman leaves her home and accompanies her husband and his male kin to his house. The next ceremony is the oven of joining, after which gifts are sent from the groom's family to the bride's. This is followed by *te anga,* the huge wedding feast, prepared exactly as on Tikopia. Only two differences were noted by Larson between Tikopian and Nukufero marriages—in Nukufero a Christian church ceremony is more likely to follow the native festivities, and the newly married woman in Nukufero does not shave her head, but instead lets her hair grow.

Monogamy is now the sole form of marriage in Tikopia as well as in Nukufero. Divorce is not permitted by the Christian mission in Nukufero, and the same applies to Tikopia.

The position of women in Nukufero is just as subordinate as it is in Tikopia, and husbands and wives share chores and responsibilities. Women are expected to have a sweet disposition; a scold can quickly acquire a nasty reputation in the community.

Marriage in Nukufero between a Tikopian woman and an outsider is condemned. In part this is attributable to the fear that the woman, following the custom of virilocal residence, will go to the place of her husband. The new husband, being an outsider, may not understand that he has an obligation to provide a man in the bride's family with the opportunity to marry one of his female relatives. This type of marital reciprocity is commonly practiced in Tikopia. Turning the matter around, Tikopians in Nukufero have no objection to a male colonist's marrying a woman of a different ethnic background, as she would be expected to stay with her husband's family and the Tikopians would gain a new member. Tikopia is so remote from the nearest inhabited island that a man from another community is rarely encountered. If one arrived and married a local woman, he would stay on, causing no loss to the community. In all cases of this kind Tikopians are very accepting, and welcome the foreigner.

Men drink alcoholic beverages in Nukufero, but rarely with their wives, unless it is a special occasion with Europeans present.

Inequities exist in the relations between husband and wife; for example, if there is only one narrow mattress in the house, the husband sleeps on it. No contradiction in attitude is felt by the husband who treasures a beautiful wife. Indeed, he is likely to seek a mate who can speak English, thereby enhancing his mobility in the outside world. Women who possess special attributes are treated better than those who do not, but such potential leverage is not a special feature of Tikopian culture.

Just as we have seen for some Tikopians, marriage among the Tlingit in the nineteenth century was an alliance arranged by the parents for economic and political purposes. Unlike in Tikopia, even the concept of romantic love as we know it seems to have been absent in Tlingit. No romantic songs or love stories have been recorded among the Tlingit, although they do exist in other cultures having parentally arranged marriages. For Tlingit, love could not possibly be a consideration in the negotiations between the parents of the groom and bride. A girl was married off very shortly after her isolation at the onset of menarche to the marriage partner that her pragmatic parents had chosen for her. Of course they hoped the bride and groom would settle into an amicable relationship, and they wished them mutual affection and sexual fidelity. The latter, however, did not mean exclusive sexual access. It was normal practice for a man to have sexual relations with his brother's wife and with the wives of his mother's and father's brothers. It followed that widows married nephews, while widowers took nieces as wives, thus preserving close family ties that would otherwise have lapsed with the death of a mate.

A man could ask his parents to search for another girl if the one they chose was not to his liking, but a young girl did not have the privilege of turning down her parents' choice. It is indicative of the superior status of men that a man said "I married," whereas a woman said "He married me."

Mating could only take place between members of opposite moieties, marriage within the moiety being considered incestuous.* It was, however, perfectly acceptable for a man to marry the daughter of his mother's brother, and highly desirable for him to marry the daughter of his father's sister, since all of these females were outside his moiety.

The mother's brother had a decisive influence in the choice of a mate for a niece, but the girl's mother managed all the negotiations. Perhaps the most important rule concerning marriage was equality of rank, and families went to considerable trouble to examine each other's pedigrees before arriving at an agreement.

The ceremony was very simple. The closest members of each family sat in the house of the bride's father, her father and uncles on one side of the room and the groom's father and uncles on the other. The groom sat on a mat in the middle, and the bride was brought to him. They were lectured on the proper relationship between husband and wife, and a promise was extracted from each to live up to it.

This was followed by a gift of blankets and copper coins to the bride's mother from the groom's family; clothing, blankets, and dishes to the newly married couple from the bride's father; gifts from the groom's mother to the bride's parents.

In the families of chiefs the bride danced to special songs sung

---

*A moiety, derived from the French *moitié* ("half"), is one of a pair of groups into which a society may be divided. Membership in such a group is usually inherited unilineally, that is, through either mother or father but not both, nor is there choice of membership. The most common function of a moiety, but not a universal one, is to regulate marriage choice: one usually marries a person who belongs to the other moiety.

at the time of the wedding. There were no contracts to sign, and children born to the young couple constituted the "marriage license."

Newlyweds first lived at the bride's house, then at the groom's. The bride continued for a long time to function under the supervision of older women in both families. The Tlingit practiced polygyny, and if a young bride had a senior co-wife she was supervised by her as well. A chief always had his eye on the younger sister of his wife, and married her as soon as she was of age. As among the !Kung, co-wives called each other "sister," yet they tended to quarrel, even if they were real sisters.

Contact with a menstruating woman was extremely dangerous and carefully avoided. The blood of a parturient or menstruating woman was contaminating to men and offensive to the spirits of animals. Could not a menstruating woman turn men and animals to stone with a glance? A woman was expected to observe the menstrual taboos, which required her complete removal from the house to a special shack for the duration of her period, lest she bear the blame if her husband returned from a hunting trip with an empty bag.

Unfaithfulness is said to have been extremely rare; if a man seduced a married woman he could be killed for it. If he escaped alive, he was expected to contribute to the support of the woman he had had relations with. Dalliance could turn out to be an expensive proposition.

Much of the foregoing has changed, owing to the overwhelming influence of the United States. Relations between young people are very similar to those to the south, and wedding ceremonies take place in a Christian church. Although the girl's or the boy's family may be vehemently opposed to a match they cannot prevent it, and they end up as seemingly happy participants in the wedding.

At one wedding Martha attended in Yakutat, the religious ceremony took place in the Presbyterian church after the mandatory Wasserman tests were completed and the license secured. The reception was held in a bar, which posed a problem, as the bride was not yet eighteen, but all obstacles were somehow overcome. The bride wore a traditional western gown and white lace veil. The groom was a member of a wealthy, high-ranking family, and the bride and her family were extremely pleased at the match. The groom wore a tuxedo, as did the best man, a non-Tlingit friend, and the fourteen-year-old boy who acted as ring bearer.

The festivities began with the cutting of the wedding cake, which had a little bride and groom perched on top. Next came the opening of the presents. A young woman, a relative of the bride, sat at the end of a long table to which the presents were brought. As the bride read the card, the young woman made a note of the donor. The bride opened each package in a careful, precise way, all the while smiling at the assemblage. When she could see the gift, she announced what it was, and her scribe made a note of it next to the donor's name. Then it was passed to the groom, who stood next to the bride. As he looked into the wrappings of the first package, his face lit up with evident pleasure at the sight of a sterling silver coffee service from his new mother-in-law, a widow. Very much impressed by her generous gift, the young man praised it to all and called out, "Hey, Mom! This is terrific! Hey, Mom! You better come up here!" He kept shouting until the woman joined him at the table, where he put his arms around her. Then he looked at the next gift, a set of sterling silver flatware from his own parents. Again he praised the gift lavishly, but he did not ask his parents to rise or to join him. He left no doubt, however, that he was very pleased at their generosity. As he examined a carton containing a highly desired object he would exclaim, "Look at this! My God, Charley (or Pete, or Joe, or Bob), this must of set you back three hundred bucks!" He radiated utter delight.

That was not always the case. Along the way, when his wife passed a box of kitchen towels to him, he tossed them over his shoulder into the air so that the box and the towels flew in all directions. "Who needs that junk?" he yelled. He repeated the performance to acknowledge a gift of bed linen and other presents of comparable kind and value. As he did this his friends scurried around the room picking up the boxes and reassembling the merchandise, placing it on the table where the recorder quietly continued her task and the bride, still smiling sweetly, neatly unwrapped the remaining gifts. The last package contained a box of disposable diapers. To some it appeared that the bride was several months into pregnancy.

After the gifts had been opened, recorded, and judged, a master of ceremonies asked all the young unmarried men to line up at one end of the room. The groom then removed the bride's garter and hurled it toward them. Leaping above the others, one man caught it and waved it in triumph. Then the young unmarried women were lined up, something of a feat, as they were swept with the giggles, showing very great reluctance to join the line and having to be coaxed, seemingly averse to appearing too eager. The bride tossed her bouquet (flown up from Seattle the previous day), and it was caught by one of the women. She was led to the man who had caught the garter, and he slipped it over her foot, placing it as high on her thigh as he could, to a raucous chorus of laughter and appropriate remarks.

There were about two hundred guests at the reception, and the bartender, aided by two barmaids, had great difficulty attending to the thirsty crowd. In most of its details it could be classified as a typical middle-class American wedding. Stripped of its religious component, it was a packaged product, turned out by a wedding mill; in that trade, small optional ethnic touches are available.

If the behavior known to the Tlingit in former times still surfaces at occasions such as weddings, it is also manifest in everyday life. There is strong continuity in the sexual division of labor. In the population directly observed, all women except the old and the sick were employed or had job histories. In 1978, a visitor to Yakutat quickly noticed the large number of women who worked. The Community Health Center was entirely staffed by women, as was the Yakutat Alcoholism Program. The Clerk to the Court of Yakutat was a woman, and so were most of the members of the Board of Education. Women taught in the elementary and high schools, worked as clerks in stores, were employed in the canneries, and ran the Post Office. Food preparation and serving in restaurants and in the old people's home were done by women. Laura Klein, an anthropologist, did a recent field study in a different Tlingit community, but many of her observations apply to Yakutat. Commercial fishing is done exclusively by men, the season lasting about four to five months. In a good year, and in 1977 and 1978 the waters were thick with salmon, a man could make $100,-000 in one season. But fishing is a chancy way of making a living, because there are lean years when the yield is not sufficient to support a family. Men tend to forget the lean years, fondly remembering the rich ones, when the catch was good and the price high. But fishing, even when done for a living, is not merely a commercial enterprise, it is a highly exciting and enjoyable sport, a manly thing to do. Given the prevalence of such views among Tlingit, it is not surprising that most of the conventional, dull, daily jobs are filled by women. When Martha questioned Tlingit women about commercial fishing, they said it was very hard work, something only men could do. Yet even among the Tlingit there are some women who are physically stronger than some men. Confronted by that fact, and by the additional consideration that such labor could be done by a group, thereby combining strengths, the Tlingit women regarded the suggestion as heresy. The idea that they should challenge men in this, their most critical activity, was to them nothing short of insane.

The division between the roles of men and women is sharp, and sometimes seems conflicting to the observer. Not unfamiliar is the Tlingit woman's attitude toward the working of simple household appliances. When a vacuum cleaner made weird sounds, a woman visitor from another state spotted the trouble as a broken drive belt. She opened the housing, confirmed her diagnosis, and explained what was wrong, suggesting a remedy to her Tlingit hostess, who was amazed at the display of such minimal mechanical aptitude. This incident was puzzling because Tlingit women run many of the services that keep the little community going, this woman among them. The men expect them to. Still, it is clear that women serve men. When asked if her husband helped out around the house, a woman who holds a very important position answered that her husband enjoyed the children and spent a lot of time with them. Asked if he ever did the dishes, the woman replied, "I'm not so ambitious that I want my husband to wash dishes!"

Asymmetry in male/female relations is clearly displayed among the Tlingit, as in the general population of the United States, by the number of acts of violence committed by men against women. Wife beating is prevalent. Health officers who treated many battered women linked the violence against wives to the high incidence of alcoholism in both men and women. But the violence is not always meekly absorbed. One close observer of the community said, "A man gets drunk and beats his wife to death.

But sometimes he inflicts physical and emotional injuries that are not fatal, but he does this regularly. She gets madder and madder and then snaps, her mind snaps, and she stabs him to death."

One divorced mother of seven talked about the trials of her marriage: "He was drunk a lot. He acted crazy. In the middle of the night he woke me up. He wanted me to make a meal for him. In the middle of the night. He would have killed me if I didn't. I ran home to my mother holding my two babies in my arms. But he sent messages pleading for me to come back. He knew how to be nice when he wanted to and I was fool enough to believe that he would keep his word and never treat me badly again. I went back to him and had more children. Things just kept getting worse. He was drinking more and more and was beating up on me. One night I got so scared, I knew if I didn't get away from him I'd end up dead. So I went back to my mother's and filed for divorce. I'm glad to have the children now, they're company for me."

There are happy marriages in Yakutat, and enduring ones. Yet when women sit around the table, sipping endless cups of coffee and smoking one cigarette after another, they often talk about the good marriages they know of as if they were extraordinary. In any event, divorce is at least as commonplace in Yakutat as in the general population of the United States. (Yakutat is, of course, governed by Alaska state law and is in no way exceptional.) Polygyny, formerly part of Tlingit culture for at least some of the men, has been long dead, replaced by our more familiar "serial monogamy," punctuated by affairs. Incidentally, one aspect of Tlingit culture that seems to hang on is a predilection for sexual relations between older women and younger men, differences of more than thirty years not unknown. Such affairs are often totally outside the matrimonial system. Relations may last for a brief while, or may continue for years.

Martha met and spoke with a number of widows of mature years. The episode of the old woman beaten by her nephews notwithstanding (see page 88), these women were self-sufficient and self-respecting. Without exception, when they spoke of their late husbands (often more than one), it was with deference to their superior knowledge of Tlingit culture. However, since Tlingit are universally tight-lipped about aspects of their cultural past, this might have been only a stratagem to avoid questioning.

Compared to Tlingit marriages, those of the Muslim Hausa are tranquil affairs. The alcoholism that clouds Tlingit family life is largely precluded by the Islamic ban on the consumption of alcohol. And there are other strains in the culture that limit intersexual violence in marriage. Before discussing the relationship of husband and wife, however, let us see how people, especially young adults, meet and mate.

The intricate courtship among the Hausa is characterized by many ceremonies and religious rituals, as well as by more secular customs backed by centuries of tradition. Incest taboos are largely confined to the functioning domestic unit. There may be no sexual relations between mother and son, father and daughter, sister and brother, half-sister and half-brother. Marriage is forbidden between uncle and niece or aunt and nephew, but first and second cousins on both father's and mother's side may marry freely.

Young girls who attend school may start having suitors around the age of twelve. A boy who sees a girl and takes a liking to her asks a friend to talk to the girl on his behalf. The *dan sako* (go-between) asks the girl her name and if she is not too shy, she tells him. He then informs her that his friend is interested in her. If she does not give a negative response, the smitten young man, in a few days or so, approaches her directly and says first her name, then *"ina sanki"* ("I love you"). Next he asks her, *"kinasona?"* ("Do you love me?"). If the girl likes the boy she says, *"ina sanka"* ("I love you"), but if she does not like him at all she says, *"bana sanka"* ("I don't love you"). A girl probably has many suitors before she makes a choice.

If she feels love for a boy, she tells her mother or grandmother that he declared his love for her, identifying him by name. They then ask, "What was your answer?" And she tells them.

Meanwhile, the boy reports to his mother or father that he has found a girl he loves who loves him also. His parents discuss the matter and go to considerable trouble to determine that the girl comes from an upstanding, honorable household that is free of serious illness or criminal record. At the same time the girl's family investigates the boy's background with equal thoroughness. If the two sets of parents find the match acceptable, the formal courtship may commence.

A *toshi* (two boxes full of gifts) is purchased by the boy's father and delivered by the boy's aunts, sisters of both his mother and father, to the home of the girl. The smaller box is filled with soap, perfume, and cosmetics; the larger one with clothing, shoes, and handbags. The acceptance of the *toshi* marks the formal beginning of the period called *samartaka,* which lasts until engagement— usually no more than a month.

Before the *baiwada sarana* (engagement), the boy's father sends representatives, usually his mother and sisters, to the girl's family, to inquire when they may bring the bride price and the *goro* (kola nuts) without which the engagement cannot take place. The girl's parents and relatives confer and, sometimes on the same day, send a representative, usually an older sister of the mother or father, to inform the boy's family of the date when delivery may be made to seal the engagement. The boy's maternal and paternal aunts take the bride price and kola nuts on the appointed day.

These gifts are equally shared by the father and mother of the girl and, in turn, parceled out to close relatives and friends. A week later, the girl's parents invite their relatives and members of the boy's family for a religious ceremony. Mats are placed in front of the house; at seven o'clock in the morning an imam says prayers and blesses the engagement.

The girl's father then sets the date for the *daurinaure* (wedding), which usually takes place a year after the engagement. If the boy's parents are eager for the marriage, they ask through representatives that the period of *baiwada sarana* be shortened.

A marriage does not require the signing of a contract or a marriage license. Only in cases of intermarriage, as when a Muslim marries a Christian, is there such a record, as those marriages involve only a civil ceremony that takes place in a court.

Before the wedding the boy's family has to deliver the *sadaki,* a sum of money (as much as they can afford), which English-speaking Hausa call the dowry. This sum will be given to the bride's father, who either transfers the cash directly to his daughter or spends the entire amount to buy something she needs. Early in the morning of the wedding day a *malam,* paid by the bride's father, comes to her home to recite prayers blessing the marriage. After this ceremony kola nuts and biscuits are served for refreshment while the bride stays in the house of an aunt. In the late afternoon, around four or five o'clock, the groom's family and friends prepare the *towon biko,* a substantial amount of food consisting of stewed chicken, cooked rice, and beef stew. The bride's family also prepares food.

About seven o'clock in the evening the bride's grandmother washes her. After this ritual bath, the bride dresses in her best garments and is taken around to her close relatives to be blessed. Then the groom's family come to claim the *biko*—collecting the bride and taking her to her husband's house.

The next day the husband's and wife's families gather in his home to consume a wedding feast that has been prepared mostly by the husband's family, with contributions of food from his wife's family. In the northern part of Nigeria the wedding celebration lasts seven days, but in the southern Hausa territory it only lasts two.

The bride's family brings furniture and dishes, a big bag of rice, bags of guinea corn and millet, *taliya* (long thin noodles resembling spaghetti), peanut and palm oil, and *manshanu* (local butter). The furniture and dishes are for the bride's personal use, the rest are given to her in-laws as a gift from her father. In some cases, cash is also given to the in-laws—as much as her father can afford.

In the evening, while the bride sits in her room in her husband's compound, the two families and their relatives and friends sing and dance. The newly married man goes away for a few days and returns after all the ceremonies and festivities are over. The marriage may not be consummated until then.

On the morning of the first day the husband will sleep with his wife (two days after the actual wedding has taken place), the bride gives the clothing she wore when she was taken to her husband's house to her grandmother, her mother, or to one of her sisters. In fact, quite a bit of her clothing is given away to her female relatives.

After she has shed her old clothes, she bathes again (sometimes her mother comes over to bathe her), and puts on all new garments that are gifts from her husband. She wears a brassiere and panties, then she dons the *rigamaihannu da zani,* a special blouse with a wraparound skirt. She then puts on her new *gayle* (shawl), and wraps her head in a *saro,* a colorful cotton kerchief with a particularly nice design. She discards her old shoes in favor of new ones, and finally puts on the jewels, all gold, that her husband has bought for her. She wears earrings, a wristwatch, a necklace, a ring (not a wedding ring), and bracelets—sometimes as many as twelve —reaching from her wrist to her elbow. The number of bracelets depends on the financial condition of her husband. A poor man may give his wife only one, a rich man can afford twelve.

The newly married man also wears all new clothes; a *babbar riga,* which is a long white shirt, or caftan. Under the caftan he wears a buttoned shirt with a collar. He puts on a white *wando* (pantaloons) and a *hula,* a cap especially made for the occasion, of white cotton colorfully embroidered. Such caps are made by both men and women. Although they can be purchased ready-made at the market, the groom wants a *hula* that is unique to wear when he is married. The groom chooses the colors and the person making the cap creates the design of the embroidery.

Both husband and wife wear these beautiful clothes all day. The bride stays in her room and receives female visitors, the groom goes about freely, wishing everyone to see him in his new, resplendent garments.

That evening, when the husband comes to sleep with his wife for the first time, he brings her more presents—blouses, perfume, handbags—to persuade her to have sexual relations with him. These gifts are called *kayan sayanbaki.* Asked if the giving of presents was the husband's way of romancing his wife, Hausa women looked puzzled and replied, "It is the custom."

A new custom, a modern intrusion, is a party given by the husband for friends and relatives. It is associated only with those who have been influenced by European culture. This party is sometimes given, with the permission of the principal, in the assembly hall of the nearest secondary school. Soft drinks and small cakes, biscuits, and candies are served.

The husband, after his first night with his new wife, returns to his usual clothes and resumes his usual work. Even in the countryside people do not live merely by tilling the soil. Each man has some special skill that he practices in addition to working the land. He might hunt and fish, be a leather worker, a tanner, or a butcher. Among the Muslim Hausa, men are the silversmiths, coopers, potters, weavers, and dyers. Men also engage in local or overland trade, and occupy all official positions in government, which is the exclusive preserve of males.

The young wife continues to dress each day in a beautiful new outfit for some time after the wedding. Some women bring to their marriage as many as seven suitcases full of new clothes.

A generation ago all girls married at a very early age. Parents were guided in the choice of a son-in-law by practical considerations, and the emotional attachments or physical desires of young people were not taken into account. A man who married a girl before she started to menstruate could not have sexual relations with her. If he had tried, she could have run back to her parents and complained. This behavior on the part of the man would have been considered scandalous, and people would have ridiculed him by saying "Look at the old fool! Can't he see that she's still a child?" When this social taboo was further pursued in conversations with Muslim Hausa women, they said, "He had no reason to even think of such a thing—he had other wives who could satisfy his needs. There was no sense in bringing social disgrace on himself." So a man waited until his child bride started to menstruate.

In many marriages, wives have to avoid speaking their husband's name. Custom also dictates that they avert their gaze when speaking to him. A wife is not supposed to be standing when she speaks to her husband, she must be sitting on the floor or on a chair. The crucial thing is for her head always to be lower than his. There are exceptions, mostly in marriages of university educated women who do not marry until they are over twenty. These women are more likely to call their husband by his name rather than *malam,* or *alhaji* if he has been to Mecca, and to face him when speaking to him. Still, a wife is expected to be sweet-tempered, gentle, and yielding in response to her husband. Her speech should never be grating or offensive, but polite at all times, even if he has spoken to her harshly. Some women give as good as they get, but that is said to be unusual.

The tradition of treating an older person with respect carries over into a May-December alliance—it is not unusual for a young woman to marry for the first time a man who is twenty or more years her senior. Such a man is likely already to have as many as three other wives.

In the case of women who have been married and divorced once or twice, the courtship is short, the parents are not involved in the decision or the arrangements, and all ceremonies are dispensed with except the wedding itself.

If the duration of a marriage is short, if there are no children, or if it is the woman who wishes the divorce, a husband has every right to demand the return of the bride price. Most men do not make this request, but some do, in which case their demands are met. Regardless of who has initiated divorce proceedings, the woman must return to her natal home and stay three months in *iddah,* a state of strict celibacy. The custom is defended as a means of ascertaining the paternity of a child she might be carrying at the time of divorce. When a marriage breaks up, the husband keeps the children, who are his by Muslim law, including any child the woman may give birth to within nine months of the divorce. Divorced women have the right to visit their children.

All our informants told us they never heard of a woman who was a spinster. All women marry, but some do not remarry after divorce or the death of their husband. Women who failed to remarry usually became prostitutes in former times. This is no longer the case today, as women have a variety of options. A divorced or widowed woman may stay in her father's house or, if she is an older woman, which is to say over thirty-five, with grown children, the children might build a house for her. She can engage in trade, sewing caps for men and clothing for women. She can become a caterer, selling prepared foods—anything from snacks to major meals. She can purchase rice, millet, and guinea corn, and sell it at a profit in her own home. If the woman has a university education, she can teach in elementary or middle school. Some women teach at university, but that is rare. Equally small in number are Muslim Hausa women doctors and lawyers, but there are some and they practice while some of their sisters still live in purdah.

A married man who is divorced or widowed may not wish to marry again, but prefer to live alone. If he has children, he looks after them. There are very few men nowadays who can afford four wives, not only because husbands have to maintain each of their wives in equal style, which has become very expensive, but also because they cannot afford to support the many children that are likely to issue from four wives. Most men have no more than two wives, many have only one.

The divorce rate among the Muslim Hausa is extremely high. "If a husband can no longer tolerate any nonsense from his wife, he can divorce her. If she can no longer tolerate any nonsense from him, she can divorce him," we were told. Some divorces are amicable, both parties wishing to sever the union, others are bitter, the result of mistreatment of wives that might have extended to unprovoked physical assault. Even though a man is carefully investigated before a match is made, he can conceal his bad traits and character flaws behind honeyed words and generous gifts. If a girl is fortunate, those who know the man well will see to it that she learns his true nature. Even when such information does reach the girl, if she is only twelve or so, her father is likely to turn a deaf ear to her entreaties to break off the courtship. He tells her, "You're just a child . . . you know nothing about marriage . . . you haven't been to his compound . . . what you hear is just gossip." The girl is forced into a marriage that cannot last. The more mature a young woman is, the better her chance to persuade her father that the impending marriage is not desirable, that the engagement should be broken. There are angry words—a father does not change his plans easily—but if the young woman is twenty or older, he may have respect for her judgment, and she will have a greater chance of winning him over.

Some women finding themselves in an unhappy situation seek solace with a lover. If the husband finds out about the affair, he beats his wife and usually divorces her. A Muslim Hausa woman must ask her husband's permission to go out visiting or marketing. If she fails to do so, she risks not only his ire but also a sharp slap to keep her in her place. "Some men are more excitable than others —they slap or beat their wives at the slightest offense . . . a woman cannot live like this and so she seeks a divorce," another Hausa woman told us.

Another reason for divorce may be the husband's inability to satisfy his wife sexually. If a man turns out to be completely impotent, his wife will complain to her mother. If the husband is realistic, he knows there is something wrong with him and seeks help. He may go to a hospital, hoping to be cured. He is thoroughly examined and the doctor prescribes medicine. Some men may simply go to the local *malam,* who attempts a cure with native herbal medicines. Others try both approaches. If none of the cures brings the desired result, his wife is likely to divorce him. However, there are women who are willing to accept dissatisfactions of all sorts, and they stay. If a man is able to have an erection but ejaculates too quickly, leaving his wife fully aroused and frustrated, she may leave him and secure a divorce. Some women are satisfied just to have children by such a man, particularly if he has many other good qualities. A man's sexual difficulties are perceived as sickness: "It is very sad, when that happens," one Hausa woman told us. Great care is taken to keep his problem a secret. A woman does not tell even her own sister or best friend about it, but only her mother, for fear that his sickness may become a subject of public gossip.

During our interviews on marriage, the one word that kept cropping up as essential to a union was "peace." Ability to get along without quarreling is considered the single most vital element in a marriage. Women want a husband who is kind, generous, understanding, tender, and a satisfactory lover. Good looks, cleverness, wealth, and social position, according to our informants, are very low on the list of important qualities.

If the husband seeks the divorce, he writes out a statement on a piece of paper: "I, [name], divorce my wife, [name], on [date], three times." If he simply writes "I divorce my wife," members of his and his wife's families will make every effort to bring about a reconciliation, but once he has written the words "three times," reconciliation is impossible, and the divorce is final. If the divorce is a particularly bitter one, preceded by harsh words and physical abuse, a wife is not likely to trust her former husband. She fears that when she wants to remarry, he may cause her trouble by denying that he divorced her. For her own safety, she may take the divorce statement to a judge, who will examine it and enter it in the court records. This precaution is not frequently taken, we were told.

If a woman wishes to leave her husband, she goes to her parents to ask for permission to obtain a divorce. If her father accepts her reasons, he grants her permission to end the marriage. Regardless of which partner initiated the divorce, the woman must go into *iddah,* the three-month period of celibacy spent at the home of her parents. Some men, after getting the divorce they sought, have a change of heart and wish to remarry their wives. This is no simple matter. First, the woman must finish her *iddah,* then marry another man. If she still desires her previous husband and wishes to return to him, she must persuade her new husband to give her a divorce. She again goes into *iddah* for three months, and only then can she and her previous husband remarry. If a woman wishes a divorce and her husband does not want to let her go, she has to give him a lump sum of money, called "alimony" by English-speaking Hausa. When she resists complying with this rule, her husband takes her to court. If the judge who examines the case finds no fault in the husband's conduct, he will order that the wife pay the alimony. In all cases, the woman gives to her father for safekeeping a copy of her husband's statement, or a copy of the court record of the divorce.

Of the six cultures discussed in this book four have permitted a man to have more than one wife and two still do. In three of these cultures a man and his wives occupied the same quarters. The Hausa, guided by the Muslim doctrine of "separate but equal treatment" in marriage, provide individual quarters for each wife. Despite this their divorce rate is high, and most men are content with one wife, or two at the most.

One observer reported that over ninety-six percent of !Kung men practice monogamy. Although having more than one wife was considered to be prestigious, even exciting, most !Kung men recognized that the accompanying strife between the women was very unpleasant and best avoided.

Eugene Hillman argues on the basis of data collected by demographer Vernon R. Dorjahn that in sub-Saharan Africa, the incidence of polygyny is about thirty-five percent of all marriages. This figure is said to be too high by Kisembo, Laurenti, and Aylward. If polygyny had a social and economic function at one time, the psychic costs were high for women and the economic costs were high for men. Most women never liked the custom, and many men were ambivalent about it. As we approach the end of the twentieth century, the Muslim Hausa, primarily because of runaway inflation in Nigeria, lean more and more to monogamous unions, and most nomadic !Kung men are content with one wife.

The rituals of marriage practiced by the Muslim Hausa are not entirely alien in Taiwan, where several thousand Muslims are found within the larger population of Chinese. The Chinese way, though, is predominant, and has affected Muslim wedding practices; on the other hand, many weddings in the cities of present-day Taiwan show the heavy imprint of the United States. Thus, in his story "T'ung pen sheng" [Born of the Same Root], Yang Ch'ing-ch'u describes a nouveau riche wedding in the lavish ball-room of a Taipei hotel. The bride wears a white fur stole over a long pink evening gown, her face made up like an actress's, while television singers entertain the noisy gathering of relatives.

Actually, there seems to be a marked preference for white lace gowns, or so it would seem from the window displays in Yenp'ing North Road, where there is a cluster of shops specializing in wedding costumes. White lace gowns were favored at most of the weddings we have attended in Taiwan over the years, including one to which we were invited while doing research on clan temples. A woman who worked in the office of one of the temples had become friendly with us, and thought that we would provide an exotic touch among the guests. We arrived in the morning at the home of the groom, which was in an old section of the city where some of the buildings predated the 1895 Japanese occupation. The groom lived in a large, three-story old structure that also housed the family business. A room in the ground floor rear had been prepared and turned over to him as a home for his new family.

The groom, a good-looking but rather fleshy man in his middle twenties, was dressed in a dark western suit. His elder sister introduced us, invited us to be seated, and offered us a small cup of tea. No sooner did we sip it than we were hurried off to pick up the bride. The groom led the entire party, about thirty of us, in honking taxicabs whose ordinary bright red paint now seemed devised for the occasion. With even more horn blowing than usual, the cabs went by a slightly circuitous route to the bride's house, which comprised three tiny rooms. It was impossible for us all to fit into the middle room where we were received; some of the party, after greetings, stood outside. The rest took seats along the walls, facing the center of the room, where a small table held dishes filled with a banquet of meats, poultry, and fish. While awaiting the bride, who was in another room having the last touches applied to her wedding costume, we were served bowls containing two hard-boiled eggs in hot water. We were instructed not to eat the eggs but merely to stir them with our chopsticks. This was an interesting variant of a more common custom, where the groom is served a bowl of soup containing one soft-boiled egg yolk, which he breaks, thereby symbolizing the breaking of the bride's ties with her family and the end of her virginity.

After a while, the bride entered the little sitting room. She was dressed in a white lace wedding gown with a hoopskirt. Pink flowers were in her hair, and she wore a necklace and earrings that were either worth an emperor's ransom or were made of rhinestone. She also wore a gold necklace and a jade pendant. An artificial rose was pinned to her gown. She took the central place at the little banquet table, that reserved by conventional Chinese etiquette for the honored guest, the place away from the door. Opposite, in the host's place, sat her father. To her left was her mother and to her right, her sister. No one else sat at the table. Her mother and sister kept lifting morsels to her lips with their chopsticks, but the girl kept her lips firmly compressed. Huge tears formed in her eyes and rolled down her cheeks. Almost everyone cried. The symbolism was evident—the bride was no longer dependent upon her father's family for subsistence. At this point, a large tray was brought in holding a huge joint of pork and a smaller chunk of meat into which folded bank notes were stuck like so many paper cloves. Surrounding the meat were a great many Chinese wedding cakes, each glistening with a patina of red sugar. Now the bride produced a number of *hung pao,* the ubiquitous red envelopes used to present gifts of money, and distributed them among her relatives and friends. Her father then placed the bridal crown and veil on her head. The groom stepped forward and drew the veil down over her features, and bride and groom left the house to the thundering noise of a long string of firecrackers. We all followed, reentering the cabs and returning, by a different but again circuitous route, to the groom's house. The bride was met at the door by the groom's youngest brother, who presented her with a plate on which rested two oranges. Then she was led to the rear of the house, to the room that was now her's and her husband's.

After an interval spent sipping tea and conversing, we were invited to inspect the young couple's room. As we knew, this was not simply a courtesy to visiting foreigners but an important part of the ceremony, a display of the dowry that had been provided by the bride's family. The room was larger than the one in her own home in which the bride had refused her last meal, and it was furnished with brand-new western furniture—a couch, chairs, coffee table, vanity, radio, electric clock, thermos carafes, a tea set, and much more. The central object was a richly covered double bed. On the embroidered bedcover was a tray with a huge cake and the plate on which nestled the two oranges presented a short while before by the young brother. Several pictures hung on the walls; all seemed to portray unusually fat babies. Also in the room were two stools close together. A pair of trousers was draped over them in such a way that one pant leg covered each stool. The bride sat on one of these and the groom on the other. It was said that this meant that two lives were fusing into one, never to part.

Because of the pressure of other commitments, we were not present at some of the most important rituals of this wedding. We missed, for example, the obeisance that bride and groom are supposed to make to the deities of the girl's house and to her ancestors. Possibly this ritual was omitted, as it usually occurs after the ritual of the eggs previously described, or it might have been carried out earlier. We know that we missed the obeisances the bride and groom offered the ancestors of the groom at the altar in his house. Fortunately, our hostess supplied an account of the procedures, and it matched records of similar events.

In the evening, we went not to the house of the groom but to the clan temple to which his family belonged. Banquet tables with bright red cloths were set for three hundred people in the middle of the temple, which was hired for the occasion, a privilege that was available even to non-members. The banquet was catered by the hotel where the groom was employed. It was considered particularly auspicious to have the celebration in the temple. On the previous day the groom had made sacrifices to his ancestors in the temple, where they were represented by a number of tablets. The proximity of the happy occasion and the feasting would certainly please all the groom's ancestors, thereby enhancing the couple's chances for a happy, productive marriage. An old man remarked that even the agnostics and Christians in the assemblage could agree on that. Along the way, speeches were made on a platform in front of the main altar, exhorting the couple to lead good lives and to observe tradition in a changing world. Through most of the proceedings the bride remained passive. At most weddings, especially those of the Hakka in Taiwan, the bride goes from table to table, filling wine cups and toasting the guests, each time to be given a *hung pao,* the red envelope containing a sum of money. At this wedding it was different. A paper screen was brought in with some of the red envelopes already pinned to it; those of the guests who had not yet given their wedding present got up, one by one, and pinned the *hung pao* to the screen. This money is usually the bride's to dispose of, and it serves as capital that may have profound influence on her own life, and sometimes on the life of her husband and the destinies of her children. For example, the money may be used to finance the education of a favorite child beyond the point where the father is willing to pay. There are other varied uses for this capital.

The banquet was also more sedate than most. Toward the end, the groom proudly escorted his wife to the platform, where, in her shy manner, she smiled at all the guests. She looked quite lovely in a pink shift, having changed her clothes at some earlier moment. Totally absent was one conspicuous feature of most traditional Chinese wedding feasts—the ribald and sometimes harsh teasing of the bride and groom that can go on late into the night. At this party the festivities drew to a quiet halt, and the young couple left not for a honeymoon but to return to their new home in the midst of the groom's family.

The rituals of a Chinese wedding are of variable length and complexity, depending on region, class, and other factors. That this should be so in China is not surprising, considering the vast geographical extent of the culture. There is also considerable variation within the small island of Taiwan, in major part due to its complex subethnic heritage, which includes people from many different Chinese provinces and linguistic areas, further complicated by urbanization and modernization. Although exceptions can be cited at every major point, there are still certain key elements that characterize most Chinese weddings. For one thing, the marriage itself is not a licensed act. No prior permission to marry is obtained from a religious or political authority, although the fact of the marriage must be reported to the local police for insertion in the household register. As for a license, the custom in recent years has been for the groom to buy two commercially manufactured certificates, each highly decorated and printed on heavy pink paper, and enclosed in a thick, quilted, red velvet-textured folder. The certificate is filled out during the wedding. Its text proclaims the marriage and has spaces for the names of the principals and their witnesses. There is nothing official about it, but it may be used as legal evidence any time the fact of the marriage is in question, as in a divorce action. For some very bold young moderns in Taiwan, the wedding ceremony has been condensed into a simple luncheon or dinner party at which the certificate is completed, signed, and witnessed. Such a ceremony is as legally binding as any other.

This casualness is far from typical, but Taiwan has undergone something of a revolution where the roles of children and parents in the contracting of marriages are concerned. Probably the least frequent type of marriage today is the marriage arranged by parents for their children, as was the custom only a generation ago. Dating has now become commonplace, although dating does not necessarily mean that a son or daughter will not ultimately be married off by parental arrangement, a practice still not uncommon. Indeed, responses to a questionnaire administered by a sociologist in recent years indicated that most people whose marriages had been arranged had been on several dates before marriage.

So rapid are the changes in premarital and marital arrangement patterns that the children in one family can display the stages of change in their own behavior. In many families, the eldest children had completely arranged marriages, before which they had not even seen their spouses. The middle children in the same family had enjoyed the halfway house of so-called *mi-ai* ("search for love") marriages, in which parents and child compromise by having a period of familiarity rather like dating between the introduced parties prior to engagement, with either person free to withdraw. Finally, the youngest children of the same family find their own mates through dating. So commonplace has dating become that one study reports only a mere one percent of respondents expressing objections to it.

With the spread of free choice of marriage partners has come an increasingly romantic conception of love. The notion that marriage should be based on romantic love has been present for some time. In a study of students in Taipei undertaken almost twenty years ago, it was found that over ninety percent of the respondents thought that romantic love should be a bond leading to marriage. Romantic love is particularly important to young women, many of whom look forward to the appearance in their lives of a *pai-ma wang tzu,* a "prince on a white horse." Actually, the Chinese phrase is said to have originated from the name given Prince Charming in the Chinese subtitled version of Walt Disney's *Snow White.*

The shift from red to white as the color of marriage is not yet a complete one, for much about the wedding remains red and gold. But the white gown has almost completely displaced the traditional red one. This change of color would be emotionally equivalent in our culture to a general shift to black wedding dresses, since for the Chinese, white remains the color of death. A variety of other traditional wedding customs have been changed as easily as the color of the gown. Most changes have involved the dropping of taboos or negative behavior during the wedding period. For example, brides were formerly secluded on their wedding day, during which time the major rituals concerned the dressing of her hair, including the depilation of her temples with tweezers. Now the bride spends the morning in a beauty salon, usually having the latest haircut, wash, and set. Where the bride' feet were formerly not supposed to touch the ground on her wedding day until she was safely in her room in her husband's house, modern brides walk about freely both inside and outside their homes, though in some rural areas a bride is lifted from her own threshold to the taxicab by one of her brothers.

Margery Wolf attributes the survival of such customs to the desire of some brides to preserve the special quality of the wedding day. They are still observed, she thinks, "for the fun of it," much like our own brides' continuing to wear "something old, something new, something borrowed, something blue." But this generalization does not apply to some of the customs being retained, at least in certain weddings. Thus one still sees doors slammed shut on the bride as she leaves her natal home, an act believed to be a means of preventing further drain on the family's wealth by her new family. There is also the custom of the bride's brother spitting at, or pouring water on, the vehicle that transports the bride to her husband's house, for "just as spilt water cannot be returned to the container, so the bride cannot be returned to her natal home."

With the breakdown of prohibitions on premarital social inter-course between men and women there has undoubtedly been an increase in sexual relations. As far as we know, however, there is no serious rise in adolescent pregnancies, or even in extramarital pregnancies, certainly nothing to match the trends in the United States. In part this may be due to the different ways in which boys and girls get together in the two cultures. In Taiwan, far more activities seem to be undertaken in groups, with couples having less opportunity to be alone. It is now fairly common, however, both in small villages as in cities, for the parents of an engaged boy to invite the girl to spend some time with them, usually for the purpose of helping her future mother-in-law prepare for some festival. After such a visit, either party may decide to call off the impending marriage, sometimes because the girl complains that the boy appears "sickly," or the boy's family discovers that the girl has expensive tastes.

What seems to be an increase in the number of women preg-nant at their weddings cannot be authenticated. Comparable sta-tistics for earlier times do not exist, even though the demographic data from Taiwan have been among the world's most accurate since the turn of the century. The picture of earlier times is proba-bly quite idealized with respect to the virginity of young wives. Still, negative attitudes toward sexual relations are commonplace among women in Taiwan, and this may reflect an avoidance of intercourse after marriage, as well as before. On the other hand, some brides are pregnant and, as far as we could determine, fear of barrenness is so great that the bride's condition is often a con-cealed cause for joy.

The fact that a bridal pair have chosen each other freely, or have participated in the choice, does not mean that they will be happier than those who have had their marriages arranged. Al-though the number of young married people moving directly to their own home has increased, patrilocality continues to be the norm, even in urban apartment dwelling. The mother-in-law/-daughter-in-law relationship, then, remains an extremely impor-tant and conflict-engendering one, even for "modern" couples.

Surprisingly, even in rural areas young women entering marriage usually lack specific preparation for the tasks they must assume. They may not even know how to cook. The mother-in-law who may have failed to train her own daughters for marriage does not hesitate to blame her daughter-in-law for identical deficiencies. She is critical even if she has played an important role in choosing her son's wife. When the bride is someone she has not seen before and knows nothing about the situation is worse. When we lived in Taiwan some years ago, Chinese neighbors of ours had met and married in the United States. The woman had lived in the United States from the age of ten, and was quite Americanized. Fluent in English as well as in Mandarin Chinese, she was a college graduate and had met her husband, an overseas Chinese student, at the school where he had worked for his doctorate. After their first child was born, they returned to Taiwan to show him off to the paternal relatives. The young mother became desperately unhappy. She had nothing in common with her mother-in-law, who spent the greater portion of each day with them. She complained of the older woman's incessant criticism, her attempt to take over the direction of the child's rearing, her constant efforts to make her son place loyalty to her before his feelings for his wife, and her plot, including allegedly feigned illnesses, to make her son take her to America to live with them permanently. By no means an uncommon scenario, it bore marked resemblance to daytime Taiwanese television programs.

The failure of a marriage may be attributed to neglect of the ancient custom of comparing the bride's and groom's horoscopes before planning the wedding, or ignoring other magical or astrological procedures. It is still common for specialists, some maintaining their practices in the streets, others in modern offices, to *suan pa tzu,* to compare the respective year, month, day, and hour of birth of a couple before their betrothal is permitted. Many regard such a practice as *mi-hsin,* or superstition, used as a face-saving means of getting out of an impending marriage when all other attempts have failed. For the believers there are additional points to be made secure. The wedding date must be auspicious. A search is made in the annual Chinese almanac to avoid the host of days reckoned bad for a wedding. Every year many days are flatly pronounced "good for nothing, bad for everything," but other days are extremely good for marriages and, on such days, one runs into one wedding party after the other, particularly in the cities. Still, the day that is good in general may not be best for a particular couple, so it is not surprising that a specialist is needed to untangle such complexities. There are, however, simpler ways, such as placing the "eight characters" of bride and groom on the family altar, each person's dates written on a separate piece of red paper, and waiting for three or four days. If no untoward event occurs, the portents are deemed favorable, and the marriage is expected to be happy and productive.

The public delivery of the dowry and its display remain an important part of wedding festivities. To provide as expensive a dowry as possible sometimes requires elaborate strategies. In former times, the father and, to a lesser extent, the mother of the bride were torn between their love for their daughter and their obligations to their sons. The latter were not merely the persons in whom the continuity of the family line was vested, but were legally entitled to an undiminished inheritance. It was precisely at such a juncture that the independent capital of a woman based on her own wedding gifts could be used in behalf of her daughter. Such customs continue, but Taiwan operates under a modern marriage law that in theory ensures daughters' inheritance rights, or at least a more generous division of assets as far as they are concerned.

Chinese marriages also involve payments from the groom's family to the bride's. Referred to in English as bride price, the payment is not called that in Chinese, but is spoken of in various ways, often as *p'ing-chin* ("betrothal gold"), which may be contrasted with the usual expression for dowry, *chia-tzu* (literally, "daughter's marriage capital"). Though some families attempt to obtain large payments for their daughter's marriage, and are aided in the effort by the widespread belief that the transaction reflects a woman's worth as well as the standing of the groom's household, it is unseemly to marry a daughter off to the highest bidder, and to do so would provide an extraordinary topic of gossip. The anthropologist Myron L. Cohen, working in a Hakka community in the early 1960s, reported a bride price of $12,200 in local currency, equal at the time to about U.S. $300. Another anthropologist, William Barnett, who lived in a poorer Taiwanese mountain village in the mid-sixties, reported the average bride price to be U.S. $175.

The negotiations to decide the amounts to be paid in "betrothal gold," in dowry, and a large number of other details are sticky enough to provide another function for an experienced go-between, whether or not the person introduces the potential spouses as well. Perhaps because their services were so vital, matchmakers have been a popular butt of Chinese jokes. Margery Wolf tells of the go-between who arranged a marriage between a young man with a bad leg and an ugly girl. To avoid complaints, the matchmaker arranged for the groom and his family to pass the girl's house at a time when they were promised she would be visible. At the appointed hour, the groom's family replaced him by his handsome brother, while the bride's family substituted her pretty sister. After the "viewing" the matchmaker piously told each family, "You've seen for yourselves. Now don't blame me if the groom is a cripple and the bride is ugly!" Howard S. Levy, who includes some matchmaker stories in his collection of Chinese sexual humor, notes the similarity between Chinese and European matchmaker jokes.

Marriage is usually consummated on the wedding night. As a rule, it is only after a considerable amount of rough and ribald teasing of both bride and groom that they are permitted to be alone in their own room. What happens then is not entirely clear, since sexuality is one area in which ethnographic accounts differ. For example, Margery Wolf says that it was very difficult to get women to talk intimately about sex; when the subject was raised, they simply changed it. On the few occasions she managed to keep such a conversation going, sexual intercourse was described as an ordeal that a good wife had to endure. But, William Barnett, who seems to have had little trouble getting his informants to talk about sex, reports that it was the source of great enjoyment for women as well as for men. Barnett's view is closer to that found in Chinese jokes about the first night. Some such jokes are built around the Duke of Chou, who is said to have established the rules of propriety three thousand years ago. For example, a woman about to be married asks a close female relative about intercourse, and is told that it is something unpleasant that the Duke of Chou ordered women to suffer for their husbands. When the two women meet again after the wedding night, the bride asks, "Where can I find the Duke of Chou?" Surprised, the other woman asks why. "To give him a present," replies the bride happily. It is also worth noting that in Chinese humor the wife is portrayed as being at least as interested in sex as her husband, and often more adept and demanding.

Chinese sexual life is a complex subject that has not yet attracted sufficient scientific and scholarly attention. Historically, the culture has oscillated between periods of extreme licentiousness and equally extreme puritanism. One scholar has objected to such an application of the concept of puritanism in Chinese views of sex, on the ground that puritanism considers sex unnatural, harmful, disgusting, whereas such views are rare among Chinese, or appear in a very different way. Sex is natural and necessary, but in a twist not unknown to puritanical societies, it may be thought more natural and necessary for men than for women. Women are believed to have much greater control over their sexual drives, although a truly disciplined male can be more than a match for the most seductive female. Chinese culture does not usually avoid recognition of sexual anatomy or bodily functions. It does, however, consistently play down a public display of sexual affection, not to say passion. Now that sexual attitudes have become more liberal, one sees lovers walking hand in hand, but a public kiss might well cause a traffic accident. What is called puritanism in Chinese culture, then, is the repression of public display of sexual interaction.

With that understanding, it can be said that there have been periods of simultaneous licentiousness and puritanism. At the end of the rule of the Nationalist government on the mainland, when the great port city of Shanghai was probably the world's greatest center of sex for sale, the Kuomintang outlawed ballroom dancing as an immoral activity. Representations of Chinese culture are ,filled with stereotypes of earthy but sexually repressed peasants and effete, sometimes perverted, officials. In such representations the theme of the sexually passive, abused woman is a constant.

Lurking behind these stereotypes is a much more complicated reality. The Chinese philosophy of health includes sexuality but, being rooted in a complete view of the cosmos, extends far beyond. The theory of sex cannot be neatly compressed into a few pages, but it does underlie the conception of marriage and the division of energies in reproduction. It is vitally related to the social positions of men and women, and frankly considers women inferior. Since that belief persists both in Taiwan and in China proper, it constitutes a large stumbling block to women's achieving far reaching changes in their position.

Put simply, men are identified with yang, the principle of strength, brightness, affirmation, and goodness. Women are identified with yin, weakness, darkness, negation, and evil. But the philosophy is not simple. No male is entirely yang, as no woman is entirely yin; everyone combines both, and each sex can be dominated either by yang or yin forces. It is in the nature of women, according to this theory, that they should be polluters through such secretions as menstrual blood. Even their role as mothers is not entirely wholesome, because of its association with such bloody contaminations as afterbirths and miscarriages. It is also in the nature of women to enter strongly knit households and subtly undermine the unity of brothers until the house is divided. Once it is autonomous, it is easier for the woman to control her own little family. In various ways, these beliefs continue, even in sophisticated quarters. There is no telling how many Chinese men delighted in the downfall of Mao's widow, Jiang Qing (Chiang Ch'ing). What is certain is that since 1976 she has been treated, in classical fashion, as the female usurper.

The same philosophy is readily discerned in beliefs concerning sexual relations. Sex is described in Chinese literature as a physical duel between the woman and the man. Her weapon is the vagina, a dangerous set of cutting edges that can amputate a man's potency if he loses control. At the heart of the fray is the woman's intention to make the man ejaculate within her. Since the male emission is the essence of yang, and since its quantity is finite, his loss of semen is a loss of yang. Ejaculated into the woman, it increases her yang. Especially for the man, to lose too much yang is to upset the balance of life forces; poor health, even death, can result. It follows that men should attempt to withhold emission as long as possible. The mythical Yellow Emperor, who is said to have written China's oldest medical treatise, *The Yellow Emperor's Classic of Internal Medicine,* is reputed to have had twelve hundred wives and concubines with whom he had sexual relations. Although he satisfied every one of them, he is said to have done so without ever having ejaculated. Such conduct is seen as ideal mainly by certain esoteric Taoist schools, but it has exemplary features for an unknown number of men. Yet the dialectics of life demand some emissions by the man, because of all unfilial acts, the worst is to fail to produce a son to carry on the family line and the worship of the ancestors.

A Chinese woman is not exclusively dependent on her husband for the fulfillment of her desires. He need not be friend, lover, confidant, father, brother, and chief financial support all at the same time. The crushing burden of trying to fill all these roles, as is expected in our own society, is eased by the wife's companionship with friends, neighbors, and other members of the family. The price of this diversification is the lack of closeness and intensity of emotion between husband and wife. The wife does her own work, is completely under the thumb of her mother-in-law, delivers sons, and thereby fulfills her role. If a man wants sexual thrills, he goes to a prostitute, and for companionship, he has his friends and sworn brothers. It is not uncommon for a man to leave his wife for years at a time to serve in a government office or pursue his education abroad. This pattern is changing, and it also ameliorates with age. Some of the couples we know in Taiwan whose children are grown and whose parents are dead are becoming truly intimate in their middle age.

There is evidence of an increasing number of marriages in which women are equal partners, sharing sexual pleasures as well as important household, financial, and other decisions, but this is not entirely new. The strong woman is a familiar figure in Chinese society, although, until quite recently, the woman's sphere was almost entirely domestic, except in the most unusual cases. Within the domestic sphere women could have a position of great power. That this situation was resented by men, and a source of anxiety for them, may be inferred by the large number of jokes about henpecked or cuckolded husbands, many of them centuries old.

Taiwan has two special forms of marriage that are now on the wane because of fundamental changes in the economical and social structures. In one of these a man married into the family of the wife; in the other a very small girl was adopted, who was ultimately to be married to a son of the family.

In the first of these irregular marriages, the groom is invariably from a social and economic level much below the bride's. The man enters the marriage because it brings him land or a shop. He may drive a sharp bargain, however, perhaps, having it stated contractually that some of his sons will bear his own family name. Sometimes the husband takes his wife's surname, but it is common for him to combine his own surname with his wife's. This accounts for the unusually high frequency of double surnames in the province. Such marriages, however, are dwindling, along with the decline in importance of farming in Taiwan.

In the other type of marriage, the parents of a boy adopt a girl, often still a baby, bringing her up in their household. The girl is often exploited as soon as she reaches an age when she can perform useful work. Her common fate is to become a household drudge. This *siaosiv* system of bride adoption is most popular among poorer families, since it avoids the heavy cost of a wedding while still providing an extra pair of hands. True, such a child has to be fed, but in the mental cost accounting of the Taiwanese farmer, savings were seen making such adoptions worthwhile. Anthropologist Arthur Wolf has made the study of such adoptions a special topic of research. He is interested in the light it throws upon conceptions of incest since, as he points out, it involves the adoption of a daughter turning into the marriage of a sister. In fact, such marriages are demonstrably less successful than other marriages. In particular, they are less fertile. Husbands in these marriages are even more likely to release their sexual drives with other women than are husbands who marry in the conventional way. Long under governmental disapproval, the custom is now in decline, as economic opportunities have opened that provide new options for those families that once would have sold their daughters into such adoptions. Closely related is the clear evidence that female infanticide, once quite common, has not been statistically significant for more than a generation.

To go through life unmarried was almost unthinkable in China and Taiwan, as census data show. Even today, the number of people in late middle or old age who have never been married is negligible. However, there were small but principled movements among women, even during imperial days, that militantly opposed marriage. Today, such movements, historically associated mainly with southeastern China, exist in Hong Kong and Singapore, where they do not come under governmental interdiction. Some such movements are said to exist in Taiwan but, being frowned upon by the authorities, they assume other guises and escape notice as formal organizations. Marjorie Topley, an anthropologist who has lived in Hong Kong for many years, has made a study of the misanthropic women's associations there. While many of the women who join such a sisterhood have refused to marry, others are drawn into the group by their resentment of the marriage they have already entered, often against their will. Although some of these associations have no physical estate, existing only in the sworn bonds of sisterhood, others have houses where the women live or where they may come when they wish. Invariably Buddhist, hence opposed to the eating of meat, the places are referred to as "vegetarian halls." Membership is formalized by rituals of swearing loyalty before a divine image, usually of the goddess Kuan Yin, in the presence of witnesses. Such a ceremony is, in fact, the equivalent of a wedding, and includes many of the points of ritual we have already described. While entrance into such a sisterhood seems to be associated with a celibate life, lesbianism is apparently not infrequent. The whole matter is quite complex and is related to a major current in Chinese ideology and social organization. An important, if obscure, Chinese religion is involved, the Great Way of Former Heaven, which is based on Buddhism but has many syncretic elements. This woman's movement also has historical ties to a secret society—White Lotus—which is known to have been in existence for at least seven hundred years. Not all of these elements seem to be active in the women's vegetarian halls in Hong Kong. Women members told Topley their reasons for joining; they covered a wide range of motivations. Perhaps at the core was the impracticality of a mature unmarried woman's remaining in her natal home; the sisterhoods provided her with an alternative.

In response to the *san ts'ung,* "the three compliances," by which a Chinese woman was subjected to the domination first of her father, then to her husband, and, finally, as a widow, to her son, some women preferred to join these misanthropic vegetarian halls that served as nunneries. One would think the alternative might have been to divorce. After all, divorce has been available in Chinese law at least since Han times, two thousand years ago.

Tai Yen-hui, an authority on the history of Chinese law, points out that where English provides only a few words, such as divorce, desertion, and separation, to describe the cessation of marriage, Chinese has at least eight distinct expressions. Most of these denote the husband's expulsion of the wife. For many centuries, the husband has had access to the *ch'i ch'u,* "seven exits," or grounds for divorce. A man could easily shed a wife if she mistreated his parents or grandparents, or if she failed to bear him a son within a reasonable time. She could be divorced for adultery, but she could not bring a comparable charge against her husband, because he enjoyed the legal privileges of polygyny and concubinage. Indeed, if she were jealous enough to interfere with her husband's taking a concubine, he could use her jealousy as ground for divorce. A wife could be divorced if she had an incurable disease, because such an illness would interfere with her participation in ancestor worship. She could be expelled for theft. (One actual long-ago case reveals that a woman was divorced after she plucked two fruits from a neighbor's tree.) Finally, and most humiliating of all, a wife could be divorced because she talked too much, since it was said that a woman's loquacity led to bickering among relatives.

A woman had no grounds for divorce, although cases through the years indicate that divorces were available to those who managed to present their causes at the magistrate's *yamen,* "office." Such pleas would be dealt with on an ad hoc basis, without reference to a code. On the other hand, women were protected to some extent against random expulsion by the *san chih,* "three restraints," which prevented a man from divorcing a wife who had performed three years of mourning for his parents, or had no place to go (no relatives to care for her), or, if he was now rich, whom he had married when he was poor.

The "seven exits, three restraints" approach to divorce, with women having no formal grounds for their own petitions, lasted until 1931, when the Republic of China activated a new code that combined older Chinese law with elements borrowed from other legal traditions, such as the German and the English.

Provisions for uncontested divorces by mutual consent are liberal, and such divorces can sometimes be had in less than a day.

Absence of mutuality, however, brings things to a halt; litigation may go on forever. In addition to previous grounds for divorce, others have been added since 1931. These include insanity, bigamy, maltreatment, and attempted murder. But the mistreatment of the parents of one spouse by the other spouse is still a major reason for divorce. The most important real change is that these grounds are now available equally to wives. Despite such alterations, inequities continue, such as preferential treatment of husbands' custodial rights, and these inequities have led to requests for reform, particularly from women lawyers.

Most Chinese we have spoken to in Taiwan, whether they are Taiwanese or Mainlanders, lack personal experience with divorce, and have no divorced friends and acquaintances. One prominent intellectual, when asked if he knew people who were divorced, thought deeply for a while. Finally he brightened, and launched into the story of a woman now a professor at a major Taiwanese university. She was married quite young to a man with few intellectual leanings but a flair for business. While he was amassing a fortune, his wife went to Japan, where she earned a doctorate. When she returned to Taiwan, she found her husband's schedule perplexing, and she finally decided to follow him. This led to the discovery that her husband had not only a mistress, but a second family, complete with children. She filed for divorce, and her petition was granted. That seemed to be the end of our friend's story, but, after a pause, he continued. "You know," he said, "now that woman is sorry. She is over forty, and will not find another husband. Now she says she acted in too much haste. She could have found some other way."

Despite changes in the law, divorce is not popular in Taiwan to the present day. In 1969, for example, the divorce rate was about 4.4 percent. The peak had been hit earlier, in 1966, with a rate of 5.1 percent. Such rates are tiny compared with the 49.9 percent rate reported for the United States in 1978, or the traditional Hausa divorce rate, which was probably higher than our contemporary rate in the United States.

The low overall divorce rate in Taiwan cloaks a more complex situation. In his research in Shulin, a northern Taiwanese community, anthropologist Arthur Wolf has had access to the meticulously kept official household registers compiled by the police since pre-Japanese occupation. For the period 1881–1915, in that part of the district known as Hai-shan, the divorce rate (the number of divorces divided by the number of marriages) was about 12.5 percent. This is surprising, because it is more than twice the current postmodernization rate, and was found in what was then a rural area. Further analysis reveals that divorce rates in that area for marriages contracted in the normal way (patrilocal, with the bride joining the household of her groom only after the wedding) were only slightly higher than the modern rate. But divorce rates following matrilocal or *siaosiv* marriages (see above) ran three to four times higher. The conventional idea of the Chinese wife's boundless passivity in the face of marital oppression is shaken by these data.

Wolf has also dealt a blow to the stereotype that in Chinese society widows remarry only in exceptional cases. Instead, his data show that between 1886 and 1940, in the same district, a major determinant of a widow's chance of remarriage was her age. Almost seventy percent of widows nineteen or younger remarried, as did more than half of all those who became widowed when they were under thirty. The rate dropped to zero above age forty.

In two essays, anthropologist Norma Diamond has raised questions about changes in the status of women in Taiwan. Flawed by the author's relatively uncritical account of conditions in the People's Republic of China, compared with her bristling hostility to the Nationalist government on Taiwan, Diamond's articles nonetheless raise important issues.

First, there is the reality of the Taiwanese woman's secondary role. The government would have us believe that women's rights are being advanced, but Diamond makes a good case against this view. Women are grossly underemployed outside the home, they do not get jobs commensurate with their education, and their access to higher or technical education is still greatly restricted. A host of related specifics lies beyond. In their own perceptions, women in Taiwan see themselves as lonely, lacking in opportunities for making friends, not having the physical mobility enjoyed by men, dominated by fashion and cosmetics, and not taken seriously by their teachers. Yet the novelty in Diamond's work is not that these observations are linked with the lingering effects of traditional marriage and family structure, but to the ongoing realities of life. In brief, Diamond shows that a move from extended to nuclear family organization is not one that frees women. As a matter of fact, families that include a working wife are found statistically more likely to include other relatives, particularly the husband's mother, than are households in which the woman is solely a housewife, possibly because the husbands of working wives are more resistant to taking responsibility for basic child care. Women either place the care of children as their unquestioned first priority, or, if they do not, they display great ambivalence, if not guilt, about it. Diamond believes that in Taiwan the "oppression [of women] has become stronger in the past decade or so despite dramatic gains made by some women earlier in the century."

If Diamond's view reflects the situation objectively, we can only interpret it as a backlash, such as the one American feminists are experiencing over the ratification of the Equal Rights Amendment and the strong gains by opponents who advocate an amendment to the Constitution to reverse the Supreme Court decision of 1973 that made abortion legally available. As Shaw so aptly phrased it in the words of the Devil in *Man and Superman:* ". . . all history is nothing but a record of the oscillations of the world between . . . two extremes. An epoch is but a swing of the pendulum; and each generation thinks the world is progressing because it is always moving."

CHAPTER FIVE

Death

"FRIEND! I who dwell here, the face of my father is never lost to me" was the sentiment expressed by one Tikopian man many years after his father perished at sea. The affection of children for their parents is very great, owing in large part to the love and care lavished on them from infancy and in part to the powerful bonds that tie together members of a *paito*—siblings, cousins, and their children and grandchildren all descended from the same male ancestor. Because the mother's brothers, the *tuatina,* play a major role in the life of a Tikopian, their group is also considered *paito,* to acknowledge the importance of the kinship bond.

The eldest son, *te urumatua,* has special status vis-à-vis his father, who consults him before making a decision that affects the family. This deference is mutual—they "listen" *(fakarongo)* to each other, even though the father is the "head" *(pokouru)* of his son and maintains a position superior to him. The respect with which a son treats his father does not merely spring from love for him, but is dictated by custom, and enforced by the severe disapproval of the community if the son should break the social and moral code. Hitting a father or a mother is unthinkable, an act of sacrilege. Children may not utter the names of their parents, nor are they allowed to touch them once they are grown. An important point of etiquette a Tikopian child learns at an early age is never to sit with his back to an elder, this being considered a sign of disrespect.

145

Reinforced through childhood, deep feelings of love and respect persist into adulthood. Tikopian offspring openly show affection for their parents and take care of them in their old age.

When a man thinks he is dying, he usually instructs his eldest son in the proper division of his estate, a larger proportion of which goes to this son, as his father's confidant and executor. The Tikopians say that "the daughter is treated just the same as the eldest male." Although it is not spelled out, we assume that they are referring to the eldest daughter or to an only daughter. The father's belongings, which cannot be used by his children during his lifetime, become cherished *tauarofa*, "links of affection," after his death.

Children take care not only of their own parents but of other aged relatives as well. Still, those couples who are not able to have children of their own usually adopt some, in order to enjoy their companionship while young and their economic contributions to the household as they get older.

So isolated and lacking in information about the world were the Tikopians in 1929 that Firth had to assure them that people in other places also wept at funerals, treasured mementos of dead relatives and friends, and could be deeply moved by the photograph of a departed loved one. Their ignorance of the outside world contrasted sharply with their exceptional sophistication in understanding the motivations of their fellow Tikopians, their keen perception of human interaction, and their perfect diplomacy in complex situations.

When illness strikes a Tikopian, his senior *tuatina,* his mother's eldest brother, comforts him, supports his body, and rubs tumeric on his neck, chest, and shoulders. If a boy or a young man dies, the mother's brothers are fully responsible for his burial, while his father and his relatives mourn and make gifts to the mother's relatives, to express appreciation for all their efforts, care, and concern. When an older man dies, the sons of his sister wail while his own sons stay in seclusion. In the old days, men cut their long hair when there was a death in the family, but as contact with outsiders increased and young men went to work for wages on other islands, they brought back not only material goods but the latest fashions. They returned wearing their hair short, a vogue that spread throughout the island. Now there is no longer any hair cutting associated with funerals.

So deeply imbued with filial respect and fear of the wrath of their ancestors are Tikopians that the breaking of a taboo may be followed by symptoms of conversion hysteria. Firth was told the story of a man who hit his mother, many years before she died. When he struck her, she wept bitterly. After her death the man suffered from a pustular infection that broke into open lesions on his arms and legs. This painful condition resisted every cure attempted over a number of years. This is the Tikopian account given to Firth: "The mother goes and announces to her ancestors: 'My son has not spoken properly to me. I have been struck by him.' Her ancestors grow angry; they speak: 'It is good that you return to men to work sickness upon your son.' She does so and the thing is done."

As we have mentioned in previous chapters, suicide used to be very common among the Tikopians and could be triggered by what might seem to us to be minor events—shame at some trivial foolishness, such as passing gas in public, rejection by a lover, openly expressed anger toward a parent—could lead to an impetuous end rather than sober consideration, apology, finding a new love. As Tikopians gained mobility over the years and were able to work and settle on other islands in the Solomons, particularly in the Russells, there has been a dramatic drop in the suicide rate. The ease with which an embarrassed young man, a jilted lover, or a momentarily disrespectful son could leave the scene and find surcease and perspective on other shores clearly eliminated the need for him to end his life on impulse. Another great influence has been the conquest of Tikopia by Christian doctrines that hold suicide to be a mortal sin. Tikopians did not fear death in the past; if they still face it with equanimity, it may be attributed to the congruence of the teachings of the native culture and the Christian mission, both stressing the eternal life of the soul.

Pagan Tikopians used to bury the dead under the flooring of the house. Someone who was very ill then could say to those nearest: "I shall be buried by you under your sleeping mat, I shall lie below while you live above, at the place where my head lies to sleep." This practice ceased when the missionaries forbade it, and since then Tikopians have buried the dead some distance from their homes, although still not in a cemetery.

Even though in the matter of the gravesite of the dead Tikopians follow the rules of the Christian mission, they continue to couple Christian prayers with traditional Tikopian rituals. A funeral is observed by all Tikopians as a syncretic ceremony, part Christian, part pagan, in which the Christian element is not the major one. After a corpse is wrapped in pandanus mats a red cross is painted in turmeric on its head. The mourners hold crosses made of leaves; these they toss into the grave along with hibiscus and ginger flowers before the earth is filled in. For ordinary people a stone is placed at the head of the grave but for people of rank a wooden cross is put up. *Putu,* a large amount of green food, was placed on the grave in the past. There used to be as many as eight sets of gifts given by mourners to the family, each requiring a reciprocal gift.

Ara manongi, the old funeral rite of the "fragrant path," required that siblings and sisters' children perform a dance to sacred songs. Food was roasted over a fire kindled by two women, and men and women danced at the same time. After the dancing was over everyone sat down to consume the food prepared by the women, who wore new bark-cloth skirts. Today, the ritual of the "fragrant path" has been almost completely eliminated from funerals, and the number of exchanges of food and gifts has been substantially reduced. *Putu* is no longer placed on a grave.

Another burial ceremony is "pressing down the grave mat"— firming the soil after interment and covering the grave with aromatic leaves. This is believed to protect the corpse from hostile spirits. In addition, the ancestral spirits of the mother's family keep watch over the grave to protect it from wandering alien ghosts. On the fifth day after death the ancestors' spirits come and take the dead person's *ora,* its soul, to *Rangi,* the spirit world. The *ora* is taken to the *Rangi* of its own clan where it is immersed for five days in a cleansing pool. The *Rangi,* of which there are several, are ranked according to status just as the clan was ranked on the island, perpetuating Tikopia social structure. The newly arrived soul is ushered into the presence of his *atua,* spiritual beings, carrying with him the grave offerings of food and bark cloth. Each chief and each ritual elder has a group of his own *atua,* ranked very much according to his station in Tikopia society before death.

Children are buried with a simplified form of adult funeral rites, but stillborn infants are buried without ceremony of any sort.

The objects buried with the dead may include a saw, some beads, calico, knives, and an adze. Although burial rituals have been shortened and the period of mourning reduced from thirty to only a few days, the basic structure of a funeral remains the same. The mourners still tear at their cheeks until blood is drawn to display grief, and some staunch members of the Christian congregation still practice as spirit mediums. The belief in the *atua* persists as well as in their *mana*, their power. The *mana* of a chief has been somewhat reduced. Tikopians say that he can no longer bring death to someone who incurs his displeasure, but he can still bring illness and misfortune. At the same time, a priest is seen to possess *mana* as the intermediary between God and man. The taboos that forbid such behavior as children's uttering the names of their parents or raising a hand against them continue to be observed, and those who break a taboo fear retribution from the spirit of the person offended.

Larson reports that funerals in Nukufero in the Russell Islands are even simpler than those in Tikopia. The relatives gather quickly after a death, the corpse is wrapped in calico and pandanus mats, and after church services the mother's relatives take care of the burial, often in the person's own orchard. Only one oven is used by the father's relatives to prepare the food offered those who buried the body. They, in turn, reciprocate with gifts. During mourning, paternal relatives signify their grief by not participating in the usual dances, one of the chief forms of entertainment in Nukufero. They also adorn their necks and hair with flowers, and some carry a fan, a symbol of personal loss.

Obedience, respect, tenderness, and compassion toward parents are enjoined in the Koran for those Muslims who would secure their way into paradise. The Muslim Hausa do not use euphemisms like "senior citizen" in discussing their elders. In accordance with their religious teachings, they are inculcated with a deep sense of responsibility for the care and support of their parents, or of any elderly member of their close family who is no longer able to work or to function self-sufficiently. While both parents are alive, their grown children support them in the home, rich with memories of their vigorous years, where they spent their lives. If they reach the point of not being able to take care of themselves, children who can afford it will hire a nurse to move in with them and look after them. If this arrangement is financially impossible, the parents are moved into a special hut built by one of the children in his own compound, and they stay there until they die. They do not have to worry about food, clothing, medical care, or spending money—their offspring take care of all that.

Children who have moved to a city usually prefer to maintain their parents in their home village, where they can enjoy the comfort of familiarity and peace of mind. There is considerable pressure on adult sons and daughters not only to support parents financially, but to visit them at regular intervals, often once a week.

If the elderly couple have no surviving children, a younger brother or sister or a nephew or niece assumes full responsibility. Although probably idealized, informants report that this is often done with devotion and grace. If an old parent has an unmarried daughter, the daughter's obligation is clear—she must live with the parent and provide complete care. The Muslim Hausa have no homes for old people; the notion of institutional care has not yet infiltrated the culture.

Belief in life after death is part of the Islamic faith, and the prerequisites for entering paradise are clearly defined in the Koran. Although the Hausa have four different Muslim sects—Malikiya the major one, Hannafiya close behind, followed by Kadiriya, and an extremely small number of Shafiiya—the differences in ritual practices are, to an observer, minor. To give one example, the Malikiya pray while standing erect, with their arms rigidly at their sides; by contrast, the Hannafiya, who also stand, cross their arms over their chests. Crosscutting such differences is their fear of ending up in hell after death, where for all eternity molten brass is poured on sinners' and infidels' heads and down their gullets. How to avoid such a fate? One begins by observing the four primary duties: to pray five times each and every day; if rich, to give alms to the poor—one-fortieth of a man's wealth must be distributed to the less fortunate once every twelve months—to fast for the thirty days of Ramadan from 5:30 in the morning until 6:30 in the evening; and, for any man who can afford it, to make the pilgrimage to Mecca; this is "a duty men owe to God." In addition, a Muslim may neither take God's name in vain nor make a graven image of him. He cannot bear false witness, be untruthful, commit fraud, and he must take care to be honest and upright in all his dealings. A woman must be obedient and faithful to her husband and conduct herself with moral rectitude in his absence. She must satisfy his every desire and never refuse him when he calls her, in return for which he must be kind and polite with her and affectionate with his children. Obviously, these prescriptions represent the ideal, yet our informants spoke as if their observance was commonplace.

"Allah never sleeps. He can always see what you're doing and know what you're thinking. If you lie, Allah will punish you; if you steal, Allah will punish you—but if you steal, the police will punish you too," said one of our Hausa informants.

Some people believe in ghosts, who tend to appear at night and throw terrible fright into anyone, but particularly a child. The Hausa cure for this is a special prayer the child must recite before going to sleep. The incantation is coupled with the drinking of *rububu,* an infusion made from the leaves of the *dinya* tree. This should ward off all further apparitions.

More common is seeing an ancestor, such as a grandmother, as one sleeps. This may be in the context of a recurrent dream in which the ancestor returns night after night to frighten the dreamer. The cure is the same as used for chasing away ghosts. Many who have such dreams also believe in the efficacy of *'yanbori* (spirit-dancers), and seek them out for help. The *'yanbori* perform a ritual dance to summon the disturbing spirits and dissuade them from further frightening the living. For their services they charge what the spirits ask them to request, usually a hen or a ram. The animal is slaughtered, its blood "feeding" the spirits, and its flesh is distributed to feed the living. The pagan Hausa have a similar practice, but Muslim Hausa we interviewed told us that fewer and fewer people believe in the power of the *'yanbori,* and report that their services are no longer sought after as they were even twenty years ago.

Paradise is cool—hell is fire. Comparing a pleasantly cool room or a feeling of great happiness to being in paradise is common parlance, but comparing a hot place to hell is not often done by those whose faith is firm and whose fear for their soul's fate after death is great.

The practical aspects of death in the family are quite simple, standing in stark contrast to the most splendid and complex ceremonies of that most celebrated Hausa transition, marriage. If a mature woman dies, her surviving husband takes care of the funeral arrangements. If the husband dies first, his eldest son or a younger brother performs these duties. When death comes to a family, a messenger is immediately sent to relatives far and near. He may go by train, bus, motorbicycle, or car to fetch them. The time of interment is decided according to how long it will take the relatives to arrive. If death strikes in the evening or during the night, the burial is in the late morning or early afternoon. If it happens in the morning, the burial is in the late afternoon. In almost no case is the funeral delayed more than a few hours.

Washing the corpse is mandatory. In the case of a male, the imam performs this task. When a woman dies, either her husband washes her or one of her female relatives. In some cases, an old woman who is also a midwife does the ritual washing. The nostrils of the deceased are stuffed with cotton and the ears are also covered with cotton. The body is then wrapped in white cotton, and the face is covered. The corpse is placed on a mat. The imam stands by it and says the appropriate prayers. He asks divine forgiveness for the deceased, and prays that the soul may rest in peace. Many men stand behind the imam. These are relatives and friends who have come to pay their respects and bid farewell to one who was loved and respected. Men and women never pray together. Whether the deceased is male or female, the men pray with the imam and the women pray in seclusion.

After the religious service, the body is placed in the *makara,* a wooden coffin without a lid, covered with a white cloth. The *makara* is carried by male pallbearers to the cemetery, where the body is lifted out of the coffin and laid in a freshly dug grave. The men sprinkle some earth on it, place on it pieces of broken pottery, then shovel the rest of the earth back into the grave. Another prayer is said, pleading for peace for the departed soul. The longest a body may lie at home is about twelve hours; it must then be buried.

Both men and women cry a great deal, although some people, though sad, are not able to cry. They merely look sad, as the occasion demands. The color of death is white only for the dead

—mourners wear ordinary clothes of any color they choose.

After the funeral the mourning party returns to the home of the deceased. They pray and receive visitors, relatives, friends, and neighbors who have come to express their sorrow and the hope that the departed will rest in peace. Again, the women mourn in seclusion. Visitors may make gifts of money to the immediate family, but this is in no way expected; it is purely voluntary. Cooked food is brought by the visitors; it is consumed by the men at the main entrance to the compound and by the women inside the house.

The initial mourning period lasts for seven days, after which everybody returns to say prayers with the imam. Forty days after the initial period of mourning the relatives again return to say prayers. At this time the food is prepared by the immediate family of the deceased. If a man dies, his wife does the cooking, with the help of relatives. If a woman dies, the food is prepared by her female relatives and female in-laws. The food is served to those who come, and portions are sent to those who are not able to attend but who, in turn, may send food and nonalcoholic beverages to the family. These simple exchanges mark the end of the period of mourning.

When a child under twelve dies, the rituals are the same, but the initial period of mourning is reduced from seven to three days. If a woman gives birth to a stillborn baby, or to one who dies within hours, her female relatives and friends come to give her comfort and sympathy. On the seventh day, which would have been the naming day of the baby, a ceremony called *fitanbakway* takes place. No man may participate in this. The grieving mother's female relatives and friends bring her presents of clothing, food, and money. If it is the woman's first birthing, she is not allowed to cry in the presence of others, not even those closest to her. Her tears may flow only in complete solitude. The infant's burial is the same as an older child's, but there is no ceremony after forty days. The Muslim Hausa never put flowers on graves, nor do they place markers on them. Graves are never visited after the period of mourning is over.

Although Muslims in other countries engage in more elaborate rituals, such as repeated washing of the corpse, stuffing of the anus and vagina with cotton, placing prickly branches on the grave, and, in some places, heavily watering the grave, even a head of state has a simple funeral.

The simplest funeral rites of the societies presented in this book are practiced by the !Kung, who are also the most egalitarian. Before we describe an actual burial, we will present some aspects of the declining years of !Kung men and women.

The respect accorded old people is rooted in the social organization of the nomadic !Kung. Once past adolescence, women are responsible for the gathering of plant foods and fruits; they bear and suckle children. The men hunt for game and participate in the care of the young. When children are ten or twelve, they move away from the parental fire and frequently move in with grandparents, or an elderly widow. Old people have the crucial function of being mentors of the young. They are the repositories of knowledge about kinship ties and etiquette, the tellers of stories, and the teachers of games. They are also the healers of the sick, practitioners of !kia, a transcendental state during which one dies and is reborn. They are capable of communicating with the spirits of the dead. At some point late in their lives they pass on these vital skills to the younger generation.

The scarcity of water in the Kalahari desert is a major threat to existence. Years of experience and expert knowledge are required to find water during the dry season, and older people possess these essential water-finding skills. Once they have established camp near a water hole, old people provide entrée to any relative who wants to join the village and share the water. They are also experienced in human relations; they are able to cool an argument before it ignites into violence. They are looked to with respect for their ability to manage water and other resources, and they are the sources of general comfort and much merriment, for most of them are very fond of playing games and dancing.

The common degenerative diseases, such as hypertension and coronary heart disease, found in western industrial societies are unknown among the !Kung. People are most likely to die from accidents or respiratory ailments, and those who manage to elude the first and resist the second grow to vigorous old age. It is quite usual to see people in their sixties jumping rope, running, and dancing with children and young people. Senility was not seen by the medical specialists or the many anthropologists who spent long periods of time with the !Kung. Caries were not found in teeth, but owing to the quantity of sand in the enormous amount of roughage eaten by the !Kung, those who reach seventy are likely to have teeth ground down to the gums. Eye problems, mostly cataracts, are quite common among the old; some have impaired vision and get around with a cane, some are totally blind and dependent. They are all taken care of, but researchers point out that those with surviving close relations get more attention. The !Kung attitude in general is one of gratitude to the old for having toiled, birthed, and reared children and taught them about kinship, mythology, and spirit dancing.

When a !Kung is ill, a *!kia-*healer is summoned to bring about a cure. If the first healer is not successful, others are called upon for help. If the patient dies, a quick burial is in order. Richard Lee observed a funeral on one of his field trips. This is his account of that event. The corpse was wrapped in a *kaross,* with a blanket obtained through barter wrapped around its legs. A litter was built of two eight-foot poles tied with six crosspieces that were secured with thong, twine, and bark. A pink aromatic powder was sprinkled over the *kaross,* and the body, lifted onto the litter, was carried by pallbearers to the gravesite. The men were relatives on the mother's side. If the mother of the deceased sobbed, his wife also cried. The nearest women to the deceased—mother and wife— were so overcome with grief they had to be supported by other mourners as they walked to the burial ground. Other female relatives also wailed, but here, as elsewhere, the proportion of tears required by the situation could not be distinguished from those shed in deeply felt grief.

The grave was several hundred yards from the village. It was dug with metal spades to a depth of five feet, six-and-a-half feet long and three-and-a-half feet wide. The body was lifted from the litter and handed by the pallbearers to men in the grave who placed it on its back and folded its arms over its chest, slightly flexing its knees. The litter was then broken and laid in pieces on the left side of the body. The earth was shoveled back into the grave and built into a mound. The men chopped away the bush and built an enclosure around the grave.

Aromatic powder was rubbed on the lips and blown into the

ears of young mourners to erase the visual image of the corpse and its burial, and to prevent their ever hearing the sound of its voice again. If successful, there would be no disturbing dreams. With no further ceremony everyone returned to the village. The men washed their hands and bodies in front of the dead man's hut to eradicate all association with his spirit. The possessions of the deceased were given to his surviving children and close relatives.

It is essential that the name of a person be carried on after death. The first child born to a man after the death of his father must be named after that deceased grandfather. If a man has three sons, and each has a son after his death, each will name the baby after him. If the grandchild is born while the man is alive, only the first son of a first son need be named after him. The !Kung believe that a child will tend to have the same qualities as the person he was named after. However, even a lazy, dull-witted, stingy man's name is given to the first son of his first son for fear the //gangwasi, spirits of the dead (plural of //gangwa), will come after his death and threaten the living, bringing illness and misfortune upon them, perhaps even killing them.

One of the frequent cures the !kia-healers are called upon to effect is ridding a person of a //gangwa. Elderly !Kung are expert at this and are very much in demand. A //gangwa can be a dead woman as well as a dead man, but the greatest //gangwa of all is the one who created all people and kills all people. When some !Kung mourners were asked after a funeral if this great //gangwa was good or bad, the answer was: "He must be a very cruel person because he gives life and takes it away."

There were no offerings placed on the grave. A dead person is remembered in conversation, but there is no further mourning—no looking back. As previously seen in Chapter Four, widows and widowers remarry quickly.

A Tlingit funeral today is a pale, westernized affair compared to those of long ago. Wailing has been considerably toned down and the body is buried in a grave, usually in a coffin made by a local carpenter, unless the family has sufficient wealth to have an expensive one flown in.

When Aurel Krause visited the Tlingit in 1881–82, a death in the family involved not only all the relatives, but the larger community. The lamentations of the family could be heard far and wide as the women dressed the deceased in his finest garments and propped him up in a sitting position against the wall of the house, which had been elaborately decorated. A wooden hat was placed on the corpse's head, his face was painted, and he was covered by a blanket richly decorated with buttons. The finest Chilkat blankets were put on his knees and on the blankets were placed a packet of letters of recommendation, requesting good treatment for his soul once it reached its ultimate destination. His most precious belongings were set down at his side, and his wife mutely kept him company.

Important features of the costume were durable shoes and gloves, because the newly dead were expected to traverse very rough terrain, "to go through a lot of devil-clubs and bushes and nettles," before arriving in the other world. The corpse remained in the house for three days, members of the opposite moiety keeping a close vigil, until it was cremated on the fourth day. Delicacies were served to these watchers by members of the dead person's clan, and a special dish was set out to feed the ghost.

Logs were piled in crisscross fashion about four feet high, and the body was placed in the center and covered with twigs and brush. Seal oil was poured on the whole which, when lit, created a fierce and rapid fire. When the ashes had cooled, the bones of the dead were extracted, cleaned, and then wrapped in a blanket to keep his body from catching cold. Although there was a considerable amount of wailing accompanying each stage of the ritual, all was not grim. The mourners, members of the widow's clan, sang to make smooth the passage of the ghost, and danced, holding branches, during the actual cremation ritual. Both men and women, members of the deceased's clan, cut off or burned their hair in the fire of the funeral pyre.

The widow's hair was cut with a mussel shell by her late husband's sisters. Eight days after the shearing the women had their hair washed in the juice of blueberries to prevent its turning white in old age.

There was great feasting the night after the cremation. The elaborate meal served the dual purpose of feeding the dead spirits and those who had attended to the details of the funeral. After cremation those who built the pyre and handled the body had to take a ritual bath. The widow, in particular, was the prisoner of taboo. She had to abstain from speaking for twelve days after the death of her husband, and was not permitted to do work of any sort. She could use neither a knife nor a cup—if she broke a cup, it could cause the death of her next husband. Her clothing and bedding were taken from her and burned with the clippings of her hair, saved for this occasion. She was then given new clothing and bedding. A rock was placed in her bed and a rope tied around her waist. The rock assured long life for her next husband and the rope around her waist guaranteed long life for her relatives.

It took several months to build a grave house to contain the bones and ashes of the deceased. When it was completed, there was another feast at which the estate of the departed was divided. Now the surviving spouse was allowed to marry the person chosen by the family of the deceased. The culmination of the death ritual, the potlatch, was sometimes delayed as much as several years, as a great deal of property had to be accumulated for distribution.

In most cases not only a new grave house was built but also a new house in which the potlatch was to be held, or, at the very least, the old house had to be completely refurbished and restored. Food and gifts were given to members of the opposite moiety; friends, neighbors, and even clans and lineages residing in another place were invited as guests. Food was placed in the fire not only for one particular deceased in whose honor the potlatch was being held but for all those who had died before. In addition to fasting, tobacco was provided for smoking or chewing, and special songs were sung to accompany the dancing. All those who worked on the grave house and the house in which the potlatch was held were handsomely paid.

The fate of the soul depended on the mode of death. Those who died of old age or sickness walked to the land of the dead over a river through woods full of devilclubs and thorny underbrush. They stayed there until they could be reborn in the body of a new infant. A mother can recognize who her baby was in its former existence by birthmarks and behavioral characteristics. Those whose end was violent went to the Land Above; bad characters, murderers, thieves, and witches went to Dog Heaven; those who drowned or were lost in the woods became Land Otter People. The Tlingit concept of heaven was one composed of several layers located "above."

Kiwa'a, the Land Above, is entered through an opening in the clouds that quickly closes up once the spirit is safely inside. It is a wonderful place, its ground covered with rich green turf on which a variety of delightful games are played. One game is a variation of golf, another requires jumping over rocks, still another is played with a ball. The occupants of this celestial domain are the Northern Lights, and when they are seen, people claim to recognize those of their relatives who died by violence. The Tlingit can even see the activities their departed loved ones are engaged in. "Look! There is grandfather, getting water!"

At the entrance to *Kiwa'a* stands a watchman who questions each newly arrived ghost and calls out his name. The newcomer is judged on the basis of his mode of death and moral conduct while on earth. If death was peaceful, the spirit is told that it is lost and must return to earth; the soul of a wretch is directed to Dog Heaven. The inhabitants of *Kiwa'a* know when a man is going to be killed, and they quickly close the opening in the clouds to prevent the violent deed, although they do not always succeed. The Tlingit watch to see the Northern Lights, and when they are close together and appear reddish, it is a sign of an impending death.

"Dog Heaven" is where the truly wicked go after death, the place "between Earth and where the Northern Lights are." It is believed by some that the inhabitants walk on their hands for all eternity. The sky is envisioned as having several layers, Dog Heaven being located in the lowest. There is also a belief that the wicked float among the clouds for all eternity, never finding a resting place. As no one whose spirit ends in Dog Heaven can return to earth inhabiting the body of a newly born infant who could at some time tell what it was like, the place is surrounded by much mystery and speculation.

The concept of a causal relationship between a life of perfect integrity on earth, and a safe passage to greener pastures and ultimate reincarnation, results from an attempt to reconcile stories handed down from generation to generation with the teachings of Christian missionaries. The mixing of conflicting mythologies, not unique to the Tlingit, is rarely thoroughgoing. A number of beliefs, contradictory as they may seem, are frequently held by people at one and the same time. Such a situation is common in cultures subject to change.

The Tlingit Indians warn their children "never take food from a stranger." They tell them that the Land Otter People, who appear disguised in the form of parents or relatives, like nothing better than to snatch children who stray into the woods to pick berries. The Land Otters do this to take revenge against people who shoot them or trap them for their luxurious fur when they have assumed their animal form. But the Land Otters also need a fresh supply of people to maintain their constantly diminishing population. Any child or adult who is captured may be retrieved with the aid of the intercession of a shaman if the food preferred by the Land Otter People has not been consumed. There are other measures that can be taken to avoid such an awful fate. Carrying a piece of metal—a coin, a knife, or even a nail or a ring—may provide protection. All one need do is quickly pop the metal object in one's mouth, and the Land Otter People become frightened and immediately return to their animal forms. Children are also told to defecate and urinate in the presence of these creatures, as they cannot endure the odor of human excrement and will flee from it in disgust. On the other hand, people who die by drowning become Land Otter People, marry Land Otters and have children with them. Drowned people are not considered really dead, but if their bodies are found washed ashore, they are given a funeral like anyone else. The mourners throw food in the water to feed their spirits.

Over the years Tlingit funeral practices have changed considerably, but they still have a decided Tlingit coloration. In the mix of old Tlingit and new Alaskan, the dead are no longer cremated but buried in a western-style cemetery after a Christian funeral service. The body, although dressed in fine clothes and wrapped in a fine blanket, is no longer propped up in a sitting position but laid flat on a stretcher, its face covered with a scarf. The watchers still stay with the body for three days and are fed, as previously, by the relatives of the deceased. They pass the time playing Monopoly or checkers, and swap stories during the vigil. Mourners no longer cut their hair. On the fourth day, the body is placed in a coffin, the face covering lifted so that everyone in Yakutat may take one last look, and then the pallbearers carry the coffin to the cemetery as final prayers are offered. The night after the funeral, members of the deceased's family give a feast to members of the opposite moiety, but this may be held in a local restaurant. Instead of burning food and throwing valuables into the fire they inter such items with the corpse.

A month after the funeral, relatives and friends in Yakutat come to the house of mourning, bringing cooked food. Although the timing may seem odd, the custom is very much in the spirit of mainstream America—friends and relatives cheering up and feeding the bereaved. It is this they now refer to as a potlatch. Sometimes later a tombstone is erected by the family at the head of the grave, which has been covered with plastic flowers. Part of the Memorial Day celebration is devoted to a picnic at the grave site, which usually ends with the singing of hymns led by one of the local Christian ministers.

Do the Tlingit still believe in reincarnation, Dog Heaven, *Kiwa'a* and Land Otter People? Only they know. Do they still commune with the dead? It is unrewarding at best even to ask such a question. The American presence is heavy and deeply resented. If the Indians do still believe in the old-time religion, they confine its practice to the privacy of their homes. Some people we talked to believed that some families still practice ancient Tlingit medicine and probably other rituals as well. They could not document this—nor can we. The Tlingit, then, at least outwardly, have warped their funeral practices to current American Christian norms. This has involved a simplification as well as an alteration of older rituals and behavior.

There are few places in the world where comparable changes have not occurred, but in Chinese culture, as represented in Taiwan, changes have been less profound. Even with the streamlining of many modern Taiwanese funeral rituals and practices, the local Chinese procedures remain colorful and complicated. It is difficult to forget a lavish Chinese funeral.

One sultry summer day in Taipei, in 1964, an ethnographer and his associate, nodding over the records in an inner office of the Virtuous Star Temple on Ninghsia Road, heard the distant sound of music. A procession was approaching. The noise grew in volume, indicating that the parade had turned off the main thoroughfare and into the side street leading past the temple. They dropped their work and hastened outside. Old Mr. T'u was already there making sure that the front gates were closed. As it turned out, the gatekeeper had been warned the day before that the funeral procession would be passing, since it is extremely unlucky for all concerned to have the invisible ghosts and demons that cluster about a funeral enter a temple along the way.

Although the funeral had not yet rounded the corner, its vanguard was already on the street. A few men, dressed in ordinary clothing but with hempen armbands showing that they were with a funeral party, were making little piles of spirit money at widely spaced intervals along the curb and putting a match to them. This was to placate the homeless ghosts who would be attracted by the procession. They also asked vendors and other people whose business was in the street to move to the side, and gave them small payments of currency to do so.

Now came the funeral itself, led by two men in Chinese dress blowing Chinese woodwinds. Behind them was a Buddhist priest, wearing rich saffron robes, riding in a pedicab slowly pedaled by a rather ragged unwashed man. This was the first of five Buddhist priests in the parade. They were likely all repeating over and over again the name of Amitabha Buddha to warn off hostile spirits and to pile up additional merit for the deceased. Flanking the first priest were two men in Chinese shirts and trousers, carrying large white funeral lanterns marked with the name of the dead man, a prominent restauranteur and owner of several magnificent wine houses.*

Behind the lanterns came the first of several musical ensembles, this one a band of Chinese instruments—pipes, woodwinds, flutes, drums, bells, cymbals, and gongs. Further along in the procession were more splendid Chinese orchestras that included stringed instruments. The musicians walked beneath white cloth canopies held aloft on bamboo poles by lines of people. There were also a number of bands with western instruments playing compositions occasionally recognizable despite their lack of

*Elsewhere, in most Chinese settings, "wine house" designates a restaurant, but in Taiwan, only a certain kind of restaurant is thus denoted. The Taiwanese wine house offers female companionship as well as food and drink. The women who work in a wine house usually provide conversation and a moderate amount of physical contact while on the premises, but arrangements can be made for additional services on the outside. In fact, the man whose funeral was being celebrated was involved in prostitution and probably in other rackets as well.

rhythm and melody. The musicians were mostly men, mainly of middle age or older, but there was a sprinkling of women if one looked very closely. Those who played western instruments were dressed in uniforms, quite similar to those associated with high school or college bands in this country, but much seedier. There were no drum majorettes; indeed, drum majors were not discernible. Every musician seemed to be on his own. Despite this casualness the use of music at Chinese funerals is an extremely ancient custom, described in ancient classics of ritual.

Perhaps the longest part of the cortege was taken up by a single file of pedicabs, each carrying a large wreath perhaps four feet in diameter, and made up of white, lilylike blooms or other flowers of similar pale color. The wreaths were mounted on tripods made of bamboo; they had been on display at the mortuary or at the house of the deceased, and would be left at the grave. In the center of each wreath were praises and condolences, with the name of the donor prominently displayed.

Now came the main part of the procession, led by a pedicab on which was arranged a large portrait photograph of the dead man, taken some years before. Behind were two special vehicles that have to be hired for such occasions. These are built on metal frames that permit one man to draw a small platform suspended between a pair of bicycle wheels. On the platform was a cylindrical structure of finely carved wood, rather like filigree, standing about six feet high. Through a window in the front could be seen a shelf holding a ceramic incense burner, from which wafted thin ribbons of smoke and a pleasing aroma. Just behind, in a similar vehicle, was the temporary spirit tablet of the dead man. To each side was a person dressed in mourning, marked by a combination of white and hempen cloth, and carrying a mourner banner made of a hoop of hemp-covered bamboo about fifteen inches in diameter from which fluttered seven long thin strips of white fabric, the whole held aloft on a thin bamboo pole. This was followed by an ordinary flatbedded motortruck, which carried the coffin. Several mourners rode with the coffin, but most brought up the end of the procession, a straggling group of several score moaning and sometimes crying individuals whose differences of mourning costume marked the closeness of their relationships to the deceased.

Although some of the features of the funeral procession just described have recurred for a long time in certain areas of China, they cannot be represented as typical. To begin with, the funeral described was for a very wealthy person; for the poor, ritual can be cut to such a degree that little is left. What is more, the kind of funeral described has become increasingly rare in present-day Taipei, as in other large cities in Taiwan, but may be seen, on a smaller scale, in the countryside. For the most part, however, whether in cities or in the rural areas, the funeral procession tends more and more to be confined to one or two motortrucks—one for the coffin and the immediate family, and the other for more distant mourners and a few musicians.

On the other hand, it is still possible, though very rare, to see a funeral of even grander scope than the one described. Added to such a funeral would be a number of bamboo and paper offerings to be burned at graveside. Each object thus committed is believed to be of use to the dead in the other world: servants, sedan chairs, automobiles, furniture, tape recorders, television sets—paper replicas of anything one can imagine are being made by the dwindling number of specialists who still make a living at this craft. This aspect of the Chinese treatment of the dead is part of a larger complex that requires sacrifices of food, wine, and other material things at the grave and in special shrines in the home or at the temples. Even as this is being written, the Chinese festival of grave visitation and cleaning, Ch'ing Ming, which falls on the third day of the third lunar month, is sufficiently close that one could go to any of the several New York City cemeteries patronized by Chinese and find at certain graves the remains of food sacrificed to the dead (and eaten by the mourners as a picnic), plus ritual goods, such as spirit money, or things the dead might enjoy, such as decks of playing cards. (But in China or Taiwan, such things would be found only rarely, since it is better understood there that the structure of the afterworld requires most things, food being an exception, to be transmuted to the world of the dead by burning.) But, to get back to marks of an especially lavish and conservative funeral, perhaps the most spectacular is the addition of exorcists, who frighten off trespassing, hostile ghosts by dressing up as gods, or walking on stilts, or doing acrobatics, or juggling as the cortege moves through the streets. When all this is added, the funeral takes on the air of a circus procession. No wonder it is watched by thousands as it makes its way up narrow streets and then out to the grave.

Just as people of different wealth and status receive different funerals, so differences of age, sex, birth order, and cause of death may affect not only the quality of the funeral but the ultimate fate of the soul. In China, including Taiwan, until quite recent decades, it was the custom to dispose of the bodies of infants who died in the first few months of life with extreme casualness. But the basis for what seems an uncaring procedure can be explained. Such children were believed to be not the genuine offspring of the stricken parents but evil spirits, in the form of children, seeking to insinuate their way into a household. Received as proper children, they would have devastated the household, mainly by spreading disease and bringing death to the other children. To avoid this, they had to be treated for what they were—strangers, aliens, interlopers, noxious spirits. Such a child had to be buried in the shallowest of graves, for it was hoped that the little corpse would be eaten by a dog or some other animal. The spirit would then have been trapped in that animal, a reasonable fate for both ghost and beast.

After a child has been fully recognized and taken to the bosom of the family, there may be considerable grief at death, yet there will be little public display. No funeral such as that described above would ever take place for a child, unless, of course, that child was of special status, for example, the child of a reigning monarch. Funerals of great elaborateness could celebrate the deaths of women, particularly those of advanced years whose sons had great wealth and power. The largest funeral in memory in Ch'uhsien, Anhwei (Chuxien, Anwei), during Mort's residence there in 1948–49, was that of a woman in her late seventies who had died several years earlier. The long delay leading up to her funeral was not untoward. Ostensibly, it was due to the inability of a frequently changing team of geomancers and astrologers to come to a positive decision on a favorable gravesite. Actually, it may have had something to do with the straitened circumstances of the war years. By 1947, however, the woman's son had become a tremendously wealthy Shanghai businessman, and a favorable spot for her burial was then found. Her coffin was retrieved from its temporary brick mausoleum in an open field, and the town was treated to a lavish spectacle, the funeral procession taking half an hour to pass a particular site.

While women may receive ceremonious funerals, their second-ary status continues to be manifested in more ordinary Taiwanese funeral ceremonies, although with less emphasis now than in the past. It was not long ago that women mourning their husbands were required to walk behind the coffin as they had walked after their living husbands, while in the reverse situation, the man walked in front of the coffin of his wife, or perhaps alongside it. It is still not unusual to find that the streamers attached to the memorial portrait or flying from the funeral banners read "faithful and devoted" *(chung hsin)* for a man, but "chaste and submissive" *(chen shun)* for a woman, as was reported a century ago. Sex differ-ences are also of great importance in establishing the type of spirit one will be after death. Women who have died in childbirth com-prise a category of particularly malevolent ghosts. It should not be thought, however, that women are uniformly belittled in funeral rituals. William Barnett, the anthropologist who made a study of Sanlei, a village quite close to Taipei, found that a woman who had married into a family and borne children would be given a more expensive funeral than a male of equivalent age in the same fam-ily, provided that the latter had remained unmarried.

In Taiwan, as elsewhere in the modern urban world, death at home is becoming less and less common, because people who are seriously ill are taken to hospitals. In the United States it is a remarkable hospital that does not severely curtail visiting rights and treat the relatives with little concern. While similar patterns are definitely seeping into the picture in Taiwan, a much more relaxed attitude still prevails. Many hospitals, including the Na-tional Taiwan University Hospital, encourage relatives to stay with the patient twenty-four hours a day, rendering services be-yond those supplied by the nurses. Patients so attended do not die in isolation but as they would at home, surrounded by a roomful of kin, including children.

As the number of people dying outside their homes increases, so does the popularity of the mortuary parlor, especially in cities. It is obviously difficult to carry out traditional rituals, such as washing the body and laying it out, in small apartments. To bring so many mourners and condolence callers to such a small space would be quite uncomfortable. Still, as we ourselves have seen, there is a solution that makes only limited use of the services of a mortician. Where the house is too small, a shed may be built outside; in the city this is done sometimes in the adjacent street, although a nearby vacant lot is preferable. In either case, a shed is thrown together of hempen mats on a bamboo scaffold. Inside, an altar is built. The coffin rests upon a trestle of planks and sawhorses in front of the altar.

When funerals take place from the home, the dying person is usually moved to the central room where one expects to find the family's ancestor tablet or tablets, plus other religious paraphernalia—perhaps an idol or two, a censer, candelabra, and other objects too numerous and varied to list. As soon as the person dies, pains are taken to cover the tablets with white cloth or with hempen mats and baskets, on the somewhat surprising ground that the ancestors are averse to the sight of death.

Traveling through the back roads of Pingtung County in southern Taiwan a few years ago, we noticed first one dead cat hanging from a tree and then another. Over several days we must have counted more than a dozen, in varying stages of decay. There are many beliefs about house cats in the Taiwanese countryside; one of the most interesting has to do with death. Should a cat leap upon a corpse as it awaits placement in its coffin, the corpse would be invigorated with demonic life, and would become a monster. To avoid such unpleasantness, in many locales corpses awaiting burial are never left alone. In more traditional families, members take turns through the night sitting in the room with the deceased. In mortuary establishments this is a task now more likely, but not invariably, to be done by a professional corpse watcher. (It is not unusual in New York City or other cosmopolitan places to have the caskets of observing Jews watched overnight by a hired prayer reader.) In any event, even a dedicated watchman can nod off, and the stealth and ability of cats is well known. Better to catch a cat, strangle it, and hang it from the branch of a tree, thereby obviating the possibility of a nasty revival of a newly dead spirit. This is only one of many beliefs surrounding death that are still held by an undetermined portion of the population.

Incidentally, if so many dangers lurk in delaying a funeral, one may wonder why the process is often so long drawn out? It is true that in recent years funerals in Taiwan have not only been getting simpler but also less protracted. In former years, the interval between death and burial was rarely less than a few weeks. Despite the penchant for making preparations well in advance of the funeral (including the purchase of a coffin that might well have been proudly displayed in the house of its intended occupant), many things were still to be done, of which the most important was the regulation of the episodes of the funeral by astrological and other calendrical portents. Just as was seen in the arrangement and scheduling of weddings, it is important to calculate precise moments for such events as placing the body in the coffin and moving it to the grave. Deciding the site of the grave or tomb, for example, is believed to have effects that will be felt for generations.

Just as one can tell in advance, by consulting a Chinese almanac, when there will be a day of many weddings, so the same source will reveal days particularly auspicious for funerals. Scheduling the funeral remains complicated for a great many conservatively religious Chinese in Taiwan. They continue to consult a variety of specialists, including the *yin-yang hsien-sheng,* or geomancer. This is a person trained in reading the character of the landscape at a particular site, its *feng-shui,* or "wind-water." Some aspects of *feng-shui* seem obvious. A lineage of the surname Ch'en had its ancestral tombs in the area of the town of Nei-p'u, and things had gone moderately well for them until an interloper bought up some land adjacent to their tomb. Shortly after, the new owner built a pigsty immediately facing the lineage plot. Although this led to some grumbling, it was at first resented only as an aesthetic intrusion. But then complaints of other kinds of trouble began to accumulate—children of the lineage getting poor grades in their entrance examinations, minor officials failing to get promotions, business men experiencing reverses—the ancestors were displeased. The lineage entered into negotiations with the owner of the pigsty. It was a difficult matter, complicated by the inability of the lineage to act as a corporation, owing in major part to restrictive laws tied to land reform. Finally, a few wealthy individuals came forward and a settlement was reached, the pigsty was dismantled, and peace was restored.

The family or lineage having a permanent burial plot is spared the recurrent investigation that goes into locating suitable gravesites, but the initial search for a site for such a large multiple-use tomb is correspondingly more intricate and elaborate. Efforts to find such tombsites go on in Taiwan today, spurred by the island's industrial prosperity. A modern transistor tycoon is quite likely to devote part of his profits to buying a favorable grave site and building an impressive tomb, likely of the conventional, omega-shaped type known not only throughout Taiwan but over much of southeastern China.

Most people cannot afford magnificent graves, and are increasingly driven to buy plots in municipally controlled burial grounds. Even under such circumstances a geomancer may be used, either to select a particular site from a restricted set of options, or to confirm the suitability of the available grave. An alternative procedure is to ask the ancestors themselves. This may be done by the custom known as *suan pei* "reckoning the blocks," the blocks being crescent-shaped pieces of painted red wood, flat on one surface, round on the other, usually about three inches long and an inch or so wide at the widest point. They are held to the forehead or at least raised high by a petitioner who asks, usually silently, a question that calls for a yes or no answer. The petitioner then drops the two *pei*. If one of the blocks lands flat side down and the other flat side up, that is an affirmative reply. Both flat sides down is a negative response, and two rounded sides down is called "playing a joke"—it is an indefinite response and must lead to a recast.

The persistence of belief in geomancy was brought home to us when we were being driven to one of the southern suburbs of Taipei by an old friend, a distinguished university professor. As we went by the hills that flank Taipei to the west, which are one of the principal sites of graves for the city dwellers, our friend remarked that his father, whom we had known, was now buried on such and such a hill, and he pointed to it. From the gravesite, he said, the street on which his own house stood, perhaps even the top of his house, could be seen. He thought the placement of the grave would have made—or would make, since such a distinction is not normally forthcoming in Chinese grammar—the old man happy. The family had certainly been prosperous since that interment.

The idea that the dead are at least as important as the living, if not much more so, is basic to much of Chinese belief, behavior, and social organization. For that reason, the apparently swift changes of attitude that have been remarked in the People's Republic of China deserve careful study and comment. As we will see, the situation is not entirely clear on the mainland with respect to current burial practices and beliefs about the dead. Certainly the government minimizes the desirability of lavish funerals, impressive tombs (except for Mao's), or observance of ancestral ritual. One anthropologist born in China, who returned to the old family home after residing in the United States for more than thirty years, found himself reacting with ambivalence to the extensive use of cremation and the minimal display of concern about the ashes of the dead or their receptacle.

Although graves of the omega type, previously described, are common throughout Taiwan, they are not the only form of grave. Indeed, there are a variety of such constructions, ranging from the kinds of mound one is accustomed to seeing in north and central China, through western-style graves, and beyond to concrete mortuaries, where the bones of the dead can seemingly be kept forever. Actually, the phrase "bones of the ancestors" is highly appropriate to Taiwan burial customs. Although many people on the island prefer massive wooden caskets much heavier in design and construction than we are accustomed to, these are associated with once-and-for-all interment. A major proportion of Taiwanese proceed otherwise. These people exhume the remains of the dead after the passage of five or six years, and find that much of the soft tissue has rotted away. There follows a practical and ceremonial cleaning of the bones, usually performed by the sons and daughters of the dead person. When the bones have been cleaned and polished, they are placed in a new receptacle, this time a ceramic urn, and they are reburied. If possible, some members of the family will return at least once a year, at Ch'ing Ming, the festival of graves, to sweep the grave, sacrifice to the spirit of the dead, and enjoy a meal at the site. Very important ancestors, such as the founders of active lineages, are also likely to have their graves visited on the anniversaries of their deaths.

Many of the dead who receive sacrifices are feted in two or more places. They may be sacrificed to at home, before the domestic shrine in which their spirit tablet may be found, in the lineage hall, where they may also be represented by a tablet, and in a clan hall, an even larger temple where yet another tablet to them may be found. They can also be worshiped at their graves. How does the Chinese conception of the soul accommodate such practices? It is indeed quite complicated.

As fits a culture so deep in time and so broad in space, variation has been great, and the differences from region to region are profound. Still, it may not be too much of a simplification to say that the minimal belief, apart from that which holds that the soul does not exist at all, is in a dual soul. The two components of common belief include the yin soul, a dark and potentially malignant spiritual essence closely associated with the remains, and usually to be found at the grave. The other soul is yang, bright, benign, and thoroughly spiritual. This soul may take abode, at least temporarily, in one of the several spirit tablets (ancestor tablets) commemorated to it, or it may reside in the Western Heaven, a realm of bliss sharply contrasted with hell. The concept of hell, in China, derives mainly from Buddhism, hence is an important and ancient one. Hell itself is complex, having ten layers and a bureaucratic structure that reflects the complicated government of the ancient empire.

While no theology is completely consistent within itself, Chinese belief is conspicuously uneven, owing to a variety of conditions. For one, there is an absence of focus of doctrinal authority. Then there is the long history of eclecticism and syncretism. We also note the mosaic character of Chinese culture, which includes a wide variety of local cultures. Finally, we must point to the exceptionally long stretch of time all these systems have been in operation. So it was that when we, during research in clan temples, asked various people whether the souls of the ancestors resided in the tablets bearing their names in the temple, we recorded many disparate replies. A fairly common response, however, indicated that sacrifices at the temple were instrumental in maintaining the soul substance of ancestors. Failure to gain regular subsistence through such sacrifices would lead to the gradual attenuation and impoverishment of the ancestors. There is some disagreement among students of Chinese religion about how widespread the belief is that ancestral spirits are capable of doing damage to derelict descendants. This probably reflects a split in Chinese belief.

Some of the people with whom we talked described their participation in both collective ancestor rites and individual worship as
a matter of social conscience, a classic Confucian response. But
other informants admitted more personal reasons, including fear
of reprisal. Ancestors experiencing reduced standards of living in
the other world could be nasty. They were capable of bringing
illness, domestic strife, or failure to mundane projects. Of course,
one made sacrifices to the ancestors out of respect or love, but
there were other motivations also.

Recent studies of Chinese mortuary customs, including the
worship of ancestors in the home and in the lineage hall, have
indicated a significant economic framework for such practices and
devotions. Not everyone within the families committed to the
practice of maintaining ancestor ritual receives a tablet when he
or she dies. As we have already seen, children who die very young
may be regarded as demonic visitors collecting long overdue debts.
Such children receive no tablets; most people who die young are
denied tablets unless they are associated with fairly violent post-
humous activity, manifested by illness in the house, failing projects, familial discord, a run of bad luck. A shaman may be consulted. Whether or not by seance, it is determined that a child of
the house, let us say a young woman of perhaps only fourteen
years who had died some years before, was now intensely dis-
tressed because she had never had the opportunity of being married. Her family now seeks a groom for her and, by posting an
attractive dowry, may find someone suitable—often a poor young
man who is already married. He marries the dead girl and gives the
dowry, or those portions of it that are explicitly for the bride—the
clothing and jewelry—to his living wife. The dead bride will not
be jealous, but she will expect to have intercourse with her husband on her wedding night. Arthur Wolf, raising this matter with
informants in the village of San-hsia, was told that a man who has
intercourse with a ghost has a fantastically exhilarating but also
exhausting time. The ghost, being entirely yin, is completely female, hence sexually ferocious. The man ejaculates repeatedly, and
the next day, utterly worn out, can do no work. The performance
cannot be repeated, for the next day the dead woman's spirit tablet
is consecrated and placed on the new husband's altar. She is no
longer a ghost *(kuei)* but now a divinity *(shen)*, no matter how

minor, and has lost her sexual appetite. If it be queried why spirits lose the appetite for sex but not for food, confusion is likely to be the response.

As funerals have tended to shrink among the urban population, it is becoming rare that one can see the diversity of mourning dress that was once so common. It might surprise a Western audience that has learned to identify Chinese funerals with the color white that one recent observer has described Chinese mourning dress as colorful, and an earlier sinologist has even denied that white is a color of mourning. To deal with the latter question first, the sinologist's view was that it was not white that was appropriate to certain situations, but a natural color, or a bleached one. What is involved is a technicality. We and native informants see these colors as "white." It is true, however, that this color is not the only one seen at funerals. Mourning dress runs the spectrum from whites and the natural brown of rough hemp to red and yellow. But describing specific styles of mourning dress would be a ponderous subject. Wolf, for example, says that he has seen at least a hundred variant costumes.

Variation in the mourning costume is based along one vector on the concept of mourning circles, the *wu fu,* or five degrees of mourning. The first of these was for one's parents, and also for a wife mourning her husband. In this degree, the appropriate basic costume is a gown of hempen sackcloth, very rough to the touch. In the second circle are grandparents, and usually a husband mourning his wife. For this degree of mourning the costume is of a lighter, finer, hempen cloth, or one made of yellow gray flax. Incidentally, it should not be thought that grandparents would wear such mourning for a grandchild, because senior generations do not publicly mourn members of younger generations. Seniors do mourn juniors when they are both of the same generation; in such a case, it is usually explained that the deceased, of whatever true age, becomes the senior by predeceasing the others.

The third degree of mourning is for sisters and brothers, and is subject to the previous stipulation about relative age. For this grade, which includes mourning for great-grandparents, the dress is of course muslin, dyed blue. At the level of this category, however, the system may be broken down into contemporary ceremonies. People in this category and below will now usually appear in ordinary dress, but will have swatches of the appropriate cloth pinned to their sleeve or lapel. This is even more likely with relatives of the fourth degree, a large category of father's and mother's siblings, or the fifth, the generalized category of remote relatives. Yet even more color was seen (and still may be glimpsed in the countryside) when great-great-grandchildren were garbed in the color of joy, red. The rationale for this is that to have great-great-grandchildren, a person would have to be extraordinarily fortunate and probably very good, something to be commemorated with public joy. This would be more pronounced in the extraordinary case of someone's being mourned by a fifth-generation descendant. For this, yellow, the color normally restricted to use by the emperor, would be appropriate.

The entire complex structure of the cult of the dead and the usages of mourning is under severe attack in contemporary Taiwan. This cannot be attributed to a general decline in religious activity. On the contrary, the rituals associated with local divinities are growing ever more lavish. Yet burial rituals, in particular, seem to be diminishing. On the mainland, the curtailment of funeral rituals seems to have been extraordinarily effective, although through the years reports have been made of extravagant funerals provided by high-ranking officials, such as the purported great funeral given by Liu Shao-ch'i for his mother. In any case, apart from the uncertain testimony of the graves seen in Gueizhou (see Chapter Six), the mass of the Chinese population seems to have accepted with little struggle a move from funerals that were perhaps the world's most ornate and complex to those of the simplest. We will return to a consideration of this problem in the final chapter.

CHAPTER SIX

Socialist Countries

 Birth

MATERNAL and infant mortality in Russia on the eve of the
Revolution were very frequent but, during the half century leading up to 1963, maternal mortality was reduced to one-fifteenth
of that recorded in 1913. One Soviet source reports that immediately prior to the Revolution no fewer than 30,000 women a year
died from postnatal diseases.

Birth was not merely dangerous but painful. According to the
Great Soviet Encyclopedia, it was not until the 1930s that "pioneer"
administration of anesthesia in childbirth was used in the Soviet
Union. In the 1940s, an English traveler, Ada Elizabeth Chesterton, described her visit to a maternity home (lying-in hospital) in
the Soviet Union. She was particularly impressed by "a deep,
fathomless peace, unfretted by any ripple of apprehension." She
further commented on the cheerful and devoted ministrations of
the nurses and "the anticipation of joy [by the parturients] which
transcended physical agony." Many years later, another observer
in Soviet labor rooms commented, "I could see from the heavy
perspiration on their faces that the women in the labor rooms were
suffering, but they did not moan." Also noted were the constant
presence and patience of midwives and nurses, and "the relaxed
pace of the entire procedure" that, in their view, created an "atmosphere of assurance." In both accounts, the assumption of pain and
suffering could have arisen in the minds of the beholders. Accord-

175

ing to Dr. Maurice S. Miller, a physician who visited the Soviet Union in the early 1950s, "In the last two months of her pregnancy, the expectant mother is prepared for what is known as psychological delivery or 'painless childbirth.'" Doctors explain the process of childbirth, assure women that it is a perfectly normal procedure for those who are not crippled by fear and ignorance, and prescribe a set of exercises to prepare the women for the work of delivering a child without pain and complication.

To some Russian women (as well as to women of other countries) the component of physical pain in childbirth still serves some purpose and, hell-bent on having it, they do in fact experience it. A Russian woman, herself a doctor with two children, told an American visitor: "Still, I am a woman and you are a man. You can advance the most marvelous theories, but I will eventually have to bear my children in agony and in anguish. Socialism cannot change this fact. And no man can feel what a mother feels—or can even imagine her feelings."

This highlighting of pain is all the more curious because research in techniques of painless natural childbirth has been vigorously pursued since the 1930s. The late Dr. Fernand Lamaze, the well-known practitioner and proponent of the psychoprophylactic method of childbirth, visited the Soviet Union in 1951. He witnessed many deliveries in a variety of hospitals during his stay, and was tremendously impressed by the absence of pain during parturition. This was the result of work by Bykov, Velvosky, and Nicolaiev, "who started from the theory of the upper nervous activity elaborated by Ivan Pavlov during fifty years of experimental and clinical research."

In Leningrad, in 1951, during a conference on the use of pain relief in parturition, sponsored by the Academy of Medicine of the USSR and of the Ministry of Public Health, Velvosky, Platonov, and Nicolaiev "explained the principles of the psychoprophylactic method and presented their results of its experimental application" in three major Russian cities. The Soviet Government was so impressed with their results that it "decreed in July 1951 that the psychoprophylactic method should be applied in every maternity unit in the Union, from the biggest city to the most distant *kolkhoz* of Soviet Asia."

Lamaze returned to the Soviet Union for another visit in 1955, and was gratified that he had been able to practice in France what he observed again as the Soviet method of painless childbirth.

The glorification of motherhood, including the notion that the role of mother remains to some extent one of self-sacrifice, is an important Soviet theme. Women carry the burden of child rearing, often culminating in a return, late in life, to the role of nurturing grandmother, or *babushka* (although a revolt against the automatic adoption of that function is in progress).

As soon as a woman knows she is pregnant, she is expected to visit an appropriate health facility. The motivation to do so is high. It is a matter not merely of planning the delivery, but of handling the possibility of abortion, for the Soviet Union has fairly strict regulation of such procedures. In the first trimester, abortion is available virtually without cost and on demand but thereafter, for medical reasons only.

The ease of obtaining a first-trimester curettage has not eliminated illegal abortions in the Soviet Union. Motivations for terminating pregnancy after the twelfth week are not clear, but likely ones include the souring of relations between the woman and the man with whom she is involved or a growing awareness in the woman that the coming of a child can affect her life-style. Although protected by law against discriminatory treatment in the workplace, pregnant women are sometimes treated shabbily by their bosses, and this may be discouraging enough to spark a late decision for abortion. If she aborts herself, a woman is not subject to legal penalty. Anyone assisting her, however, risks imprisonment. Soviet law distinguishes illegal abortions carried out by persons with "higher medical education" and those obtained from persons with lesser or no medical training, but both are punishable offenses.

The high rate of abortion distresses the markedly pronatalist Soviet government. It has sought to reduce the number of abortions by different means at different times; for a period, under Stalin, they were almost totally unobtainable. It should be remembered that at that time most of the world was at least as repressive in its legal posture toward abortion, a posture that has only begun to ameliorate on a large scale in the past decade. Against this background, Soviet policy on abortion has usually been liberal.

Without interfering with the right of a woman to obtain a

first-trimester abortion, Soviet policy against abortion shows itself in the barriers that are encountered after the twelfth week of pregnancy.

There is increasing recognition of the fact that major motivation for abortion arises from the unequal demands made on a woman's work contrasted with those made on a man's. Women bear almost the entire burden of child care plus almost all of the housework, even when employed full time outside the home. Precisely because of this, the Soviet Union is pressing relief efforts in many directions: an attempt to increase the availability of "labor-saving" machinery for the home, an effort to make more flexible the conditions and particularly the hourly schedule of work for employed mothers of young children, and a constant campaign to encourage men to do more at home. The situation is somewhat improved, as will be seen, by a much more extensive availability of crèches and nurseries than can be found, say, in the United States.

Starting in the third month of pregnancy, a woman is encouraged to see her doctor once a month, and more often if any special conditions are known. After a flurry of interest in the late 1960s, practical concern with genetic defects in the human embryo seems to have tapered off. Ambitious plans for a network of genetic counseling offices have not been implemented. There is undoubtedly sincere interest in the subject, but, as perceived by the Kremlin, it is clearly of much lower priority than the task of raising the low birthrate.

While prenatal care and methods of childbirth are quite similar to those in the West, the one great exception is the general exclusion of the husband not only from many of the preparations for delivery but from the labor room itself. Usually, the husband cannot even get into the hospital or other facility where his wife has delivered, and he may not see the baby until ten days after its birth, when it finally goes home with mother.

Early in her pregnancy, a woman begins to enjoy certain privileges that speak to the importance the delivery of a healthy child has for the Soviet state. She obtains a certificate of pregnancy well before her condition shows in her appearance. This enables her to go to the head of the line when shopping or taking public transportation. It also should enable her to get off from work an hour early and to obtain understanding and permission to miss work on days when she doesn't feel up to it, which can happen, despite the stereotypes of dogged women workers staying on their shifts regardless of personal hardship. During the early months of her pregnancy, the worker will apply for paid maternity leave. She is entitled to 112 days of it without question, and is usually advised to take the first half before the baby comes. Beyond the 112 days of paid leave there may be extensions, but with growing complications: pay may be sharply reduced or, more often, entirely foregone. Women's wages are generally at par with men's (a more common technique of exploiting women is to inhibit their promotions so that they lag in status and pay grade). Both are low, though equivalencies are difficult to provide in international comparisons, since Soviet rents are low, medical fees negligible, and transportation costs quite reasonable. On the other hand, most clothing is expensive, food is not cheap, and, in general, the disposable income of a worker is not great. This means that families have to struggle to get by on the income from a single job. However many women work for ideological reasons in the Soviet Union, we know that more work for the money. Of course, a great number work for both reasons. In any case, the strong pressure for women to work is not merely political but born of economic necessity. It comes as a bit of a shock, then, to discover that some working mothers encounter barriers when they seek to return to the job that was held for them, according to law, after they have given birth.

A pregnant woman who remains on the job as she moves into her seventh month is protected by provisions that shorten her work day. She is allowed to leave an hour early, and may take more frequent breaks. If she works at a physically demanding task, she may be transferred to something less arduous without salary penalty. In her eighth month of pregnancy, the woman leaves her job, although some carry on almost to the moment of delivery. In earlier days, that was considered to reflect a proper attitude for a revolutionary woman, but today one hears considerably less about it.

Long before her ninth month the woman should have made arrangements with some lying-in hospital or other obstetrical facility. Robert Kaiser tells a few stories about women whose origi-

nal bookings for obstetrical services went awry—hospital closed
for repairs, that sort of thing—and who had a frantic time trying
to make arrangements elsewhere. Even when such problems do
not exist, bureaucratic emergencies may be created. Yuri Druzhnikov, an émigré writer, has described the conditions of his own
birth in a syndicated newspaper article:

> "I was born in a line. My mother was in a maternity hospital at the
> time, waiting to be registered. Unfortunately, she had forgotten to
> bring along her passport—the internal passport required of all adult
> Soviet citizens. My father raced home to get it, but by the time he
> reached my mother again, I had already arrived—in the corridor."

Some private rooms are available for deliveries, but these are
for particularly complicated cases. We are told that most women
prefer to labor in the company of others undergoing the same
experience, the women offering each other support and encouragement. After the child has emerged and has been shown to the
mother, they are taken off in different directions, the former to the
nursery and the latter to the recovery room. When she is ready,
the new mother will be returned to the ward, but she probably will
not see her baby again until a full day has passed. Thereafter, she
will see it regularly for nursing.

When the new baby arrives for nursing, it is likely to be tightly
swaddled, bound in garments so tight that it can hardly move its
face, and its limbs not at all. Soviet doctors occasionally rebel
against this means of wrapping the infant, but by and large it
remains very popular. Volumes have been written by western
anthropologists in an explication of theories about the effects of
this tight swaddling on the earliest character formation of the
Russian child.

According to the *Great Soviet Encyclopedia,* "almost 100 percent"
of infant births were medically attended as early as 1965, thus
accounting for the marked decline in both infant mortality and the
death or disabling of the mother. Even fifteen or more years later,
this does not mean that every birth is attended by an obstetrician.
Midwives serve in many Soviet deliveries, sometimes in the absence of more highly trained medical doctors. The Soviet medical
system itself classifies a midwife as a "middle level" medical staff
person, one who has had only a three-year course of training.

Midwives are also prepared to assist pregnant women at home if complications have been diagnosed, and they appear in the homes of new mothers during the early postnatal period, mainly to make certain that everything is proceeding smoothly.

The mother of a newborn baby usually remains for at least eight days in the hospital after giving birth, and a ten-day stay is not unusual. During that time she may not be visited by her husband, a custom that is usually explained by fear of infection, but is also perceived as a means of keeping the maternity service running as smoothly as possible. Husbands and other relatives nonetheless come to the facility and smuggle gifts of food and other small prizes to the women inside, sometimes by attaching them to cords the women drop from the windows. New fathers are not shy about letting the public at large know what is going on, and may make general announcements while riding a bus or in the subway. A cheery, congratulatory response can be predicted.

The mother returning home with her first baby is usually facing a problem. If she is married, she and her husband will have less space than they require with an infant—some couples still live in dormitories or in rooms in shared apartments. They probably have long since been listed for an apartment, and the baby's arrival will probably raise their priority and hasten the day they can occupy a small apartment of their own. A number of couples still continue to move in with the baby's grandparents. This was formerly the most popular solution, providing, as well as a place to live, a *babushka* to take care of the baby and the recuperating mother. It has become less popular in recent years, in some part through the reduction of necessity, but also because the older people, particularly older women, are no longer so accepting or proud of the role.

The Soviet Union tends to obfuscate statistical and other information about the religious behavior of Soviet citizens. According to Hedrick Smith, however, Soviet periodicals, such as *Science and Religion,* have revealed that in recent years, more than half of the babies born are being baptized, seemingly a great increase from the low number in the Stalin years. Robert G. Kaiser is more informative. He tells us that, according to an unnamed Soviet periodical, "60 percent of the babies born in the industrial city of Gorki in the late 1960s were baptized." The same author says that conversation with priests in Moscow supplied a comparable figure of about 33 percent. In any event, says Kaiser, baptisms are a common sight in Moscow's more than 45 active churches. Overall estimates of the number of believers in the USSR are from 30 to 50 million, and this figure applies only to Christians. Religion is far from dead in the Soviet Union.

According to William Mandel, "The Soviet Union provides day care or even twenty-four-hour care for virtually every urban child whose parent desires it." Usually more restrained in his generalizations, Mandel seems to have considerably overstated the case. A more recent Soviet spokesman says that in 1976 throughout the Soviet Union as a whole one-third of the children in rural areas and half of those in the cities were in nursery school or kindergarten. Needless to say, those figures are far greater than those representing conditions in the United States.

Hedrick Smith confesses that when he first went to the Soviet Union he expected to find most babies to be turned over "almost automaticaly" to a state nursery. Instead, he discovered that of the roughly 30 million children aged one to six, 10 million had been accommodated, or about a third. The difference between the figures given by Smith and those by Batygin a few years later may indicate a rapid increase in the provision of such facilities, which is not unlikely, since it had been a focal point of discontent, as was revealed in newspaper articles and public correspondence with periodicals.

One who does not follow Soviet developments closely may be surprised to learn that women in particular are often ambivalent about sending small children to state crèches or kindergartens. Anxiety is much higher with respect to the placement in nurseries of one- or two-year-old infants. Women complain that the standard of care is not satisfactory, and this may be borne out by statistics indicating that the staff in such places is close to the bottom of the Soviet wage scale. It seems that female nursery attendants are so usual that even to suggest that a man might work at such a job is a joke.

Steven P. Dunn and Ethel Dunn note that Soviet social scientists distinguish "elementary child care" *(ukhod za det'mi)* from "upbringing" *(vospitanie)*. Where the former includes such basic caretaking as feeding and cleaning, and is usually applied only to infants and toddlers, the latter includes not only education in the formal sense, but most processes of enculturation and socialization. Calling attention to deficiencies in this simple dichotomy, the Dunns remark that it can be utilized to describe the sexual division of labor in child rearing. Men play some role in the upbringing of a child, but hardly any in the basic work of diapering, bathing, or feeding it. This "tendency does not show much variation either geographically or between urban and rural populations." Soviet sociologists, however, have asserted that male participation in the care of young children varies with education—the better educated a man, the more likely he will be to share tasks of child care and housework with his wife. The Dunns take exception to this generalization, pointing to at least one concrete Soviet study that challenges the conventional wisdom on this question.

There are indications that a significant portion of the staff in nurseries comprises young women whose first job this is since leaving school. Actually, apart from the usual hierarchy, such as directress, teacher, and nanny, the more fundamental split in nursery and kindergarten staffs is between those who have special training for their jobs and those who have not. The latter are known as *vospitatel*, "upbringers," and include relatively young women who have dropped out of formal education as soon as they could, or sometimes more mature women, who take such low-paying positions for diverse motives. Hedrick Smith mentions his encounter with Zoya Lissner, a nanny at Kindergarten Nursery No. 104 in Moscow. Comrade Lissner left a good job at an automobile plant after her son was born because she couldn't take the daily hassle of getting the baby to the only available nursery she could find, a long distance away. Instead, she devoted herself to housework and child care for three years. When it came time to put the child in a kindergarten, she managed to get a job at No. 104, where she enrolled her child. Her salary was about a third of what she had earned at the automobile plant.

Urie Bronfenbrenner, a leading American specialist in early childhood education with special reference to the Soviet Union, provides what appears to be a somewhat idealized view of upbringers. His observations, although made at several localities in the Soviet Union from Leningrad to Alma-Ata, seem invariably to have been made in remarkably well-staffed, carefully programmed institutions. He says, for example, that nurseries admitting babies as young as three months provide one upbringer for each four babies. He describes intense personal interaction for each infant. Yet, in 1979, several years after the observations published by Bronfenbrenner, critical comments in the Soviet press revealed that such ratios may have been unusual. Certainly the ratio of upbringers to children falls off dramatically in the ages past three, and the resulting conditions are often distressing to parents. An article in *Trud* in November 1978, written by a faculty member of the Rostov Teacher Training Institute, acknowledges the reality behind such complaints. Working on a project sponsored by the USSR Academy of Pedagogy, she finds merit in some sharp complaints about the system:

> ". . . A. Ilyushina's letter about the overcrowded conditions is entirely accurate. The instructresses and nannies wear themselves out just getting the children's shoes on, feeding them, and keeping them clean and occupied. So that the fine points of character building are completely out of the question.
>
> "It would be naive, however, to believe that the problem can be solved overnight. . . . Thus we must expect kindergartens to continue to focus primarily on children's social development, with individual development being primarily the family's responsibility. After all, not even the finest preschool can replace Mom, Dad and Grandma."

The same article acknowledges that there is too high a rate of turnover among unskilled nannies. The physical burden of the job far exceeds the low wages; if other opportunities are seen, they are quickly grabbed. As for trained personnel, some of them are admittedly unsuited to the work.

Observers of infants and small children in the Soviet Union report, seemingly without exception, the close nurturance of these little citizens. Bronfenbrenner declares unequivocally that "Russian babies receive substantially more physical handling than their American counterparts." At home, babies are fondled, dandled, and constantly held, even as household chores, such as cooking, are being done. The disparity between the treatment of children in the public and private sectors, so to speak, and in the years between infancy and late adolescence, is a source of difficulty, and many Soviet pedagogues have expressed anxiety about it. At the crux of the problem is the contrast between the diminished family, which now often includes but one child and rarely more than two, and the crowded nursery or kindergarten or classroom. In the latter situation, the number of "upbringers" per child is, except in certain apparent showplace exceptions, almost never in ratios of fewer than fifteen or twenty to one, and often is much higher. Structurally, this provides a situation of automatic contrast with the home. The Institute of Pre-school Education of the USSR Academy of Pedagogical Sciences issued in 1974 a set of "Brief Guidelines" stating the expectations for each age level beginning at two years of age. Children in the youngest group, aged two to three,* are expected to be toilet-trained and to take a role in dressing themselves, although provision is made for a range of abilities in mastering the complex muscular tasks of buttoning or shoelace-tying. Still, the guidelines manage to sound fairly tight: The child "learns to take off and put on his clothing in a certain order, to fold it, to button and unbutton his clothing from the front, and to untie his shoelaces." Yet the next sentence eases the pressure: "This is a great effort for a child." The teacher and her assistant must help. "The child should be taught to take care of himself gradually."

It is of great and pointed concern that the child be instilled with respect for labor at the earliest time of life. "The inculcation of a love of labor in the children requires no less attention from the teacher of the youngest group." Even from age two, children help in cleaning up the nursery by picking up papers, taking toys from one place to another, and helping to push chairs into place. The child is encouraged to feel a part of a "children's collective."

> "Children are taught to observe habits of cleanliness and orderliness; to wipe their feet carefully; not to litter; not to spill water on the floor while they are washing; not to throw and break toys; . . . to greet one another politely, to say good-bye, to express gratitude, to ask for things, to leave the table only when the meal is finished, not to bother one another, not to take toys from their comrades, to share toys, to pick

---

*This is not the youngest group in the system. Infants of three months, but usually of six months or older, may be placed in crèches providing twelve-hour service, but places are limited. On the other hand, this does not appear to be the place of critical shortage in the system. There seems to be considerable resistance to sending the infant out of the house for care until two or three years of age.

up toys and put them away, not throw them on the floor, and not to
break them."

Children of three and a half are instructed to set and clear the table
for nursery school meals, and they take shifts under the teacher's
supervision. Contrast this with the behaviour at home of little
Vita, who is being addressed by his father in the following domestic scene recorded in a Soviet journal of pedagogy:

> " 'Do you see how much your mama works?' Vita's father tells him.
> 'She worked at her machine tool all day at the factory. She came home,
> tidied up the apartment, prepared our supper for us, and is washing
> the dishes, and you don't even want to carry your plate out to the
> kitchen.' 'I don't want to,' his son agrees and continues to play."

Vita's behavior is compared with that of Leva, a boy of six, who
"has been brought up to perform useful chores." He has been
known to carry a chair from one room to another and to bring
babushka her eyeglasses. Leva receives lavish praise for each helping act and the Soviet pedagogues frown on the abuse of such
positive reinforcement. In their view it does not work. So we are
not surprised to find that in the end Leva's behavior is rather like
Vita's. ". . . Leva renders . . . aid depending on his mood and,
having performed the task, he considers that he has rendered a
great service." Oleg is the seven-year-old son of a street car conductor. His teacher exclaims what an interesting job Oleg's mother
has and asks Oleg what he likes about it:

> " 'Mama has a very good job. She works one day and spends two days
> at home. And she manages to do everything—to do the laundry and
> housecleaning.' 'Everything?' the teacher says in astonishment. 'And
> she even manages to prepare dinner for papa and us.' 'And do you help
> your mama?' 'Why should I? She does everything herself. That's the
> kind of job she has.' "

The conversation may appear stilted, but its content has been
recorded so often that there can be no doubt that it gets to the
heart of a significant Soviet reality. As will be seen, the Soviet
system has a share of deviants, albeit running at considerably
lower percentages than is known in the United States. It should
not be assumed, however, that we accept the Soviet piety that sees
the school on the side of the angels and home to the contrary. The

interface is much larger and more complex between the molding of public character and private character. What seems evident is that there is slippage between the models of Soviet rectitude who are said to populate its schools and the more free-wheeling pragmatists engaged in the moderate corruption of daily life.

Indeed, it is not unlikely that from the age of seven, when children enter the now universal elementary educational system of the USSR, awareness grows of the differences between school life and real life. The latter, as indicated, is not unlikely to be organized to the satisfaction of the child, who is often the pampered center of attention. On the other hand, that child is subject to strong discipline and extensive criticism in school, not only by teacher, but by fellow students as well. There is some indication that negative intersexual attitudes may arise at this age. Girls are described, in general, as more precocious than boys, leading them in work and in holding positions within the student authority structure. Tattling is to some extent institutionalized within Soviet educational arrangements, such as in the appointment of *zvenovoi,* group leaders, who report to the teacher about the conduct of the other members of the group. This institution may be less widespread than imagined, for it seems to have been absent from the school attended by the children of an American reporter. The same correspondent notes, however, that whatever the apparatus of social control in Soviet schools, it does not obliterate undesired behavior. From the age of about fourteen, students, markedly more often males than females, smoke and drink, often in the school lavatories. They also get into mischief, escalating from minor infractions inside and outside the classroom to "hooliganism," which is a category of criminal behavior worthy of more extensive discussion in the following section on adolescence.

School and home are not the only institutions that mold Soviet children, there are also the renowned youth organizations that claim as members high proportions of the available boys and girls. In the view of Nigel Grant, a specialist on comparative education at the University of Edinburgh, who has written a study, *Soviet Education,* these youth organizations, although voluntary, are better considered a part of formal Soviet educational structure. The Soviet youth groups have many points of resemblance to comparable youth organizations elsewhere, the Girl Scouts and Boy Scouts coming most conspicuously to mind. Nor can the comparison be lightly eluded by asserting that the Soviet youth organizations are politically inspired where the Scouts are neutral—that would take a naive view of the very basic ideological orientation that participation in scouting brings. In any event, there is no problem in identifying the Soviet youth movements as politically based, for they proudly define themselves in political terms. The first rule of the Pioneers is: "A Pioneer loves his Motherland and the Communist Party of the Soviet Union."

The youngest of the youth groupings is loosely structured. The Octobrists, celebrating in their name the premature revolution of 1905, comprise girls and boys seven to nine years old. Membership is not exclusive, whole classes are enrolled without particular ceremony. Activities within the school include communal tasks, such as cleaning the classroom, but some emphasis is placed upon games. During the children's last year in the Octobrists, the teacher spends a certain amount of time encouraging them to move on with the youth organization by applying for membership in the Pioneers.

Much more selective than the Octobrists is the *Vsesoyaznaya Pionerskaya Organizatsiya imeni V. I. Lenina,* the Pioneers, which recruits girls and boys between the ages of nine or ten and fourteen. Induction into the Pioneers is ceremonial. The initiate recites a pledge ("I, a Young Pioneer of the Soviet Union, in the presence of my comrades, solemnly promise to love my Soviet Motherland passionately, and to live, learn, and struggle as the great Lenin bade us, and as the Communist Party teaches us"), and receives a badge bearing the inscription *"Vsegda gotov"* (Always Ready). The initiate is also given a triangular red scarf. There usually follows a program of speeches, and the setting for the occasion is sometimes the school or, if it can be arranged, an even more impressive location, such as a local factory or one of the thousands of Pioneer Palaces found in the cities and towns. The ceremonies are solemn, usually carried out before audiences of parents and relatives, and they come close to providing a universal experience of initiation into the Soviet culture.

The Pioneers are organized in the school formation: each school is a *druzhina,* or brigade, within the larger structure of the Pioneers. The classroom is a unit in itself—the *otryad,* or detachment—within which is the *zveno,* or "link," also equivalent to the "row" in a Soviet classroom. It is the *zvenovoi,* "link leader," who is responsible for telling the teacher anything untoward that has occurred among the children in the row.

While the Pioneer organization carries out many tasks of indoctrination and management, it is often associated with pleasure in the minds of its members. In addition to sports at levels from the spontaneous to the international competition, there are also nonathletic activities such as touring, chess, and the arts. Still, some children prefer not to join, and resist all pressures to.

Before transferring our interest to the next major period in the life cycle, a few brief glances at two other examples of birth and childhood drawn from socialist countries may be instructive. It must be realized, however, that one of these—the People's Republic of China—has at this time of writing existed for only some thirty years, a bit less than half the duration of the Soviet state. The other example, Cuba, is even younger as a socialist country —a matter of ten years—succeeding in its revolution only at the beginning of 1959. China, in the brief span since Mao Tse-tung's rise to power, has already undergone various revisions of its policies regarding treatment of the young. Cuba has been more constant within its shorter time span.

Both countries began, marvelous to say, at even lower levels of technological and economic development than was represented in the Russia of 1917, which has had marked effect on their development. China and Cuba, despite subsequent differences in their political alignments with the Soviet Union, both show much convergence with it in their treatment of children. This can be attributed in some measure to direct borrowings by both countries from the USSR. Differences can be partly attributed to markedly different bases, resulting from totally disparate histories, and to differences of scale and internal complexity between China, the world's largest country, and Cuba, which, with its population of less than 10 million, would come at the bottom of the list of Chinese provinces.

Similar to that of prerevolutionary Russia was the low rate of medically assisted child delivery available to most Chinese and Cuban women. Contemporary Cuba has already developed an extensive system of health-care delivery that extends into the countryside, and most women are afforded clinical precare once pregnancy is established. Working women in Cuba, as in the USSR, are released from work but continue to receive their pay during a period that begins six weeks before delivery and extends for twelve weeks after. A sliding period of two weeks is provided for lateness of actual delivery. Differing from both Cuba and the USSR, China supplies leave with pay for only half as long— fifty-six days. This, however, probably applies largely to women employed in state enterprises, that is to say, factories or other workplaces operated directly by government. By far the greatest portion of Chinese labor, including women, is employed in non-state enterprises, such as locally based production teams and brigades that have operated more or less successfully where the earlier attempt to leap to the large unit of state control, the commune, failed. To most intents and purposes, the lapse of the commune as a production and accounting unit has had much effect on the medical system, including the treatment of maternity. Even in those cases in which an operating commune medical system had developed, it returned to lower level control. With that came great variation in details such as the amount of paid leave due a pregnant or recently delivered woman. For most, it probably meant no paid released time at all.

If the standards of released labor time for pregnant women and recent mothers varies between socialist countries, so do the amenities of care. China again probably has the broadest spread of conditions. Where the USSR and Cuba have been more or less successful in providing maternal and infant care based on modern western medical practice, the Chinese, particularly in rural areas, have resorted to a mixture of traditional procedures and modern innovations. Trained doctors (M.D.s) and trained midwives continue to be thinly distributed over the countryside. As is well known, the Chinese have sought to fill the void with paraprofessionals having limited training, the so-called barefoot doctors. In a manual for such personnel originally published by the Revolutionary Health Committee of Hunan Province in 1970, there is a brief section devoted to "new methods for delivery of the newborn." This, in the main, offers a straightforward description of a relatively antiseptic procedure, stressing certain safeguards not

always found in traditional Chinese procedure. Deliberately omitted is a variety of traditional practices not entirely compatible
with, or even contradicting, the new procedure. While deliveries
at home are still common in rural areas, prenatal care emphasizes
the identification of expectant mothers who may encounter complications. If possible, such cases are moved to better equipped
facilities, perhaps in an urban center. Still, according to one study
conducted among Chinese informants who had recently left China
and were residing in Hong Kong, it is clear that many births do
take place at home, attended by midwives, barefoot doctors, or
even untrained older women. The same research indicates that
paid leave for childbirth is far from widespread in rural areas (the
study in question pertains specifically to Kwangtung Province),
and women work almost until delivery, resuming their work
within forty days, although with a reduced load. Ceremonies
marking the birth are maintained, in particular the "full month"
(man yüeh and *tso yüeh)* described earlier, in the context of Taiwan.
It appears, however, that little religious symbolism is now displayed, such as making an announcement to the ancestors. What
remains is a substantial feast for a fairly sizable company of
friends and relatives. It is worth noting that these feasts are most
frequently held, and are most lavish, when celebrating the birth
of the first son.

Three decades after the Chinese Revolution, various customs
associated with previous regimes continue to be found among the
peasantry. It is not unlikely that some of these observances have
percolated into sectors of the society that previously lacked the
means of supporting the large families and lineages that are their
usual accompaniment. Thus we may still find in rural China villages where many people of the same surname also share one
character of the usual two-character given name. In a village with
a Wang lineage, one would run into Wang Pei-yun, Wang Pei-ho,
Wang Pei-fu, for example. In such a situation, the common character "pei" marks a generation of males in the lineage.

Quite distinct is another previously widespread naming practice that is reported still in use, especially in the countryside. As
recently as the 1940s, infant and child mortality was so common
in China that the agency of wandering, homeless ghosts was
thought to be responsible. To mislead such vengeful spirits, par-

ents gave their newly born children temporary "milk" names such as "Little Dog" or "Little pig," indicating that the child was not worth much to them. The persistence of this custom seems at odds with the marked decline in infant and child mortality in China, and it is likely eventually to disappear.

If there are marked continuities in relatively minor customs of naming in China, equally noticeable continuities may be discerned in most areas of daily life, including facets of education. Actually, a major break between traditional modes of education and those presently in use took place around the turn of the century, approximately at the time that imperial rule was coming to an end, and the republican form of government, preceding the victory of socialism, was coming to the fore. The governmental shift, of course, did not bring complete change, much less changes that fully penetrated the countryside. All the more remarkable, then, was the acceleration of events in Chinese education that followed Mao's rise to power. Changes were particularly evident in the preschool program. Once again, it was less a matter of innovation than of the percolating of existing institutions, often after minor alterations, throughout the society, where previously they had been confined to a small class of favored people.

The same comment applies to Cuba. There was an extensive system of education, including some preschool facilities, in operation long before the Revolution, but these facilities penetrated hardly at all into the countryside or, indeed, into the lower classes of the cities. One of the first and most remarkable triumphs of the Cuban Revolution was its 1961 campaign to eradicate illiteracy, which was pronounced a great success and may have reduced formal illiteracy in the population from about twenty-two percent (and perhaps over forty percent in the countryside) to about four percent.

Even before its crash program of combating illiteracy, Cuba had been building *circulo infantiles,* child care centers for the young who range in age from forty-five days to five years. By 1973, such centers accommodated some 50,000 children; the intention was to provide for 150,000 by 1980. To give some perspective for evaluating these figures, Karen Wald notes that early in the 1970s, New York City, with a population somewhat smaller than Cuba's, provided day care for only 18,000 children. The services available in the Cuban *circulos* are also much more extensive than those provided in government-financed child care centers in New York.

Children enter the *circulos* at different ages, the youngest being infants less than two months old. These receive medical attention, meals, and mothering. (Men are not found on the staffs of these centers.) As the children grow, or as older children are admitted, they play in the large elevated cribs familiar in Soviet baby care. In general, what appear to be Soviet influences may be detected, but there are differences. Not the least is in the artwork produced by the children. Where Soviet nursery and kindergarten children alarm western observers by turning out identical copies of the same theme, the Cuban children display great variety in their creations.

While there is basic age-grading in the *circulo,* it is not very rigid, and mobile little ones may be found in groups of older children, a practice rarely or never observed in the equivalent Chinese setting, where there is little intercourse between children of different ages. This is in marked contrast to older Chinese patterns of child rearing, especially among workers and peasants, which saw very small children, usually but not invariably girls, charged with care of younger siblings. Significant is the inclusion of children through five years of age in the *circulos.* Elsewhere, in the USSR and the People's Republic of China, this span is usually divided into the nursery period (age infancy* to three years) and the kindergarten period (three to six or seven years of age), although the physical plants may be combined. The differentiation of nursery and kindergarten coincides with the Soviet psychologists' consistent finding that clear self-awareness develops at about the third year, but is not automatic. In the Soviet view it can be facilitated by social interaction in the kindergarten:

"When a three-year-old first goes to kindergarten, for the first months he does not appear to notice the other children and he acts as if they did not exist. But later the situation changes. As a result of the development of group activity and the formation of the children's society in the preschool class, earning a popular appraisal and popularity among his peers becomes one of the genuine motives underlying a

*The minimum age for admission varies. In Cuba it is forty-five days, in the People's Republic of China it is two months, in the USSR, three months.

child's behavior. . . . The motives of *self-esteem* and self-affirmation develop in preschool childhood. They initiate at the point of the separation of the self from other people and the formation of the child's perception of an adult as a model of behavior, which occurs at the beginnings of preschool age [that is, at about the age of three—Eds.]."

For the Cubans such divisions are not entirely necessary. For some time in the late nineteen-sixties and early seventies, a kind of minimally structured kindergarten, the *jardines,* contended with the *circulos* for support. The *jardines* for the most part provided supervision (two women for twenty to thirty children) for play-groups of children. Often located in public parks, functioning with minimum plant and amenities, such kindergartens saw heterogeneous groupings of children in all activities, a necessity that was called the "free play method." In any event, the *jardines* have lost the contest with the much more structured *circulos;* the emerging pattern is more like the Soviet one.

Few social programs have had more of a bootstrap quality than that devoted to the expansion of public education in Cuba. Following the preschool period, which may be encapsulated in attendance at a *circulo* or may be divided between a day-care center (forty-five days to four years), followed by kindergarten, which is housed in a *circulo* or an elementary school, or with no previous exposure to education, children enter the primary grades. The usual age of entrance is seven, and as there are six grades, most graduates will be thirteen. Those who go on will enter an *Escuela Secondaria Basica* for grades seven through ten. There are several types of these secondary schools—day schools, boarding schools, and schools that combine studies with serious labor. Still beyond are grades eleven to thirteen, which are preparatory for university. That last stage, the university, offers four- and five-year programs.

Parallel to the lower grades of the formal educational system is the Union of Pioneers of Cuba, obviously modeled along the lines of the Soviet Pioneers. As in the USSR, the general organizational scheme is based upon the school, but again there are differences of detail. One difference: where the Soviet child experiences discipline by threat or reality of refusal or withdrawal of membership, the Cubans use the Pioneers as a means of reeducating delinquent youth.

When we again add observations and other data about education and the ways of handling children in the People's Republic
of China, we are struck by the range of variation that exists within
the broadly defined socialist camp of nations. To be sure, there are
basic similarities. When resources are available, the state, or its
lower level units, provides some facilities for children from infancy through university. It may come as a surprise to some readers, however, to learn that it is highly improbable that all children
in China manage to attend all six years of primary school. There
is still a marked distinction between educational facilities found
in cities and those in the countryside, particularly in areas truly
remote. Subdivisions of rural communes, units such as brigades
and often the much smaller components known as production
teams, are the active suppliers of educational facilities, particularly
in a financial sense. They are often responsible for their own
staffing, hence the remarkable range of quality and preparation of
the teachers who often are drawn from the resettled youth *(hsia-
hsiang chih-shih ch'ing nien)* or the "returned youth" *(hui-hsiang chih-
shih ch'ing nien).* * In neither case is the level of educational achievement clearly specified, and for good reason—it was diverse. Even
if the recruitment of such students had been attached to the completion of courses, there would have been three such cutoff points:
ninth grade (completion of Junior Middle School), twelfth grade
(completion of Senior Middle School), or eleventh grade (completion of the then recently introduced five-year High School, which
combined the work of the senior and junior middle schools). From
this sketchy context may be seen just some of the problems beset-
ting elementary school education in the Chinese countryside, considering the pronounced discrepancies in preparation of these educated youth from whom a goodly portion of rural teachers were
drawn. Added to these problems were a host of others. For example, some of the educated youth were evidently reluctant to accept
teaching jobs in the country for fear it would kill their chances of
transfer to an urban job. Teaching jobs were not the only ones that
were declined, one might add.

---

*The Chinese characters indicate that the first of these groups originates in the
cities and is relocated "down" to the farm; the second group comprises those who
left the farms for secondary education and returned when they completed their
courses.

It is impossible to estimate with any confidence the extent to which nursery care is available in contemporary China. Recently, the government has indicated that despite the use a couple of decades ago of such slogans as "inadequate labor in the country-side," it has now embarked upon a decided antinatalist policy, and will attempt to limit births to one or two per family.

Shifts in Chinese attitudes toward population planning are not unlike their shifts of policy concerning the supplying of early child care and the method of access to education and educational policy at every level. It is to be expected that the attitude of the state toward general questions of population size, and toward the birth rate in particular, will have important consequences in the provision of subsidized child care. As indicated earlier in this chapter, the Soviet Union has invested in nurseries and kindergartens as one means of encouraging fertility. In China, as this is being written, explicit population policy has tipped the other way, and diminishing access to nurseries and kindergartens can be expected to become one of the means of lowering the fertility rate.

Actually, the use of nurseries seems never to have approached the levels achieved in the Soviet Union. Ruth Sidel was told that nurseries could accommodate about half the children aged one to three in urban China, falling short of that in the countryside. Quite possibly the figure given for the urban setting is accurate. Some facilities that have been described by observers are minimal. At one factory visited by the American Delegation on Early Childhood Education, in the winter of 1973, members were taken to see the facilities for the care of infants whose mothers worked in the plant. They describe a "feeding station" that served some thirty swaddled nursing infants arranged on a huge *k'ang* (a raised hollow platform, heated with warm air from a stove that may be some distance away). Two "caretakers or nurses" held infants who had been picked up because they were crying; when their cries subsided, they were put back on the *k'ang*. How diapers were changed or babies were cleaned is not mentioned. We are told, however, that each infant is breast-fed by its own mother, who receives breaks from work for this function.

The range of variation in facilities and procedures associated with crèches and nurseries in China is immediately evident when this account is compared with Ruth Sidel's. Some differences may be ascribed to the different seasons of the year in which the visits were made. Sidel came through Peking at a warmer time, when the *k'angs* were not used. The twenty-seven babies in the nursery through which she was shown were in cribs or carriages. Most were under the age of eight months, although there were some older babies, up to perhaps eighteen months, who were in play-pens. These babies, too, received most of their nourishment from their mothers, who came twice to nurse them. Sidel, however, did establish that if a supplementary feeding was required, one of the the nursery's four attendants would provide a bottle rather than summon the mother. Ruth Sidel questioned one of the "aunties" concerning the frequency of picking babies up. It is interesting to note that even though this nursery had four adult attendants, she was informed that it was impossible to pick up every crying child; instead, babies might be put into carriages and wheeled back and forth.

Crèches for nursing infants are less in demand in rural areas. Indeed, informants from Kwangtung Province interviewed by Parish and Whyte made it clear that most peasants prefer to make their own arrangements which, as described, differ little from the pre-Communist norms we observed in Anhwei over thirty years ago. The more common pattern in the countryside, then as now, saw nursing infants carried to the fields or wherever the mother was going, usually held on her back in an elaborately decorated cloth sling, which held the baby in snug contact. Women carrying babies in this way pursued most tasks as if unencumbered. If the mother had to leave the house on some task or errand that would find the baby's presence unwarranted, the likely solution was a grandparent babysitter, probably the father's mother, if she lived in the house. If there was no grandparent, a young child, prefera-bly female, would do, even one who herself seemed only recently released from her mother's back. There were other possibilities— a neighboring woman being the most likely. Of course, to some extent these possibilities have now changed. The use of an older sibling would seem precluded by the likelihood that such a child would be involved in educational activities most of the day. As for the neighbor, she would probably be at work. Still, the available accounts indicate that to a considerable extent the old patterns persist in the countryside. Thus, the Parish and Whyte study found that only some nineteen percent of the villages on which they collected data had their own nurseries or kindergartens; this was not the casual result of a process that had yet to run its course but the product of retrenchment following an expansion of nursery and kindergarten building that peaked in the Great Leap Forward of 1958. Apparently the area being studied had sharply reduced nursery and kindergarten care in response to a poor reaction to the facilities previously offered.

Since the rise to power of Teng Hsiao-p'ing there has been less reluctance to acknowledge variations. Similar variations also mark available accounts. Two items are worthy of specific mention. In Ruth Sidel's observations we find the establishments efficiently run, and quiet. By contrast, a woman who had been employed in a Kwangtung kindergarten in 1968 told her interviewer: "Children were crying all the time. When all collected in one place they got bored, but once you let them out they would run away and you would have to spend your time chasing them down. . . . Unlike in the city, there is no schedule of activities. Things just happen." In a similar vein, the account of the Delegation of Early Childhood Education specialists includes episodes not merely of confusion but of mild corporal punishment. Sidel remarks that while people told her of the use of corporal punishment at home, she never observed anything other than tender loving care in either nursery or kindergarten.

The life of the kindergarten takes on a variety unknown in the nursery. Still, it remains a compressed world. A comparison of the daily schedules taken from two different kindergartens by two different observers shows very little discrepancy. The largest single difference is found in the time of retiring, varying from 7:30 P.M. in the Sidel account to 8:30 in that edited by Kessen. The children rise about the same time—about 6:30 A.M. The one-hour difference in retiring time reflects a period of free play after dinner in one of the nurseries.

Apart from specific political symbols, a casual visitor and perhaps even a professional observer would find little to distinguish between kindergartens in the People's Republic of China and Taiwan. Schedules are very much the same and activities are identical. Most visitors to China who have not been to Taiwan are amazed at the performances put on by the children, consisting of songs, recitations, skits, and tableaux, and they assume mistakenly that these performances are a product of the new regime. Similar programs, differing mainly in political content, are staged on the other side of the Taiwan Straits.

A similar remark about elementary schools would be risky. Even in the small province of Taiwan there is a noticeable variation in their quality. This pales beside the range of quality that can be observed during a relatively brief trip outside the province, suggesting the much greater range of quality to be found in such a vast country. Indeed, it has become clear after some obfuscation that the completion of elementary school is by no means universal in China. In August 1979, Deputy Prime Minister Chen Muhua, in an interview with a *New York Times* correspondent, stated that "6 percent of Chinese children do not go to primary school." She asserted, however, that only 12 percent of elementary school graduates did not go on into junior middle school, although more than 50 percent fail to enter senior middle school. She also indicated that only 5 percent of senior middle school students enter college.

Each entrance into a higher level school would have marked something of a transition for students in the old days, as they still do in Taiwan. But we have no information on how such events are marked in contemporary China. Quite likely, such transitions were unmarked during the period running roughly from the late 1950s through the Cultural Revolution and terminating with the ouster of the "Gang of Four"—Chiang Ch'ing (Jiang Qing) and her associates, in 1976. We surmise that during that period it was wiser to be discreet about academic achievement. The need for such discretion has waned in the past two or three years, and more public celebration of a student's progress is now countenanced, if not encouraged.

China's youth movement differs considerably from those of Russia and Cuba. In brief, it lacks the Octobrist-Pioneer complex of the Soviet Union and the comparable organizations in Cuba. Instead, the Chinese have taken the Red Guard movement of the sixties, itself derived from earlier prototypes, and adapted it to school children, mainly at the elementary and junior middle school level. Like the Octobrists in the USSR, the Red Guards or "Little Red Guards" are a mass organization preferably encompassing whole classes of students. But there are criteria of membership, including quality standards of behavior and academic performance, and students may temporarily lose their Red Guard membership—usually a spur to improved performance. Red Guard activity also goes on outside the school, partly in athletics and athletic competition (the latter quite muted), and, more prominently, in music, singing, and dancing. In 1977, with the Delegation of Applied Linguists, Mort attended an elaborate vaudeville program put on entirely by Red Guards who appeared to be under twelve years of age. It was a far cry from the politically active Red Guards who had moved from major city to major city during the Cultural Revolution, creating a definite impact on adult political life. The movement now functions primarily as a source of student leadership and a model for emulation. There do not seem to be any important ceremonies concerned either with induction into, or graduation or expulsion out of, the Red Guards, such as those concerned with the Pioneers or Komsomol in the USSR.

 Adolescence

UNTIL recently, complaints about the behavior of adolescents and young adults were commonplace in the United States and other countries with capitalistic economies, but less frequently heard in socialist countries. As far as is known, adolescent crime in the USSR still lags well behind that in the United States, but it is clear that recent years have seen a burgeoning delinquency in the Soviet Union. According to Victor Nekipelov, a Russian dissident who at the time of writing is still living near Moscow, the ten years leading up to 1979 have been "ten years of deepening chaos, militarization, catastrophic economic disorder, increases in the cost of living, insufficient basic food products, increases in crime and drunkenness, corruption and thieving." Written by a self-identified opponent of the regime, these charges may be thought extreme, yet at least some of them are readily verified—if the materials published in the *Current Digest of the Soviet Press* are reliable. Of particular interest is the seemingly continuous rise in delinquency and "hooliganism" among older adolescents and younger adults.

Consider, for example, a letter to *Izvestia* published in the issue of March 27, 1979, written by one A. Ryabukhin, identified as a Deputy to the Grozny City Soviet and a mechanic in the Soviet oil industry. He is unhappy over the rising hooliganism that surrounds him: "Take the Jubilee Movie Theater. It's not a year old but look what's been done to it. Seats have been slashed with knives, seat numbers have been torn off, and the floor is littered with sunflower seed husks and candy wrappers. . . ." But what most disturbs Comrade Ryabukhin is the violence. "A hooligan thinks nothing of insulting a woman, pestering a child or assaulting a person standing right by the doorway of his own home. Here's a recent case: two technical school students, V. Korneyev and D. Magomedov, assaulted a citizen 'just for the hell of it' . . . in fact, it's unsafe to go out on the street at night in some parts of the city."

As in the United States, problems of this kind are sometimes linked with behavior in the schools. This may come as a surprise, considering the emphasis previously placed on collective discipline. Reality, however, may depart from the ideal as readily in the Soviet Union as anywhere else. Hedrick Smith relates his conversations with some teachers in the Moscow system. One eighth grade teacher of mathematics spoke of his "dead souls," the fifteen of eighty eighth-graders he regularly met who had medical slips identifying them as victims of various kinds of severe learning disabilities. Others in the classes who were not so identified nonetheless had great difficulty doing the work, especially the homework. This was blamed in part on "broken families or alcoholism at home." Another teacher told Smith that many of her eighth- and ninth-grade students were "illiterate," which might have been an exaggeration. She did say that in a class of forty, about five of the boys were "real hooligans," drinking, smoking, and fighting. Outside the school, they were picked up for robbery, and at least one girl was convicted for prostitution. Pregnancy was not unknown.

It is, of course, somewhat unfair to begin this discussion of adolescence in the Soviet Union by paying so much attention to delinquents who represent only a small proportion of the age group. The vast bulk of Soviet citizens move through their years of education obediently, even diligently. Still, the system is highlighted by its failures as well as by its successes.

Until 1966, school was compulsory in the Soviet Union only through the eighth grade, which was usually completed in the student's fifteenth year. In 1966, compulsory education was extended by two years, thereby taking the student to the end of the normal secondary education course, although alternative means of education were provided. The academic path is preferred both by students and by the government. The Ministry of Education, which supplied the figure of sixty percent for the proportion of eighth graders who went on to academic high school, also predicted that the figure would rise to seventy-five percent. On June 3, 1976, *Izvestia* indicated that the figure had indeed risen to sixty-four percent for the class embarking upon the ninth grade in the fall of that year. Perhaps more interesting is the information from the same source that not a few students departing the eighth grade the previous year had complained of difficulty in obtaining access to programs in one of the two alternatives to the general high school, namely, the technicum and the vocational-technical school. The complaints were invariably from the countryside, where, according to *Izvestia,* strong traditions continue to pressure youngsters to acquire practical skills rather than uninterrupted academic knowledge. Partly out of self-interest, and partly because they are striving to realize the early government goal of seventy-five percent senior high school enrollment in general education, the heads of rural schools apparently delay sending documents of applicants to the vocational schools, or otherwise interfere with many attempts to enroll in such schools. According to *Izvestia:* "Among those who complete the eighth grade are youngsters who for a whole series of reasons must go to work, continuing their education in schools for young workers. Usually these are children of disadvantaged families. Education was difficult for them. . . ." Such a student, according to the same piece in *Izvestia,* often hears a categorical rejection of his request. The school bureaucrat is likely to say, "Enter the ninth grade, and let's hear no more about it." In contrast to the rural attitude, in the cities "the predominating and customary tendency is to enroll in the ninth grade no matter what."

If there is something of a problem in the transition from junior to senior levels of secondary education, there are also problems in the movement from secondary to higher educational institutions. It is, however, the reverse of that just seen. This later step is not merely pro forma, but requires success in negotiating an entrance examination. The way in which many students approached and performed on these exams was discussed scathingly in the spring of 1979 in an article in *Pravda* written by Prof. D. Chkhikvishvili, the Rector of Tbilisi State University. According to him, "The competitive exams for secondary-school graduates are beginning to resemble a contest among programmed automations to determine which one has the most reliable working memory." The fault, according to the professor, is not entirely that of the students, for the questions are such that each "year more and more written compositions on entrance examinations are alike as two peas in a pod, repeating each other word for word and comma for comma." The system regards this as a kind of plagiarism and mandates the grade of 2 on a scale of 1 to 5, where 5 is A. Whether closely parallel essays by candidates are indeed the result of copying or of common mechanical preparation is not made clear by Prof. Chkhikvishvili. It seems, however, that the culprit is private tutoring, very much like the tutorial schools known as *pushipan* in Taiwan. In such tutorials the candidates learn to write "answers that cannot be faulted from a formal standpoint. They are all smoothly written, precise, impeccable. However, they are as uniform as carbon copies." One suggestion for solving the problem was to substitute an oral examination, specifically for the Russian examination or for the region's native language (for those candidates in one of the Republics having another official language), for one of the three written examinations that comprise the major barrier to university admission. Another suggestion was to do away with the written examinations altogether, deciding admission by a thorough competitive screening of the candidates' high school achievements.

There does not appear to be much difference between elementary and higher grades in the way subjects are taught, or in the relations between pupils and teachers. There is strong emphasis on committing to memory extensive portions of a semester's work. American students who have lived in Russia and who have been subjected to Soviet schools often find themselves ahead of their classes when they return to the United States. Hedrick Smith tells about the son of another *New York Times* correspondent who found himself in a secure and enviable position vis-à-vis mathematics and the natural sciences when he entered Columbia College after having attended a Moscow school for a significant part of his education.

Of course, there are important differences in curricula as the Soviet student proceeds through the grades and, for the most part, their system is not unlike ours in its overall emphases at different levels. Heavy tutoring in Russian (or the national language) predominates in early years, but courses in literature are given greater weight toward the end of high school. Mathematics runs through the entire ten years of general education. History starts in the fourth year, continuing through the tenth. Art and music are in the program through the sixth or seventh year and then are dropped. The sciences are phased in, beginning in the fifth year with biology. Physical education is required in every grade. Though homework is theoretically restricted to about an hour a night in elementary grades and two in higher grades, teachers do not coordinate their assignments, and the pupils often have very heavy loads, said to run regularly to four hours a night. On the other hand, there are reports indicating that teachers tend to bark rather than bite. It is not merely a matter of the outlawing of corporal punishment in the classroom (though some instances of cuffing in the lower grades are alleged), but it seems that however badly the pupil does, he or she is almost always moved to the next grade, a not unfamiliar complaint about our own system.

Just as in Taiwan (or in the United States, for that matter), the Soviet middle school grades run a gamut of quality. Beyond the variation in the ordinary schools, however, is a much greater leap to the special school, which is usually identified by some indication of specialization. Thus there are middle schools specializing in mathematics, or in biology, or in other subjects, mainly in the sciences. Robert Kaiser spoke with a student in such a school. She was one of a class of thirty-two—four were children of ordinary workers, the rest had parents who were "officials and intellectuals." They had all entered their school through competitive performance and they looked down upon ordinary schools. This particular school specialized in biology, and its graduates expected to go to Moscow State University or to an equivalent institution of higher education. All but three students in the girl's class were members of the Komsomol (Young Communists League). According to Kaiser, this was less a matter of ideological conviction than, as the student put it, "a credential you have to have to get into the university."

Another journalist, Fred Hechinger, who was formerly specialist on education for the *New York Times,* walked into a chemistry class while visiting a Moscow high school, only to find one of the students before the class. She was running a Komsomol meeting. The order of business was the induction of a new member. A boy was being asked if he wanted to join. Described by Hechinger as "flustered and ill at ease," the student replied that since only a few of his comrades had not yet joined, he thought he might as well become a member. On this flat note a vote was taken on his admission, and he was inducted "with only a few abstentions." In Hechinger's view, this represented "a ritual that no longer was taken too seriously." On the other hand, Professor Wesley Fisher, a Soviet specialist at Columbia University, remarked to us that Komsomol activity is not always such a routine and so seemingly inconsequential, but has many active and enthusiastic participants.

Somewhere between are additional observations by Robert Kaiser, who spoke with one young Russian who entered the Moscow State Institute for International Relations in the middle 1960s. The Institute is one of the main passageways to Party and governmental status, and to excellent positions in the diplomatic corps, the KGB, or to jobs as journalists or Party officials. Advancement requires character references from the candidate's regional Young Communist League committee. This is associated with an intensive regime of lectures and examinations that are used to select the best and most dedicated candidates. Immediate family background may play a role; certainly hurdling the barriers to membership seems more likely for the children of people who have already embarked on successful Party careers. Yet with the routinization of the Party there is also evident opportunism and careerism, described in some detail by Kaiser's informant.

Induction into useful labor remains a surprisingly uneven process, especially in the view of American observers of the system. In the general curriculum, every school grade, from first through tenth, provides for two hours per week of "labor training." According to Grant, such training may take place in workshops inside the schools, but perhaps more often the school is linked with one or more nearby factories where the work is carried out. At one time, prior to 1964, the emphasis on such work was stressed to the point that the school course was extended a full year to permit more time for such work. It seems to have become a largely time-serving and unproductive exercise, however, because sharp retrenchment followed. Now, concentrated "labor training" is found in perhaps one out of three schools. Elsewhere, the basic concept seems to have evolved; some schools devote the time to "theoretical" courses about work, while others may even accept driver education as a substitute.

One of the surprising things about work in the context of Soviet formal education is the persistence of sexual divisions. Summing up her own observations, which repeat in this detail what others have also reported, Susan Jacoby says that by the seventh grade (when children are about fourteen), " 'labor' means metal-working for boys and home economics for girls." In discussing this situation with a Soviet school principal, Jacoby brought up the contradiction between such school practices and the reality that Soviet factories, including those involved in metal work, have a significant proportion of women workers on the line. The principal replied, "Yes, yes, but the woman still has the responsibility for the home. She needs to learn something about cooking and sewing and caring for her family. The boys certainly wouldn't like to take these classes." Adding to Jacoby's remarks, Richard B. Dobson notes that student military training sees the boys oriented toward combat, while the girls train in first aid; furthermore, while the boys' extracurricular activities stress sports and technical specialties, the girls are involved in music and dance.

Dobson also refers to the work of V. D. Popov, a Russian sociologist, who asserts that in the USSR boys are twice as likely as girls to be truant or to violate school rules. Boys are more than six times as likely as girls to get into serious trouble, including the familiar category of offenses called "hooliganism," but also extending to theft, hard drinking, and worse. Another Russian sociologist has pointed out that twice as many boys as girls are likely to be inert in school with respect to assuming active class or other social roles. Girls are much more likely to be class officers or to take seriously Pioneer or Komsomol activities.

It should not be simplistically concluded that boys are invariably less compliant, less cooperative, than girls. One means of expression for female resistance in the context of the school has been in details of dress. Until 1963, both male and female students wore school uniforms, that of the boys being quite military in appearance. The boys were then put into ordinary suits and the military cap was replaced by a beret. The girls, however, continued somewhat longer to endure a costume described by one Scots observer as an "antiquated (and hideous) dark brown serge dress, with frilly collars and cuffs and black aprons for ordinary days, white ones for special occasions." That costume, curiously, is said to have been based on the school dress of proper young ladies in czarist times. It has been replaced, somewhat more gradually than was the boy's attire. Now one dress, a navy pinafore, is worn by little girls, and a totally different outfit, a navy skirt, blouse, and blazer, by older girls and young women.

Changes in required dress provided an opportunity for unofficial self-expression, and tiny variations that might scarcely be noted by outsiders began to appear in students' dress. Probably the most conspicuous deviations occurred in the wearing of jewelry, a practice previously forbidden that became known in the seventies. The issue actually rose to public discussion in 1977, in an exchange of letters and editorial views in a major newspaper in the Turkmen Republic. The central issue was earrings—was it proper to wear them to school? Noting that the Turkmen Republic had only recently (October 1976) issued a new, fashionably up-to-date set of school uniforms for girls, the paper contended that the wearing of jewelry in school would be injurious to school performance by altering attitudes toward work. However, it saw no reason why girls should not adorn themselves outside of school.

Concern about the clothes and accessories worn by teenagers extends beyond the school, and may be reminiscent of earlier struggles in the United States. Indeed, there is a connection between them—for example, in the well-publicized Soviet youth craving for jeans. Teenage fads have been discussed since 1975 in various Soviet newspapers and periodicals such as *Literaturnaya gazeta.* In one such story, a young woman is quoted as remarking about people in her age group that "they talk only about their 'rags' ['threads'], their 'hot plates' ['platters'] and their drinking, and they dress as alike as a football team, in 'uniforms' of jeans and T-shirts." In the same story, a seventeen-year-old Moscow boy complains, "You adults get your guard up as soon as you see our T-shirts, blue jeans, and air of independence—yet you tell us not to judge by appearances." The fad for this costume continues, and high prices are paid for items of clothing made outside Warsaw Pact nations, despite the increasing accessibility of similar items made, say, in Poland.

A final quirk of adolescent and young adult adornment may be mentioned. Until we began background research for this section, we had never heard of a fad that seems to have started in the Black Sea resort country of the Soviet Union and may still be continuing despite official reprobation. We refer to the penchant for the wearing of small gold and silver crucifixes by youths of both sexes. The Soviet journal *Science and Religion* responded with alarm, quoting one teacher who took exception to the practice. Denouncing the new fashion as offensive to both atheists and believers—the former for obvious reasons, the latter (gratuitously?) on the ground that it was a travesty of religious faith—the teacher provided an alternative. Maidens might wear "a dainty swan, sea gull or swallow . . . on a delicate chain." They were also advised to give their boyfriends "a miniature anchor, dagger or sword as a symbol of manliness and courage."

The clothes worn by adolescents and young adults may stir uneasiness in adults, but much more disturbing are the activities that were mentioned at the beginning of this section—the loose category of actions that the Soviet people refer to as "hooliganism." Included in this package is drinking. As described by Robert Kaiser, drinking in the USSR tends to be by the bottle, rather than by the individual drinks bought in a bar. Drug control in the USSR is obviously tighter and infinitely more successful than in the United States. Most mentions of drug arrests we have been able to collect deal with transient foreigners, often those attempting to take drugs from a point of origin in non-Soviet Asia to a place of sale in western Europe or North America. Also, as far as we have been able to discover, readily manufactured or synthesized drugs, such as LSD or angel dust, are used little or not at all, and are certainly not produced in school laboratories.

If bathtub vodka is a problem, we have not found it mentioned. This may be because it is unnecessary to go to such lengths. Not only can adults find ample supplies of liquor if they have the rubles, but so too can youth, albeit illegally. Fairly typical are the remarks of one S. Makarov, a special correspondent writing in *Komsomolskaya Pravda* about the town of Chapayevsk, in Kubyshev Province, which had attracted attention because of its high youth crime rate. One of the centers from which such activities seemed to radiate was State Vocational School No. 38, which drew students from many other cities. Making pistols and sawed-off shotguns was a popular activity. Delinquency was such that the Young Communist League, in collaboration with the militia (police), staged some eighteen raids on legitimate liquor stores to discover if the clerks were making illicit sales to youngsters.

> "It was established that sales clerks in liquor departments do not sell alcohol to teenagers. But the entries in the book of visitors to the sobering-up stations indicate otherwise: Among this institution's 'guests,' one frequently encounters the names of minors. Moreover, they are picked up not only on the street and at beer stands. The tenth grader Aleksandr Kovalenko was brought in, intoxicated, straight from School No. 8 [School No. 38?]"

On the other hand, perhaps because of the persistent belief in the Soviet Union that youngsters do not really drink, it is not uncommon for a shift of workers, a factory team, to celebrate the arrival of a new worker, particularly one for whom this job is his first real employment, to make a ritual occasion of it by drinking, often until the young recruit gets sick or passes out.

By no means are all such rituals of transition marked by drinking. A suggestion was recently made, for example, that young people becoming collective farmers, something that can still be done as early as sixteen, should experience an impressive rite of transition to enhance the importance and memorableness of the occasion. It was proposed that an initiation ceremony should be developed and perpetuated that would include "the solemn presentation of the deed transferring the land for use in perpetuity." The ceremony was to involve the handling of the actual deed held by the collective, thereby providing a real use for a document that otherwise simply lay on a shelf in the administrative office, gathering dust.

Shifting our view to postrevolutionary Cuba, we note strong similarities to the way youth is treated in the USSR, but with a great many differences at all levels of detail. Given the divergent base cultures, the great differences in the sizes of territories and populations, and the four-decade time advantage of the USSR, it would be simple-minded to expect Cuba to display itself as a replica of the country to which socialism came first. On the contrary, those directing the Cuban Revolution have already made it clear that their sociopolitical distance from the Soviet Union is a variable. As this is being written, Cuba and the USSR have been enjoying a special relationship for several years. Cuban youth are affected by such orientations. The recent tendency toward the militarization of Cuban society, for example, has a marked impact on the structure of schooling and the disciplining of the entire population, especially of the youth.

Still, to utter statements about Cuba can be hazardous. One Cuban-born scholar who devotes himself to its study has put it this way: "The Cuban Revolution is a phenomenon in such flux that to write about it always involves a risk: what appears as solid after some years of accumulated evidence can dramatically change in a few weeks or even days." With respect to the treatment of youth, that passage is borne out in a number of ways. Of particular interest is the development of the educational system on the Isle of Pines, which began in 1965. One major objective of the Revolution was to speed the country to communism; another was to have students include real labor in their schooling. The Isle of Pines, renamed the Isle of Youth, was to be a showcase demonstrating at least partial attainment of these goals. Choice of the island as the locale for this social experiment was deliberate: Castro had spent more than a year there in the old prison after his 1953 attempt at revolution collapsed. The island was long withheld from Cuban rule, the United States having used it as a naval station well into the twenties. After it was formally returned to Cuba, its primary use was as a gambling center. The island sustained hardly any agriculture. The scene was set for a smashing revolutionary victory. A call was sent out to youth—students in the seventh through tenth grades in particular—to come to the Isle to combine heavy production of grapefruit and beef cattle with daily continuation of their education. It was to be half a day in the fields, the remainder in the classroom. As described by Karen Wald:

"The old prison was converted into a school. Many students who went for six months or a year volunteered to extend their stay. Some got married and began raising their families on the Isle. Others moved in, and several new communities were built. The tiny island that had been a prison and a gambling resort was reclaimed by the Revolution. As with other areas of Cuba, the School went to the Countryside and made it prosper."

Another view of the history of the development of the Isle of Youth is told by a writer who lived in Cuba from 1969 to 1976 and who is still extremely friendly to the regime. Nonetheless, this account departs from that of Wald:

"The young people worked hard and displayed many of the characteristics of the new man and woman of the future—but the Isle of Youth experiment did not succeed. The Cubans quickly realized that the transformation of society involves much more than mobilizing the enthusiasm of youth. . . . The 'communist enclave' on the Isle of Pines failed not because of the youth, but because it was fundamentally out of step with the realities of underdevelopment and socialist construction."

Confusing the picture still more are the comments of Fred Ward, a writer who has visited Cuba on seven occasions, totaling six months, and who has had an audience with Castro. Ward toured the Isle of Youth not long before he wrote his book about Cuba. He reports that the teenagers combining work and school are very much in evidence, as is their work and its fruits—"mile after mile of cleared land . . . planted in grapefruit trees, all tended by the students. Over 3 million trees surround the schools and another million are being prepared." With production said to be twenty thousand metric tons [of *grapefruit*] per year, most of it exported to Canada, the experiment seems to be doing quite well.

Just as the Isle of Youth represents perhaps the most advanced development of school and agriculture, so the Lenin Vocational

School in the outskirts of Havana shows a similar fusion of school and factory, albeit with some student labor in the vegetable gardens that surround the school. Constructed as a showplace, its typicality may be judged from the two Olympic-sized swimming pools and another for diving that are part of its facilities. As in most other schools, the day is so divided that half of any particular class is in academic session while the other half is at work. The Lenin school is unabashedly elitist. A grade average of 85 percent or better must be maintained from the fourth grade on, in order to secure admission. Each student is evaluated on the basis of academic work and performance, "attitude," and relations with classmates. Each year, perhaps fifty of the top students are rewarded with a one-month trip to the Soviet Union.

From the exemplary schools such as Lenin to the general run of schools in the cities, and even more profoundly, to the ordinary country school, appears to be as much of a leap as anything that can be found in the United States. Available visitors' accounts seem to concentrate on Cuba's better schools. How else to explain what seem to be extraordinary dropout rates?

One commentator, for example, asserts that in 1971, some 300,000 children under seventeen were neither in school nor at work. The introduction of an antiloafing law is said to have reduced this truancy to about 215,000 the following year. In any event, the rate of school dropouts continues to be a major problem in Cuban education. Almost a quarter of the children who are fourteen years old leave school. This leaps to 44 percent at age 15, and 66 percent at age 17. Not all these are permanent leave-takings, since some will resume their education in night schools when they are regularly employed. These dropout figures are so high as to create concern about their accuracy. Fred Ward reports, however, that Castro himself certified the problem in one of his speeches, in which he acknowledged that only 21 percent of the children who had entered school for the first time in 1965 had reached the sixth grade. Only 13 percent of the class that started junior high in 1966 went as far as the tenth grade.

Against the background provided by these figures, it is difficult to understand repeated statements of those who attest to a Cuban policy that mandates school attendance through the sixth grade, and who declare that heavy social pressures are applied to those leaving before sixteen.

The problem has been attacked legally from the other side; that is, since 1971, a vagrancy law has been enforced against those not in school who do not work. The second provision of the law states simply, "All men from 17 through 60 and all women from 17 through 55 are presumably physically and mentally fit to work." The first provision states that all citizens who are fit should work as a "social duty," but no penalty is prescribed. That is covered by the third provision of the law: "All male citizens of working age who are fit to work and not attending any of the schools in our national system of education but who are completely divorced from any work center are guilty of the crime of loafing." Penalties begin with a warning, but escalate from confinement to one's home to as many as two years at forced labor in a rehabilitation center.

Some people have pointed to the law as sexist, because it fails to provide penalties for "loafing" women. Supporters of the regime declare, however, that much pressure is directed at young women who defy the intent of this law. On the other hand, as will be seen, equality of the sexes is defined somewhat differently in Cuba, but remains a finite social goal rather than an attainment.

In 1963 Cuba began to operate under Law 1129, which required all males between the ages of 16 and 44 to register for military service. The agency directing the draft was the smallest effective unit of government, the Committee for the Defense of the Revolution (CDR), which issued Obligatory Military Service (SMO) draft cards. Whether those drafted into military service had completed their educations or not, part of their activities in service returned them to the classroom, and they received academic credit for such work.

During the 1970s, efforts have been made to reduce the military' dependence on conscription by supplying a major educational road that leads from early military training, to service, and ultimately to the career of military officer. The specialized schools for such training are known as Camilo Cienfuegos Schools and their pupils are known as Camilitos. While such schools include both male and female students, women play less than a full role in the Cuban military. There is evident ambivalence about this matter. In the Revolution that brought Castro to power, there was one unit of women, the Mariana Grajales Platoon, an exemplary combat unit of twelve persons, including one man, Eddy Suñol, who took command reluctantly, only to end up singing the praises of the outfit, as does Castro himself. Yet, in the same speech in which he extolled the Grajales Platoon, Castro dwelled at length upon the theme that "Nature made woman physically weaker than man, but it did not make her morally and intellectually inferior to man. (APPLAUSE)."

Castro celebrates the maternal role, or the female capacity to assume that role, and he demanded that men compensate women for their actual or potential assumption of maternity. He was concerned that the movement toward sexual equality might lead to the loss of certain female perquisites: "the struggle for women's security and full integration into society must never be converted into lack of consideration for women: it never means the loss of habits of respect that every woman deserves. (APPLAUSE) Because there are some who confuse equality with rudeness. (APPLAUSE)" Those who think that a proper manner between the sexes is bourgeois are mistaken. According to Castro, "instead of bourgeois and feudal chivalry, there must exist proletarian chivalry, proletarian courtesy, proletarian manners and proletarian consideration of women." As an illustration, Castro urged men to accept as an obligation the giving of seats to women in public transportation, not merely to old or pregnant women, but to all females. This certainly could not be confused with current behavior in the United States.

This brief treatment of the way in which youth and adolescence are handled in Cuba reflects a less changeable climate than we might have been led to expect. Certainly there have been changes, but the general outline and direction have suffered little alteration. In this respect Cuba resembles the Soviet Union much more than it does China. In the three decades of the People's Republic of China there have been a number of mercurial changes affecting very basic concepts of education and of the role of youth in the society.

Neither Russia nor Cuba has ever had anything remotely resembling the Great Proletarian Cultural Revolution. Although the term was early in use in the USSR, only China has known a period in which masses of young people, ranging in age from preteen to early twenties, moved about the country demonstrating, demanding change, and disciplining those who opposed their programs. This is a matter of some significance, since the youthfulness of the Cuban leaders in 1959, compared with the leaders of Russia in 1917 or China in 1949, might have been expected to predispose the Cubans to greater radicalism. There is only ten years between the Chinese and Cuban revolutions, yet the second generation of Chinese leaders remains older than the surviving members of the first generation of Cuban revolutionary leaders. Another blow against simplistic generalizations about society. Youth is not necessarily more radical than age. The received knowledge of the 1960s, "trust no one over thirty," is no longer viable, if it ever was. Even before the 1960s, Mao Tse-tung referred to this situation in a remark that found its way into the "little Red Book" that brought together the essence of his thought:

> "The young people are the most active and vital force in society. They are the most eager to learn and the least conservative in their thinking. This is especially so in the era of socialism. We hope that the local Party organizations in various places will help and work with the Youth League organizations and go into the question of bringing into full play the energy of our youth in particular. The Party organizations should not treat them in the same way as everybody else and ignore their special characteristics. Of course the young people should learn from the old and other adults and should strive as much as possible to engage in all sorts of social activities with their agreement."

Although little has been heard of it since 1976, there has been one theme that appeared pivotal to internal Chinese struggles concerning both the broad goals and immediate problems of education. The critical issues are summed up in the slogan "red and expert." The cutting edge is the reality that for most of the past twenty years or more it has not been a question of red *and* expert, but of determining the relative importance of these qualities. There have been periods during which emphasis has been placed on the absolute priority of ideological purity ("red"), while other periods have seen the predominance of technical proficiency, whether industrial or agricultural ("expert"). The latter philosophy, more dominant at the time of writing than at any previous period in the history of the People's Republic, replaced the strongest assertion of "the primacy of politics," which encapsulates the program of the Cultural Revolution and that of the so-called Gang of Four faction led by Chiang Ch'ing.

A simplified sketch of the vagaries of Chinese educational and youth policy may be useful. From the victory of the Communist revolution in 1949 until the Great Leap Forward in 1958, the main educational efforts were devoted to an expansion of the system, especially in lower grades. There were also various drives to "reform the thinking" of teachers and other intellectuals, partly by participation in *hsüeh-hsi* (study) groups, partly by reliance on other and sometimes harsher methods. While the overtly political and ideological content of the curriculum was changed, this did not represent a substantial departure from the system which had existed under the Nationalist government.

A brief interval in 1956 was devoted to a sudden liberalization that affected all intellectuals and, to a lesser extent, the schools. This was the period of the "hundred flowers" which, in retrospect, brought forth the blooms of intellectual diversity only to identify them for cutting. By 1958, the tendencies forecast in the repression of 1956 came to the fore in conjunction with the "Leap Forward," which glorified peasant efforts to move directly and simultaneously into industrial and advanced agricultural production. It was also the period in which the communes were instituted as the new basic unit of the society. Education at every level became part study, part work. The failure of the Great Leap, denied at the time but now generally acknowledged, saw a brief reversion to the encouragement of expertise rather than ideological fervor. However, by 1962 a new campaign swept the country that again placed educational stress upon "redness." This was the Socialist Education Movement that may be seen retrospectively as the harbinger of the Great Proletarian Cultural Revolution. An early symptom of what was to follow came with the reduction of the number of students—the higher the level, the larger the slash. Those who remained in the schools found the academic curriculum greatly reduced because of the increase in the proportion of time devoted to physical labor, and the growth of "ideological" instruction.

In 1966 the Cultural Revolution began at National Peking University (Peita) symbolizing the key place of education in the struggle for domination between the factions. The spark at Peita jumped almost immediately to other universities and, more importantly, to middle schools all over China. By November of the same year, China was witnessing the most colossal children's crusade ("youth crusade" would be somewhat more accurate, although no one knows how many preteen children were involved) in history. It has been estimated that well over ten million Red Guards came to Peking alone, and many millions roamed the country. Since one of the key goals of the movement was the purge of political institutions and the radicalization of Communist structure at all levels, the movement could not be considered a Party venture. Although not officially closed, most schools, especially at the senior middle school and university level, were empty of students. The government sought to order students to return early in 1967, but most remained in wandering Red Guard units, lecturing workers in their factories and cadres in their political posts.

The schools were effectively closed for varying periods of time. The elementary schools were the first to reopen, the universities the last. In the interim, many teachers were subjected to "reeducation," sometimes by their students. When schools opened once again, it was with greatly reduced enrollments and somewhat altered organization. Replacing the former educator-dominated structure, in which principals and other professional teachers and administrators led in making key decisions, was the Revolutionary Committee, usually dominated by activist students, leaders in the Red Guards. By this time a clear trend emerged throughout China with regard to educational institutions. Politics was emphasized over technical abilities, and the higher the level of education, the more important was it for a student to be in ideological step rather than proficient. Admission to higher levels of education, particularly university, was in only a few special cases a matter of direct transition from senior middle school. Other graduates were expected to spend two or more years in factories or on farms, working full time, before they might even be considered for advancement to a higher educational institution. During this period, until 1978, youth wishing to attend college were almost entirely dependent upon the recommendations of their comrades in the workplace for referrals. In any case, the work unit had absolute veto power and could prevent a worker from returning to an educational institution other than a night school or special short-term school. Not irrationally, many work units penalized the best young workers. Fearful that, once given more education, such workers would move on to other assignments, many units deliberately nominated less skilled candidates.

To some extent the quality of candidates for higher education did not matter, since the education being dispensed was of conspicuously reduced caliber. Examinations were sometimes entirely eliminated or transformed into group performances. Graduation was not necessarily a ticket to a great job. For once in recent Chinese history, there was a principled attack on the old policy of *tu-shu tso-kung* (study and become an official).

The contest for control of China during Mao's physical decline and immediately following his death on September 9, 1976 was won, as we all know, by Teng Hsiao-p'ing, an old Communist who had previously had difficulties with the ultra-leftists. Within less than a year from the time of the ascendancy of Teng's wing of the CCP, China instituted a new version of the examinations that had been a major feature of the Empire. Where the old examinations had led directly to the conferring of degrees, the new ones dispensed admission to higher and highest levels of the system, now refurbished even to the point of the return of fine distinctions of academic rank. With the return of the examination system came a return of the predominance of direct transitions from senior middle school to college. Factories and agricultural units were stripped of their previous power of preventing particular candidates from pursuing higher education.

Rushing through this history, we have skipped many points, but one is important enough to warrant separate mention. Beginning as early as 1956, the inability of the system to absorb all senior middle school students who desired higher education, and all junior middle school students who wanted industrial jobs, had led to a system known as *shang-shan hsia-hsiang,* "up to the mountains, down to the countryside." The total number of young people who have been sent down is not known with certainty, figures ranging as widely as 12 and 40 million being offered. Thomas Bernstein, who has made a special study of the problem, favors the former figure. The process of transfer to the countryside is complex. One variable is assignment—voluntary or involuntary. Many youths of both sexes came forward, particularly in the late nineteen-sixties and early seventies, and presented themselves for such service. Some, often the children of Party officials, did so apparently for direct ideological motives. Others resembled American youth during World War II—volunteer, and you had some choice of service; wait to be drafted, and everything was out of your hands. In the Chinese case, possible choices included the nature of the assignment (to a basically military unit, to a farm run as a quasi-military unit, or to a People's Commune, the last being the most civilian alternative), and the location. Volunteers frequently were assigned within their own provinces, sometimes within visiting distance of their homes, as we were told by a woman in Kweilin who went through the process.

Like the USSR and Cuba, China has organized its youth into mass organizations and at times has had a two-tiered arrangement of Pioneers and Young Communists. The history of these organizations is complex and discontinuous. The Young Pioneers, said to have had a membership of 100 million in 1966, seem to have been replaced after the Cultural Revolution by a very loose, school-centered organization known as the "Little Red Guards," older members of the Red Guards no longer being in evidence. The ages of the Pioneers, nine to fifteen, do not quite fit the span elsewhere but the differences are small. Members of the Communist Youth League range in age from fifteen to twenty-five. This organization was almost devastated during the Cultural Revolution, sometimes being directly attacked by Red Guards. It has since been restored.

There are many accounts of the violence of some Red Guard activities, and we had visual evidence of it at several places we visited in 1977. In Sian, for example, there is a famous collection of large stones engraved with various literary and graphic classics, including a series of stelae on which a famous work of Confucius was reproduced. During the Cultural Revolution, the Red Guards broke into the building housing this collection, known as "the forest of stelae," and vandalized many of the stones. Other accounts, such as that of Ken Ling, describe acts of physical violence against faculty members. Yet when we met and interviewed scores of teachers at all levels in 1977, many of them claimed to have only secondhand knowledge of such events, and not one admitted to having been personally attacked. At the same time, we were impressed at every level by the discipline shown by the students.

From the lowest grade to the upper college classes, for example, the entrance of the teacher was the occasion for the top-ranking student, sitting by the door, to stand and cry, *"chan!"* ("attention!").

The vicissitudes of the educational system make it difficult to generalize about the nature of adolescence in the People's Republic of China. Even for the great masses of youth there have been periods of strong control and times when youth dominated and directed age. Still, it should not be thought that these patterns have controlled everyone's behavior. There has been a steady trickle of stories from various parts of China indicating a low but chronic incidence of disaffection and delinquency. For years there has been an intermittent flow of young defectors who make a dangerous and long swim to Hong Kong from adjacent parts of Kwantung. There are also those who defy the system from within, perhaps even by robbing banks. Although on a much smaller scale, we saw some "Wanted" posters pasted to trees and lightposts in some city streets. These referred to petty thieves who had stolen bicycles or committed similar small crimes.

Compared to Russia and Cuba, the Chinese appear to be extremely conservative with respect to sexual relations among young people. One area of absolute similarity, if not identity, has to do with homosexuality. It is simply not recognized in any of these regimes. Jose Yglesias writes of one homosexual he encountered in Havana who had a good job, but was not making public, much less flaunting, his amatory preference. As for China, we attempted in 1977 to draw a number of professional psychologists working in various Shanghai universities into a discussion of homosexuality. Politely but firmly they declined to speak about it.

In relations between unmarried males and females, the Chinese seem puritanical. Sexual relations among young teens seem nonexistent, and are apparently not significant among older teenagers. The exceptions occur in rural areas, where marriages still take place between men and women in their late teens and early twenties, although with greatly diminished frequency compared with prerevolutionary days. Although "barefoot doctors" and other sources dispense contraceptives, indeed, make great efforts to get them used by married couples, no easy access to these materials is provided for the unmarried, the young people least of all. Still, pregnancies do occur in young, unmarried women, although it seems that the rate is extremely low. Reprobation of such activities is quite vicious, if the reactions reported to us privately by young people who have left China can be credited. These informants stressed the uneven bestowal of wrath by parents and neighbors—women receive much harsher judgment than men, and marriage with a woman known to have had sexual affairs is avoided.

While the average age of marriage, even in rural areas, has risen well above prerevolutionary norms, in most other respects sexual life seems little changed. One area of great change, however, is prostitution. Although one American psychologist who has done extensive interviewing among Chinese exiles in Hong Kong asserts the prevalence of teenage prostitution in Kwangtung, confirmation of such practices is not yet forthcoming. The recent shifts in Chinese economy and ideology may well presage the growth of such sexual practices.

Marriage

A SOVIET futurologist, Dr. I. V. Bestuzhev-Lada, Chief of the Department of Forecasting Social Processes of the Institute of Social Research, Academy of Sciences, expressed concern during 1976 about a problem alluded to earlier in this chapter. Her focal point was the declining birthrate in European portions of the USSR and the areas of Siberia populated mainly by Europeans. Dips in the birthrate are the product of many forces, among them a tendency to delay marriage, which itself is the product of still more basic changes. Thus, the birthrate has dropped in response to the massive entrance of women into the labor force, the extension of education for both men and women, and significant alterations in perceptions women have about themselves as social beings. Yet there are other factors, such as those that have to do with the time of marriage and the availability of marriage partners.

Of course, marriage is not a prerequisite for sexual activity. A sociological study carried out in Perm, a city of about 850,000 in the Urals found that sixty-five percent of males, but only twenty-eight percent of females, engaged in premarital sex. Perm has a very high rate of unwed motherhood. No such attitude exists in the Soviet Union and such an intrusion into what are considered a woman's personal rights is heavily penalized. On the other hand, there are private opinions of the propriety of bearing children out of wedlock and these may clash with official views. At any rate, the number of babies born to unmarried mothers in the USSR fluctuates around 200,000 a year. That is merely a fraction of the birthrate among married women of childbearing ages. Given the availability of abortion, it is clear that for some women, single parenthood is a matter of personal ideology. Such women have children deliberately, with every intention of raising them on their own. In our culture, some women who have children under such conditions are self-identified homosexuals. It is impossible on the basis of available data to evaluate this phenomenon in the Soviet Union since homosexuality remains a null category. However, such evidence as is available—postnatal marital frequencies, polling, and letters to the editor—indicates a marked preference for the married state. In all, combining never wed and divorced, unremarried mothers, and adding the relatively small number of currently unmarried men who live with one or more of their children, one-sixth of all Soviet families, about nine million, are of the single parent type.

Whether never married or divorced, with children or without, there appears to be a marked preference for marital status among both Soviet men and women. Such evidence as exists indicates that the former major cause of a decline in marriage rate—lack of housing—has been reversed but not entirely overcome. What has apparently taken the place of the housing shortage as a depressant of the marriage rate is the absence of places where prospective marriage partners can seek each other out. Speaking as a historian, Bestuzhev-Lada puts it this way: "Ritual carnivals are no longer held and no new rituals have been developed . . . one has to depend only on the dance floor."

The difficulty arises in good measure from the greatly increased mobility of Soviet citizens, particularly those in their twenties and early thirties. Upon taking leave of their educational institutions, at whatever level, there is much moving about to seek appropriate and desirable jobs. Longtime friendships, including some that might have developed into romances, are suspended—broken off, as it often turns out—and the young people find themselves in the company of strangers. What is worse, there is a tendency for young male workers to be attracted to different locations from those preferred by women. One such example is towns dominated by textile production, which involves predominantly female workers. Conversely, there tends to be a surplus of unmarried men in mining towns. There is also a fairly regular movement of young women from rural areas to the cities, while young men who are agronomists and engineers move to the countryside.

One of the Soviet Union's outstanding sociologists, A. G. Kharchev, coupled a study of vital statistics from several different locations including Kiev, Tumen, and suburban Leningrad, with a questionnaire study of 500 newly married Leningrad couples. He found that 9 percent of the married pairs had lived in the same building or neighborhood since childhood, and had known each other a long time. A much larger number, 21 percent, had met at work, and 17.5 percent got to know each other while attending the same school. By far the largest single category comprised those who had met in some kind of a recreational setting, ranging from a private party in a dormitory room or an apartment to a chance meeting at a skating rink or dance, or at a vacation resort, especially in summer. Such meetings came to well over a third, or 37.9 percent. Introductions made either by relatives or friends added 8.5 percent, with successful introductions being made more often by friends than by relatives. There remain a small scattering of miscellaneous categories. Casual meetings "on the street" accounted for 1.8 percent of eventual marriages, which was twice the number recorded for persons who met because they happened to live in the same dormitory. The final category is quite a hodge-podge—couples who met on trolley cars, or in hospitals, or (in an unspecified number of cases) "at a mathematical elimination competition."

The picture provided in Kharchev's data of twenty years ago has not changed. An article in the journal *Molodoi Kommunist* concerning the possibility of establishing "get-acquainted" services was reprinted in another journal, *Nedelya,* and quickly garnered over 10,000 responses from readers, an unusually heavy flow. Overwhelmingly, the letters pleaded for such a service. The reason was evident:

"Indeed, where can people get acquainted? Not at home. Sociologists have ascertained that 80% of the residents of large cities have no contacts with their neighbors. Even people who share the same building entrance may not know each other. Nor is it easy to meet someone at work, on the street, or in a recreational setting."

Soviet sociologists have also discovered that in their survey data well over half (58.5 percent) of all marriages take place after an acquaintanceship of two or more years. Conversely, 12.2 percent of couples marry after knowing one another only from a few days to half a year, and those who have not known each other for more than a year total 18.5 percent.

One consequence of the decline in the traditional means of getting couples together has been some pressure to increase state services that may provide opportunities for meeting and dating. Some of these are already evident in the greater significance accorded recreational activities, in part precisely because they provide such occasions. But there is some public demand for modern versions of older, discarded institutions. The matchmaker was not unknown to prerevolutionary Russia but fell quickly from grace because of the association of such persons with monetary gain and for the implication that motives other than love were behind the pairing. Somewhat surprising, then, is the emergence in the late 1960s and early 1970s of a groundswell of opinion in favor of the development of computer-assisted introduction agencies. To sample the public reaction to such a development, *Literaturnaya gazeta* opened its pages to a discussion of the possibility of encouraging the process. The editors received a flood of mail. The great bulk of it was in favor of such a move. Also interesting was that in those letters that gave an indication of the writer's age, the very young and the old proved the least favorably disposed. People from their mid-twenties to late forties were invariably favorable, if not openly enthusiastic. Unfortunately for the preponderance of the favorably disposed, the editors indicated that it would be some time before any extensive use could be made of such facilities. It is quite evident that the concerned authorities are not only alarmed about the mounting Soviet divorce rate, but skeptical, perhaps fearing that quick marriages based on computer predictions of compatibility will have an accelerator effect on that rate.

The age of parties to first marriages has undergone interesting fluctuations since the Revolution, and also reflects different cultural backgrounds among the Soviet people. In general, however, a rise in the average age at marriage of both men and women is known to have followed the Russian Revolution, but then the trend reversed, and the age of first marriage dropped again. Other general characteristics can be reported, such as the continuing tendency of women to marry at younger ages than men, reflected in the relatively small proportion of couples whose ages are the same (that is, falling within a twelve-month period). Although the data are twenty years old, studies revealed that the proportion of marriages between persons close in age hovered at about 11 percent of the total. Marriages in which the bride was older than the groom ran a wider range, from a high of 29.5 percent from a district near Leningrad to a low of 17.5 percent in Kiev. As for preference for the husband's being older, about one-third of all husbands in the sample were more than six years older than their wives, and about two-thirds were more than a year older.

We know some of the reasons why marriage rates are depressed in some parts of the Soviet Union, now we turn the question over: What motives do people give for getting married? Both popular and scholarly treatments of this subject in the USSR contrast the pre- and postrevolutionary attitudes. In general, the older view was that nonromantic considerations should control so serious a matter as marriage. The new view is that love is the most important thing in contracting a marriage. This may come as something of a shock to readers who have been told that marriage in the Soviet Union is arranged at the convenience of the state. Quite to the contrary, the evidence indicates that individual marriages tend to be of no interest to authorities unless there is domestic violence or other unusual behavior. The Soviet attitude is consistent with its conception of privacy. Invading many areas that our culture assigns strictly to the individual, the Soviet state stays clear of most familial matters unless direct violations of Soviet law occur. Thus, attempts to maintain customs of payment of bride-wealth are suppressed, even in parts of Central Asia and other regions where payments of animals, jewels, or money to the family of the bride-to-be was for centuries considered the essential means of entering a betrothal. Soviet newspapers continue to run articles from time to time in which court cases involving such payments are reported. Penalties can be harsh. Beyond confiscation of all property in such a transaction, the principals may receive jail sentences.

Apart from considering such dealings as public business, Soviet legal authorities tend to stay out of domestic affairs, to the point of avoiding intrusion into family fights involving moderate violence. This is consistent with the policy of drawing a curtain about the domestic lives of high officials and celebrities of all kinds. Compared to *Pravda* and *Izvestia,* the *New York Times* looks like a scandal sheet.

Returning to the question of motives for marriage, the official attitude is expressed by Kharchev: "a socialist economy and the entire system of social relationships existing under socialism create the atmosphere 'most favorable' to marriage for love and sharply reduce the opportunity for 'marriage of convenience.'" Kharchev backs up this assertion with data drawn from an interview and questionnaire administered to a total of 800 Leningrad couples in 1962. About three-quarters (76.2%) gave as "the prime condition for a lasting and happy marriage . . . love or love plus a community of views, mutual confidence, sincerity, friendship, etc." Another 13.2% cited "equity of rights and respect." And 4% named "love and housing conditions; 1.6%, love and material well being." Only half of one percent gave as the main reason the presence of children, and two-tenths of one percent said, "a realistic view of life." The remainder (4.2%) did not answer.

Without criticizing the methodology of that pioneer study, it may be sufficient to say that some students of the subject remain unconvinced. Gail Warshowsky Lapidus has specialized in the study of women in Soviet society, and she is inclined to find fault with such research results. Recognizing that there is a special problem in areas in which bride-wealth is still customary, even if illicit, she notes a variety of situations elsewhere in the USSR in which material considerations play major roles. Perhaps most important are cases in which marital choices are based upon occupation, access to housing, or a chance to remain in a large city.

We know from Soviet sources that among the reasons given for divorce are strong parental pressures (albeit indirect ones), economic considerations, and other unromantic factors. Still, it is at least as difficult to pursue the question in the Soviet Union as in the United States. Perceptions of motivations may change dramatically with the years. Also, whatever the feeling that existed at the outset of the marriage, it might not survive the housing conditions that most Soviet citizens must accept.

The plot of *Nochnoi Trolleibus,* a Russian story current in the mid-1970s, illuminates the feelings of some women about marriage. Rita, the heroine, lashes out at the contradiction between idealized marital roles and their reality:

> "I know intelligent, talented women whom the family has turned into day laborers. It ate their talent. . . . With borsch and cutlets. . . . And here's the way it turns out: people get married in order not to eat in restaurants and carry clothes to the laundry, in order to have a cook and a laundress at home. But I don't want it!"

Russian fiction has undergone some changes since the zenith of Socialist Realism under Stalin. The portrayal of marriage in novels and short stories does not coincide with their depiction in sociological writings. Brittle relationships, sexual incompatibility, and even mental breakdowns are now to be found among the themes.

However they meet, the couple may elect to marry or not. Longstanding nonregistered pairings are not uncommon, but have several disadvantages. Not the least is the fact that such a status is of no help whatsoever in the contest for housing. There is also evidence that living together outside marriage has lost much of its chic. In part this is due to the ironic dialectic of history. The people who have been coming of age since the late fifties and early sixties are the children of parents who came of age after the Revolution and who themselves lived through a period of greater social radicalism than is known to the present generation of young adults. Such parents are unlikely to react with shock to pre- or extramarital sexual activities. Whatever satisfactions there may have been in the use of such behavior as a punishment for parents is therefore obviated. The same generation of parents is refusing on a mass scale to assume the role of surrogate parents for their grandchildren. Women in particular decline to act as *babushkas* and this, in turn, is one important reason why the birthrate is crumbling.*

---

*This trend was continuing at the moment of writing. See Craig Whitney's

While thousands of couples marry in the most perfunctory way, simply registering at the nearest civil registry office (ZAGS), even at such offices there has been a conspicuous increase in ritual. Many people want more of a fuss than can be made at any ZAGS office; to satisfy this need the Soviets have developed and continue to increase the number of "Palaces of Weddings." The earliest of these had previously been the residences of czarist nobility, hence the accuracy of the term "Palace." More recent additions to the network have shown some fortuitous resemblance to more elaborate wedding mills in the United States, but the most ambitious and active of such institutions in America turns out only a fraction of the marriages that a Soviet establishment does. Despite the tight scheduling and the absence of catering facilities, so that the wedding party must go elsewhere if it wishes to enjoy a banquet or party, the Palaces of Weddings run behind demand. Even a weekday wedding must be scheduled several days or weeks in advance, and reservations for a Sunday, months ahead.

The increase in the numbers of small-scale rituals involving Soviet citizens is so great that a need has developed in recent years for some kind of authoritative source describing the conduct of such affairs. Our society has known such guides for a long time. The current volume is probably that bearing the name of Amy Vanderbilt. Her most famous predecessor was Emily Post, but books of this type go back into the nineteenth century, if not before. The Soviet equivalent is simply entitled *Soviet Etiquette.* It has a long section devoted to weddings.

One of the first points given attention is dress. The book describes appropriate wedding dress in the USSR as falling within European norms. The bride's dress is white or pink, her shoes are supposed to be white. The groom will wear a dark suit, black shoes, a tie (not necessarily dark colored), and a white shirt. The bride should wear a veil, or something that gives a similar impression. White gloves are recommended, and flowers are indispensable, both as adornment on the dress itself and as a bouquet.

The couple arrive at the Wedding Palace at a set time so that they may be greeted by relatives and friends already assembled for the occasion. The couple pull up in a rented limousine marked in

story from Moscow in the *New York Times* of 26 August 1979, sec. I, p. 12.

front by two blue flags and on the side by a design of two rings, emblematic of the wedding. *Soviet Etiquette* advises the groom to assist the bride from the car, and to escort her into the Palace. Once inside, they part. The bride's party leads her to a place where she may make last-minute rearrangements of her costume, while the groom goes to another room with his friends.

At the appropriate moment, which depends on the progress of the ceremonies preceding their own, the couple is summoned into the main hall by the official who will conduct the wedding. As they make their way to the "room of nuptial celebration," music is heard—usually a recording of Tchaikovsky's First Piano Concerto. They move in pairs, first the wedding couple, then the parents, relatives, friends. Usually the procession mounts an elegant staircase and proceeds through wide doors until it comes to a ceremonial table behind which stands the wedding official, who may be a woman or a man, dressed for the occasion in rich clothing with a sash across the shoulders. In addition to this functionary, there is also a representative of the local Soviet, and a director of the Wedding Palace. A seating arrangement has already been prepared, usually a semicircle. Care is taken to see that the closest relatives are nearest the couple.

The music trails off, and the ceremomial director announces that in conjunction with the representative of the Soviet, she or he has the power to wed this fortunate couple. This brief speech notes the compassionate interest taken by the Soviet state in marriage and the family, and stresses the voluntary nature of the proceedings, but it also refers to the obligations that marriage involves, and the expectation that both bride and groom will provide an example of the highest moral commitment to each other and to their marriage. Bride and groom are asked if they share this pledge and are prepared to enter a strong family tie and to care for the children who may come of it. After their assent, the ritual specialist declares them married, and indicates that this will be registered. Now the couple signs a registration book, the bride invariably signing first. The witnesses add their signatures as music is heard again—often something by Glazunov or Chopin. Again the music fades away, and the ritual specialist directs the couple in an exchange of wedding rings. Each of them places the ring on the fourth finger (counting from the thumb, which is the first finger) of the right hand, which is the common European practice.

The representative of the local Soviet now steps forward and makes a brief speech extolling marriage and the lovely couple. When these remarks are over, the ritual specialist again declares the couple married, and the music comes up once more. In the account in *Soviet Etiquette,* this moment is said to be dominated by the playing of "The Hymn to the Great City," a tribute to Leningrad composed by Reinhold Glière. Once again the ritual specialist begins to speak, urging the couple to create a strong partnership and a healthy family. They are told never to forget their parents, whose efforts led to this happy moment. The parents are summoned to be the first to congratulate the couple, and then the other guests crowd about, presenting gifts and best wishes. Usually it is the witnesses who actually take the proffered presents, as the couple would be thought to be embarrassed to receive them directly. (What would the Tlingit say about this?)

What follows such a ritual is sometimes a banquet, but often something more modest, such as a party at the home of the bride or groom. It sometimes happens that the mother of the bride or groom, if the party is to be at her home, misses the ceremony entirely, staying behind with some friends to make preparations. On the other hand, if one or both families wants to make a big display, the locale may be a fancy hotel, and the cost can run to a thousand rubles or more. Elsewhere, in rural areas or where other nationalities are involved, festivities following weddings may go on and on. William Mandel mentions an occasion in 1973 when he met a young man who described a country wedding as "Something else! Three days running! Communism for real!"

Some weddings are accompanied by lavish gift-giving, and newspaper accounts indicate that the occasion may be manipulated or even used to extort gifts from political inferiors. If discovered, such activities are condemned, the gifts confiscated, and the principals may end up in jail. On the other hand, some weddings conclude, not with a Veblenian feast but with a visit to a patriotic site, or with the planting of a tree in a park. Wesley Fisher, who has made a study of Soviet marriage, is convinced that the scale of wedding luxury and display is continuously mounting.

Once the couple is married, they will quite likely return to a place of residence already familiar to them or certainly to one of them—the parental home. A housing shortage continues to plague the Russians despite large annual additions of apartment developments. In very few cases, however, can a newly married couple occupy their own flat, let in conjunction with their marriage. They do improve their priority ratings and, with luck and (according to emigrés) a little judicious bribery, they may have a place of their own in a year or two. Other felonious means of obtaining premises are sometimes reported in the Soviet press. In one complicated arrangement, a man who had a desirable apartment in a certain city was in love with a woman who lived in another city that she did not want to leave. Since she had a reasonably comfortable place, he decided to join her. To hold on to his own apartment, he signed a contract to go off to Siberia to work for a three-year period in a lumbering camp. That enabled him to obtain a special permit allowing him to sublet his apartment during the period he would be off doing this socially advantageous work. A young married couple paid him handsomely for the right to occupy the apartment, and he went off to join his love. Unfortunately, the State lumber company finally realized that he had never appeared for work, and he was ultimately tracked down by the police. He and the other principals were tried and found guilty, and drew prison terms. The payments put up by the young couple were confiscated. Everything ended disastrously, but provided a splendid warning to others.

The housing situation is not a joke for those who face its rigors. In February of 1979, for example, from Volgograd came news (in *Sovetskaya Rossia*) that the divorce rate in that province and in adjacent Astrakhan, already the highest in the Soviet Union, had gone up again, increasing by more than half within a period of about six years. In fact, no fewer than 70 percent of newly married couples in that area were said to have filed for divorce before their first anniversaries. Various reasons were given for this situation, including "hasty decisions to marry, psychological incompatibility, ill-advised interference from parents." One in every four of the couples queried as to why they had broken up said that they didn't have a place where they could live together.

Divorce is a simple matter in the USSR, especially for couples that have no children. One woman told Robert Kaiser that she had obtained her decree within four minutes of entering the ZAGS office. Only a little more difficulty attends divorce when there are children. It was not always this way. Divorce in the Soviet Union has been of great concern to the state, and there have been fairly sharp turns in policy over the sixty or so years of the new system.

Divorce remained easy to obtain for almost thirty years after the Revolution, although the imposition of fees in 1936 represented the first attempt by the government to interfere strongly in the process. The fee for a first divorce was 50 rubles, for a second 150, and the third cost 300 rubles. For many, such costs were prohibitive. Although the courts now had the power to slow divorces down, in the final analysis individuals were not prevented from obtaining them. During the war, in 1944, the law was changed. Instead of a perfunctory hearing, the court was permitted to go much more deeply into the matter, and could do so in open session, so that one's dirty linen was washed in public. To provide time for reconsideration by the couple, divorce hearings were held in at least two sessions, sometimes before different courts. There was also an escalation of costs. Merely to file a petition required a 100-ruble fee, and the final declaration could cost 500 to 2000 rubles.

The liberalization of Soviet divorce laws in the mid-sixties was sharply reflected in the divorce statistics. Registered divorces leaped from about 360,000 in 1965 to about 646,000 in 1966. From 1.6 divorces per 1000 population, the rate went to 2.8. By 1976 the rate was up to 3.4 per 1000 population. This trailed but was gaining on the comparable U.S. figure in 1975, 4.8 per thousand population.

In addition to the felt causes preceding divorce that were mentioned above, one frequently advanced reason was drunkenness. Previously, this complaint was invariably heard from women; their husbands usually denied it, and responded that in-law intervention was the main problem, either in itself or because it was the factor that led to drinking. There is some uneasiness in the USSR over a recent increase in drunkenness among women, particularly in the cohort aged 31 to 40. Women are seen with increasing frequency in the "sobering-up stations" and such conditions may begin to affect the reasons given for divorce. However, there are indications that much drinking among women does not precede divorce but follows it, since a major motive that women mention when queried about drinking is loneliness.

Unless something extraordinary about the wife is disclosed, the custody of children is invariably assigned to her. She is also awarded child support, which usually comes to about one-quarter of her ex-husband's wages, more if there are additional children (one-third if there are two, up to a maximum of half for three or more). The father who reneges on child care payments is not unknown in the Soviet Union. At times, the Soviet police system has been accused of laxness in tracing and disciplining such men. On the other hand, the plight of women with defaulting ex-husbands is no worse than that of women who as a matter of personal ideology remain unmarried while raising a child or, more rarely, two.

According to the American commentator William Mandel, Soviet marriages based on love are more likely to be successful than those contracted for other reasons. He offers no supporting evidence for the statement. It is contradicted by the results obtained by Soviet sociologist Z. Fainburg in a study of 15,000 people in Perm. In the part of the sample that said they had married for love, a little over half pronounced the marriage unsuccessful, whereas of those who married for other reasons, only about a third thought the marriage unsuccessful.

Although political changes within the Soviet Union do not seem to be coupled with rates of marriage, there does appear to be some correlation with rates of divorce and declining birthrates. The Soviet marriage rate in recent years has hovered between ten and eleven per thousand population. But, as we have seen, the birthrate is down and still dropping, and divorce has increased. In view of the fact that the Soviet system has undergone quite basic changes in the past, mainly under Stalin, it is evident that there could be sharp new turns in the future, especially since central problems, the gross size and ethnic proportions of the population, are at stake. In whatever changes may come, it appears that a consideration will be the maintaining and strengthening of Soviet family life. Although a new wave of social radicalism is thinkable, a subtle retreat in the areas of female rights is more probable. Cost accounting is likely to prevail. The family remains the cheapest institutional means of caring for babies and small children and indoctrinating them into the system. Grand Soviet plans for absorbing such functions into state institutions have undergone deflation and phasing out. Even the boarding school for older children has shrunk as a state objective. In many respects, the dynamics of the family in the USSR most closely resembles those in the United States.

In 1950, Chiang Ch'ing, the wife of Mao Tse-tung, was working in a village where, one day, the swollen corpse of a man was found in a pool. The man's arms were tied behind his back and it was obvious that he had been very badly beaten. At first it was said that demons had done away with him, but, after a time, investigation revealed that he had met his end at the hands of his wife and her lover. Actually, the woman had not concealed her feelings for this former soldier she had married and, after the Marriage Law of 1950 was announced, she had asked him for a divorce. Only passion seems to have been involved. The husband was a poor worker; the lover an even poorer hired laborer. The lovers were soon caught and were not reticent about what they had done. A people's court sentenced them to death, but this was later commuted to a sentence of hard labor right in the village.

Chiang Ch'ing told this story to Roxanne Witke in 1972. Chiang was under no illusions about the ease with which the Marriage Law would penetrate the countryside. She remarked how ancient rituals continued to survive in the rural areas, and mentioned the crippling expenses associated with bride price, the furnishing of the bride's wardrobe, and the lavish ceremonial feasting. The interview was remarkably candid. Chiang Ch'ing let it be known that the program dealing with marriage and marital relations was far from accomplished. "Women in China still have a long way to go," she said.

Chiang Ch'ing was removed from access to power within a month of Mao's death in 1976. Barely a year later, we were speaking in Peking to a man who had known her. He had nothing good to say about her. Among many nasty remarks and anecdotes, he included one that at the time went right by us. He told us that a famous artist had been humiliated because, it was said, in a lithograph of an owl, a portrait of Chiang Ch'ing was sketched, almost microscopically, in one of the owl's eyes. It was only some months later when, for purposes having nothing to do with Chiang Ch'ing, we were reading the ancient Chinese classic, *The Book of Odes (Shih Ching)*, that we came across the third stanza of the tenth ode in Book III:

"A wise man builds up the wall [of a city],
But a wise woman overthrows it.
Admirable may be the wise woman,
But she is [no better than] an owl.
A woman with a long tongue
Is [like] a stepping stone to disorder.
[Disorder] does not come down from heaven:—
It is produced by the woman.
Those from whom come no lessons, no instruction,
Are women and eunuchs."

How representative of Chinese culture, regardless of political ideology! Despite truly great changes in its social fabric, Chinese culture continues to deal uneasily with women in power or close to it.

The Marriage Law of 1950, mentioned above, was critical to the Maoist attack on the "semifeudal, semicolonial" features in the society against which the Revolution was directed. As Mao had observed in 1927, a Chinese man was subjected to three systems of domination: political, clan, and religious. To this, a woman had to add a fourth—the marital system, in the form of domination by the husband.

Even in the countryside, despite Chiang Ch'ing's seeming pessimism, big changes in marriage can be seen. When Mort lived in Ch'uhsien in Anhwei, just before the triumph of the Revolution, marriages were still being performed in which the principals had not previously met or even seen each other. It is likely that such marriages have been eliminated, even in remote areas. But this does not mean that the Chinese have moved to a new system based on uninfluenced personal choice preceded by dating. Certainly, there are people who display a form of dating behavior that resembles American patterns of perhaps pre-War (World War I!) times. This involves participation in such group activities as picnics, or in such organized labor ventures as taking turns harvesting in the fields. In cities, there is some movie-going (but never, to our observation, anything like necking in the dark of the balcony), and, especially in Shanghai, walking in the park or along the old Bund at night (some smooching is observable).

Although the Marriage Law of 1950 provided that women could marry after 18 and men after 20, in many parts of China these ages have risen to 23 and 25, respectively. In some places, Peking, for example, we were told in conversations with ordinary people (such as an ex-PLA soldier now a cabdriver attached to the Peking Hotel) that there are pressures to hold off until the late twenties and early thirties. These are obviously suggestions related to China's huge and still growing population.

Things are much different in the countryside. Jack Chen, the Trinidad-born son of a former Chinese foreign minister, spent a number of years in the People's Republic of China, including all of 1970, when he and his family were sent down *(hsia-fang)* to a rural village, "Upper Felicity," and he has told us about that year in a fascinating book. Marriage in the village could hardly be described as revolutionized. There were, however, great changes. Couples still used go-betweens, and although parents had a major voice in arrangements, they did not have a veto. Also, "blind marriages," in which the couple saw each other clearly only after they were married, were definitely a thing of the past. The newer vogue is for matchmaker and parents together to seek out an appropriate mate, and then permit the young couple to meet and determine their own reactions. This is by no means a standardized process. In some cases, the prospective bride and groom have one meeting and hardly speak, both consumed by embarrassment. On the other hand, some young people have traveled, have been educated to secondary level and even beyond. Such people, even if they do not take the lead in seeking a mate, will defend their own interests, not hesitating to turn down several successive proposed mates pushed by relatives and friends.

Although love is now supposed to be a consideration in marriage, it has made only a moderate penetration of the countryside, as far as present evidence shows. The social statuses of the two families contracting the marriage tend to be roughly equivalent, as was previously the case. There are stories of sent-down students marrying peasants, but scarcely any reliable statistics. On the other hand, where in prerevolutionary times the worst marriages involved marked differences in wealth and status, a similar rule exists even today, but effectively reversed. A poor peasant family would be quite upset if its daughter or son wished to marry into a family that had previously been of rich peasant or, worse, of landlord background. Especially during periods of ideological puritanism, the desirability of people with previously high class standing drops calamitously. If intraclass pairings cannot be arranged, the people concerned may remain unmarried.

A similar point is made by Parish and Whyte with regard to free choice of spouse. The young person who insists on such a choice is likely to have extremely restricted access to situations in which potential mates can be found. The choice then is between strict adherence to the principles of free choice and endlessly delayed marriage on one side, or, on the other, foregoing individual principles by getting help from relatives and matchmakers, and making a fairly expeditious marriage. Remember, Chinese culture has long included an ideal of romantic love, but it is not particularly associated with courtship and marriage. Some Chinese tease American friends by noting that American marriages are supposed to begin with the parties hot for each other, subsequently cooling off. In a good Chinese marriage, they point out, the couple weds coolly, but continues through life to warm up to each other.

Despite legal reprobation, property exchanges are still common in Chinese marriages, especially in rural areas. The payment of dowries and bride price are supposed to be illegal, yet we know that in divorce proceedings, cadres have often taken the lead in sorting out the return of at least a portion of the funds and other gifts settled on the couple. In fact, Parish and Whyte believe that in some rural areas bride price has increased due to the greater significance of women in productive activities.

Another quite conservative feature of marriage in the Chinese countryside is the heavy frequency of patrilocality, although there has been a little propaganda by the government, especially in "radical" times, such as during the "anti-Confucius—anti-Lin Piao" Campaign of the early 1970s, favoring free choice of post-marital residence site. The movement of a husband to his wife's village or production team seems at least as uncommon as prior to the Revolution. As a matter of fact, it might even be rarer, because the economic motives for such postmarital residence have been eroded with the shift from private to communal land ownership.

As far as we know, the main postrevolutionary change in residence patterns has been the increase of marriages within the community, or even within the surname group.

If marriages have changed relatively little in some respects and only moderately in others, divorce shows a somewhat different picture. When the Chinese ousted the Nationalist (KMT) government, there was a spate of divorces in city and country. Old women and young girls left tyrannical or merely incompetent husbands to whom they had been joined without a moment's consultation. The anecdote previously related, in which a woman and her lover murdered the husband who would not allow her to seek a divorce, is something of an unusual case. Even in the remote rural areas the tide ran mainly the other way—in favor of woman's independence aided by readily available divorce.

One marked change concerning divorce is the mounting frequency of remarriage of the ex-wife. There was never any obstacle to the remarriage of men. Of course, as we know, men could have as many secondary wives and concubines as they could afford, at least until the republican legal reforms of the early 1930s, many of which failed to penetrate the countryside. Ironically, there is some evidence that in the new regime, it is divorced men and not women who have the more difficult time finding another spouse.

There are no legal grounds as such for the granting of divorce other than the lack of compatibility that led one or both of them to seek the termination of their marriage. Informal reasons that have motivated divorces are known from interviewing in Hong Kong; these involve very small samples, and often include materials supplied by an informant about others still in China. For whatever it is worth, such data indicate that the leading complaints are economic: the accused spouse is lazy, consumes too much, or made misleading promises before marriage.

Since the Revolution, the word used to refer to one's spouse has been *ai-jen* ("lover"). The use of this term would have occasioned the deepest embarrassment prior to the Revolution, but it was encouraged by the government, through cadres, and spread far and wide with remarkable speed. Despite the use of this term, as we have seen, love is not considered an important basis for marriage (as is asserted, for example, in the USSR), and the loss of love is not often given as a reason for divorce. It may be surprising, then, to find that sexual incompatibility is a prominent motive for divorce. More often than not, it is a woman who cites this defect in her spouse. Sometimes there is a third party, a lover who is monopolizing sexual attentions that should be focused at home. But there are many cases in which the complaint is simply of a husband's impotence.

Within one year of their assumption of power, the Chinese Communists uttered a Marriage Law that is still the guiding document on the subject some thirty years later. This was not the case in Cuba, where a comparable statement of legal rights and obligations was not put into effect until March 8, 1975. Actually, Law No. 1289 was approved by the Cuban Council of Ministers on the previous 14th of February, but held for ceremonial proclamation until International Woman's Day. Although known as "The Family Code," the document is aimed at equalizing the relations between the sexes, hence the appropriateness of the symbolism.

In the preamble, proclaimed by Oswaldo Dorticos, then President of the Republic of Cuba, is a declaration that "the family . . . is the elementary cell of society." Even before this statement, however, the Code declares war on "[o]bsolete judicial norms from the bourgeois past which are contrary to equality and discriminatory with regard to women and children born out of wedlock. . . . "

The Code sets the minimum marriage age at eighteen for both sexes; however, it immediately provides for exceptions. Females aged fourteen to eighteen and males of sixteen to eighteen may marry if they have parental permission. If refused, an appeal to law is possible. There is an absolute prohibition on marriage under the specified ages.

Marriage requires the presence of both parties before a civil registrar or a notary public, but conditions are provided for marriage by proxy. Certain testimonials, both oral and documentary, must be presented, although this part of the ceremony is waived where one or both parties stand in imminent likelihood of death. Article 16 then describes the minimal formalities:

"The marriage will be formalized with dignity and the solemn setting that the act requires because of its social significance. The parties—or one of them and the proxy representative—will appear before the official, together with two witnesses who are of age and not related to the partners up to the second degree of consanguinity. Then, after the official has read Articles 24–28 inclusive, he will ask each of them if they still want to formalize their marriage."

If they agree, the official signs the completed certificate, which is then endorsed by principlas and witnesses. The longest portion of the ceremony is the reading of the five articles of the Code that are in the section entitled "Rights and duties between husband and wife." These are worth quoting in full, since they provide one of the key loci in the struggle for sexual equality.

"ARTICLE 24. Marriage is established with equal rights and duties for both partners.

"ARTICLE 25. Partners must live together, be loyal, considerate, respectful, and mutually helpful to each other.

"The Rights and duties that this code establishes for partners will remain in effect as long as the marriage is not legally terminated, even if the partners do not live together for any well-founded reason.

"ARTICLE 26. Both partners must care for the family they have created and each must cooperate with the other in the education, upbringing and guidance of the children according to the principles of socialist morality. They must participate to the extent of their capacity or possibilities, in the running of the home, and cooperate so that it will develop in the best possible way.

"ARTICLE 27. The Partners must help meet the needs of the family they have created with their marriage, each according to his or her ability and financial status. However, if one of them only contributes by working at home and caring for the children, the other partner must contribute to this support alone, without prejudice to his duty of cooperating in the above-mentioned work and care.

"ARTICLE 28. Both partners have the right to practice their profession or skill and they have the duty of helping each other and cooperating in order to make this possible and to study and improve their knowledge. However, they must always see to it that home life is organized in such a way that these activities are coordinated with their fulfillment of the obligations posed by this Code."

Somewhat unexpectedly, for us at least, the Cuban marriage code goes into considerable detail specifying property rights within the family. Particularly notable are the individual rights that extend to items previously owned by one party or the other. Not only do such things remain the property of the spouse to whom they originally obtained, but so do replacements purchased with inherited money. Property acquired through joint action belongs to both. These will be divided equally upon divorce.

Those readers who are confused by double Latin surnames may like to remember, as stated in Article 73, that the "first last name of the children will be that of the father and the second last the first last name of the mother." Note that this more equitable treatment of surnaming is still ultimately more supportive of male descent to the extent that it selects the mother's patronym for retention.

In fact, the tilt toward male supremacy in Cuban society is still manifested in many ways by the population. It would be naive to expect things to be otherwise. One act of preparation for the introduction of the 1975 Family Code was the showing of a special documentary film "Con las Mujeres Cubanas" ("With the Cuban Women"), a compilation of clips showing women at various activities—operating cranes, serving in the militia, as students, and in other roles. One segment showed a male university student doing housework, tending the baby, and in other ways sharing domestic tasks with his wife. When the film was shown publicly, "catcalls broke out from virtually the entire audience." Some women in the audience tried to respond with applause but were hooted down.

There are few sectors of life in which socialist countries show more diversity than their treatment of sex. Compared to the Russians, and even more contrasted to the Chinese, the Cubans remain generally more permissive and relaxed in treating sexual relations. This is evident in such phenomena as nudity in films and the relative freedom of sexual activity among young people. Only a naive propagandist would expect complete and pervasive changes in a culture because a political revolution has swept a country. Mary Lou Subor, awaiting a plane for a local flight during a trip in February 1975, overheard two Cuban men conversing about the impending Family Code. The first remarked how enthusiastically his wife had come home from a Congress of Women that had been called to discuss the new Code. His companion replied that it was the same with his wife. "But it isn't fair to get them all enthused like that. It's one thing to talk about those things at a convention, but when they come to us, in practice, it just doesn't work."

Cuba has taken the institution of the "Palace of Matrimony" from the Soviet Union, and provides an ambience for the wedding ritual in great buildings that were formerly associated with the rich and powerful. As in the USSR, the services, expectedly devoid of religious symbolism, take only a few minutes, but the bride invariably wears a white wedding gown and the groom a suit and tie, sometimes purchased for the occasion with special consumer dispensation that also includes access to a variety of merchandise usually difficult to obtain. The new couple also gets privileged access to a hotel or other resort place for a few days of honeymoon. There are still some people who openly pursue their religion, and they may have a brief, truncated, church wedding in addition to the required civil proceeding. It is said that no overt interference obstructs such weddings, but only a handful now take place in a country that until recently was considered Catholic.

Articles 49 through 64 of the Family Code provide for universal and readily obtainable divorce. It is carefully drafted; the language gives no clue to any predisposition in the society to award custody of children to one or the other parent on the basis of sex. Informal sources report, however, that custody is awarded to women unless special conditions prevail. There are detailed provisions for alimony and child support, but we have been unable to locate reliable statistics or hard information on the way the system has been working. It has only been in effect a few years.

Old Age and Death

WHEN we began a serious effort to discover how people living in socialist countries dealt with death, there was a period when it appeared to us that death, like a number of other bourgeois outrages, had been abolished. Of course that hypothesis was never strong. We knew that major figures of such regimes not only were given gorgeous state funerals but were often laid to rest, although not necessarily for eternity, in a splendid mausoleum. Still, we managed to find only scant reference to death in descriptions of ordinary life in socialist countries, and very little detail about what follows in the way of ritual and mourning. Before treating the very end of the lifespan, however, let us take a brief look at the increasingly long period of old age that is its precursor.

Indeed, in most socialist countries, there is relatively brisk movement to a more modern demographic profile, which means that death is delayed for an increasing part of the population. Socialism cannot be credited with inducing the world's greatest longevity among human beings, but the population that is normally conceded this record is in the USSR—certain peoples of the Caucasus who have been described by Sula Benet, and who have been seen in commercials on American television. According to anthropologists who have worked with this population, a birthday party for someone reaching the age of 100 is not surprising even when it is attended by the parents of the birthday boy or girl. Some cynics, however, have noted that record-keeping has never been a strong suit in these areas.

When we asked Russians not long out of the Soviet Union at what age "old age" began, we received a fairly firm reply—70 or even 75. This is in line with the remarks of a Russian writer specializing on the topic of social security in the USSR. He wrote that "Soviet gerontologists classify people aged 60–74 in the middle-aged category, while those aged 75–90 are considered to be in the aged class proper." The same source makes clear that there is a calculated disjuncture between old age and retirement age, the latter being 55 for women and 60 for men, although at younger ages in hazardous industries. Konstantin Batygin indicates that pensioners can readily obtain permission to stay on at good jobs: "In a country like the Soviet Union, where no unemployment exists, there is no difficulty in acquiring it."

Despite such assurances, Comrade I. Litvinov, a 67-year-old pensioner living in Krasnodar Territory, wrote to the journal *Nedelya* to complain. He had retired in 1971. A trained engineer and economist, he applied for a wide variety of jobs, he says—in construction, as a mail car conductor, as a retail clerk, and as a seller of papers in a kiosk. "Everywhere I applied I was refused outright ('we don't need pensioners') or else simply never hired." Litvinov finally got another job—as an insurance salesman. He is beginning to feel his age, and would like to share his job with another pensioner, but "management has no incentive to work out such an arrangement."

From the commentary appended to Litvinov's complaint, a statement by the Deputy Director of Social Security Administration of the USSR State Committee on Labor and Social Questions, we learn the official view of the pensioners' situation. There are now about 30 million people in the USSR who are drawing pensions because of age, and at present demographic rates another million will be added above and beyond attrition each year for the next several years. According to the government, 60 percent of pensioners continue to work in some capacity, up from a previous level of about 40 percent. While most workers have a right to continue to draw pensions while earning salaries from jobs obtained after retirement, that privilege does not extend to white-collar workers, about 10 percent of the retirees.

Apparently recognizing some of the problems of pensioners, and perhaps in view of the inflation that undermines the retiree's incomes in socialist economies as well as capitalist ones, the USSR has experimented with various schemes of work at home. Mainly adapted to light consumer goods industries, it seems that the system works by piece wages, and applies largely to women who can produce or finish knit goods or embroidery at home.

Pensions in the Soviet Union range from a low of 45 rubles per month to a high of 160. This bald statement hides a complication: the highest pension not associated with special additional benefits comes to 120 rubles per month, but workers in hazardous industries, or working under debilitating conditions, are entitled to an additional 20 or 40 rubles per month. There are other ways of hiking the pension. Disabled war veterans get a flat 15 rubles per month above their pensions and apparently without reference to the severity of their wounds. A long continuous work record is worth 10 percent more. The number of dependents is also reckoned. One gets 10 percent additional for the first dependent, 15 percent if one has two or more dependents. Thus, some pensions may be quite good by Soviet standards: a wounded veteran who held a hazardous job and retires with two dependents could receive a pension of 215 rubles a month, much more than many people earn at full-time work.

Russians we talked to were not impressed by that kind of

arithmetic. We were told that most pensioners barely manage to scrape along, and often must cut their consumption. The most difficult cases are said to be those who live alone on the smallest pensions. Such people may encounter real hardship, even hunger. As will shortly be seen, there are not enough old age homes for those who need them, and they do not necessarily bring their clients a better standard of living. We were told by Russians that social services for the old—such things as scrip for purchasing food, home-visiting social workers, or special day centers for the old are rare or absent.

The pensioner who receives only the minimum payment is poor within the Soviet system. The treatment of such cases in books and newspapers makes it clear that no one is happy about it, and though some propagandists deny the existence of such poverty, the government would like to abolish it. But to do so would be expensive, just as it is in this country, and other things, such as "defense," get higher budgetary priority.

Pensioners have some things in their favor. By any standard, they enjoy very low rents and do not have to worry about eviction. Their apartment is likely now shared with a son or daughter and grandchild or grandchildren. Even when pensioners become seriously or terminally ill, they may remain in the apartment, except for periods of treatment that absolutely require hospitalization, such as surgery. But after the procedures have been undergone and a moderate recuperation period has passed, the invalid will go home again.

There are many reasons for this: a lack of facilities, the fact that the hospitals are really not geared to their needs, but also because old people with families are believed to be better off at home. What becomes of those who do not have families to look after them? After all, with the shrinking of the Soviet family and the soaring divorce rate, there are formidable numbers of old people who have no one to turn to. There are some excellent old age homes in the Soviet Union. They are beautiful, well staffed, well stocked, and pictures of them are forever appearing in the magazines the Soviets send abroad. But such homes are a rarity. There does not begin to be enough state-run institutions for the aged who need them.

"If you are old and don't have a family to help you . . . it's terrible." So said a Russian friend to Robert Kaiser. The official view, of course, is otherwise:

> "Most old people's homes occupy modern buildings . . . equipped with everything necessary. The home at Lyubino outside Moscow is typical . . . The two five-storey buildings situated in a big park are linked with glassed-in passages. The buildings are fitted with lifts and there are two halls on each floor where one can relax in easy chairs, read a book, watch the TV or listen to a radio programme. There is a riot of flowers in the park and potted flowers inside. Usually there is one or two inmates to a room, which contains a wardrobe, a washstand with hot and cold water and a separate toilet room."

For each Lyubino there is an unspecified number of run-down, dilapidated dormitories overstuffed with the old. Even given the cultural predisposition to keep the aged with their families, the total accommodations available in Soviet old age homes came in the mid-seventies to places for about 300,000, an obviously inadequate supply.

The miserable conditions suffered by so many of the elderly in the United States make it hypocritical for us to criticize conditions in the USSR. That is not our intention. On the other hand, from such materials as we have found, and from interviews with Russians who left the Soviet Union quite recently, we see an unhappy convergence in the United States and the USSR with respect to the treatment of the indigent old. It is this part of the population that pays heavily for such things as massive military expenditures by government.

Apart from fiction, accounts of Soviet funerals for ordinary people are somewhat rare. Robert Kaiser describes a visit to a crematorium near Moscow. His account of funerals centering upon cremation may be compared with the oral account of burial given us by a Russian who left the USSR in 1977.

At the outset, there is a clash between the two accounts. According to Kaiser, death must be certified by a physician. Our leading Russian informant was sure it wasn't necessary. He said:

> When a person dies, you have to go to the Funeral Bureau. Anyone in the family can go, and takes the person's documents, including his [internal] passport. They give you a special form and you fill it out, and it is written when the dead person was born and when he died, the

cause of death. [He is asked if any queries are raised about the reported cause of death.] I don't think so. They don't care very much about that. They don't care, because if you're coming to the Funeral Bureau, they know [chuckles] you are there to ask for a place in the graveyard and it's not easy to get. So people sometimes have to give tips. Meanwhile the body is at home or in the morgue, usually at home. Bodies may remain at home a day or two. [He is asked if the Health officials are concerned.] No, nobody cares about it. No law says you have to be buried in a certain length of time. People manage, because nobody wants to have a dead body around at home. They pay out money [in bribes], they find a place, they find room—worse or better, they find a place.

[Asked if cremation is common.] I have never been to one. I don't think they're common. They do it in Moscow, when bigshots die. Bigshots are cremated and they put the ashes in an urn and the urn is put in the Kremlin Wall, but you know this? With ordinary people, I think they don't cremate.

[Asked about autopsies.] They do it now and then, actually it's very seldom. I think they do it if the relatives insist. If the cause of death is unknown. If they think it was the doctor's fault. Otherwise they don't do it. Or it may be done from a medical point of view. For instance, if the clinic or the doctor is working on this scientific problem, and he wants to confirm his ideas. So it is done for research.

The discussion turns to cemeteries. The interviewer says that the Soviet Government is supposed to hold cemeteries on a tight rein. If not functioning, as manifested by continued use, it will be zoned for other use. The informant reacts negatively: he has never heard of that. Instead, it seems to him that cemeteries are usually expanding. There was always an increasing demand for plots. Because of the tight market in grave plots, one must go to the Funeral Bureau to obtain not only a burial permit but a receipt showing that one has a right to a plot in a particular cemetery.

You get a kind of receipt with the number of a place, a plot, where you have the right to bury a body, and a worker from the cemetery comes along to see that you don't occupy another place. But if you do want a better place, it goes this way. When you're with this worker [you see an area without graves], you know, you give him a tip and, instead of giving you that place, he gives you a better one. And on the paper he writes it [laughs].

[What is a better place?] A better one? It depends. For instance, if it has some trees, some greenery. Yes, and it's a nice place, smooth, well kept, and the neighborhood, yes, the neighborhood [laughs]. That means the dead people there, the monuments there, all these things, you know that's how it is.

Of course you have to pay for the plot. I don't remember how much. I know that in Odessa they give very much, but not legally. They want their relative who is dead to be in the central cemetery. They have to pay very much for it. Make additional payments.

[If a person dies at home, is he taken to the morgue?] No, he isn't taken to the morgue. If he dies in the hospital he will be taken to the morgue, or if you want it. I will tell you why. Because it [a funeral] takes money. If a person is poor. . . . Some people [turn the corpse over to the morgue, for perfunctory state burial] not because they don't have the money to do it, but because they don't care for the dead person. . . . But this is not the rule. These are exceptional cases. Most people, even if they die in the hospital, they take them home and then they take it to the cemetery from home. That's how it's done.

[As for the funeral cortege], they do it this way. If it is a Christian, they have the old-fashioned cabs, with the coachman in black, with horses, yes, still there are some. But now you wouldn't [be likely to] see that. Now they have special buses. You order these at the Funeral Bureau, you order a special bus. You pay the money and the bus comes —one, two, or even three, because there are too many people who want to go to the cemetery. One bus for the person who is dead. It may be an ordinary bus or a minibus. The coffin is put in the bus and the closest relatives sit on both sides and they go to the cemetery. There are even some of the relatives who come with their own cars.

[As to the coffin.] There is a special place, ah, it's the same Funeral Bureau, and they have special workshops and they just make those coffins. You pay the money and you get the coffin, yes. I think all coffins are the same for everybody. One style, you know. It's just a box that is smaller at one end than the other and with the sides [gesturing vigorously] not straight but tapered and here is the cover, not flat but [with a peak]. It's painted black and sometimes they put flowers around it, natural and artificial, it depends upon the money problem. Often, if they care very much about the dead, they buy [fresh] flowers.

Jews and Russians, if they are not religious they do their funerals the same way, the way I just described. If they are religious, the priest comes to the cemetery and says his prayers.

No, they do not do embalming. Maybe it's only in the family, when they are home [with the body] they take some chemicals so that there isn't a bad smell, you know? There is no such thing as you describe in the United States, [all that complex embalming]. But they wash the body and put on the clothing. The close relatives wash the body. There are no funeral homes such as [you have] in the United States, nothing like that. Recently I was at the funeral of a Jewish old lady here and I was in a funeral home and it was like a club! The rabbi stands up and says his prayers and all the people sit. There is nothing of that kind in Russia.

[He is queried about visiting the home of the bereaved before the funeral.] Yes. But, first of all, you are not invited to take part in the funeral, so to say. When a person dies, all their closest friends and relatives, as soon as they find out, they come. They learn about it. Some of them are given calls, you know, by friends, or the close relatives, the word is spread and those who want to take part come to the apartment. They stand for a while, they say condolences or words of sympathy. No, you don't bring a gift, but you can bring flowers. No, not vodka, or whiskey.

The Russians have a tradition. After the funeral, after everything was done, they come home and observe a tradition—this is most of the Russians, excepting maybe orthodox Communists or those who are absolutely antireligious. It's called *pominki.* A table is laid for you, with whiskey, with wine, vodka, all kinds of refreshments, and food. People sit at the table, friends and relatives who are invited. If you are not invited, you would never go. Right after the funeral, you come home and the table is laid already. They begin to say good words about the person who has died and they drink. They get drunk and they forget about the person who is dead. That's how they do it. They may even quarrel. There may be fighting. Even among intelligent people, the educated.

From death to burial it may be only one day, or two. Usually it is quick, because they don't want the body around. The casket is open. The Jews do it the same way. You come to see the family and you see the open casket. The wife or the relatives come up and they kiss him.

I think there is no problem [getting off from work to attend a funeral]. They are allowed. I think there is even, although I don't remember if it's legally allowed, a second day, two days for a funeral.

[Asked about crying.] Yes, I will tell you. That's what I was struck by here, when I was at this funeral home and everyone was silent. There was no such crying or *mischugas.* On the other hand, in Russia, everything is Russianized. It's the influence of the way of life and the traditions of the country. It depends. Intelligent people, I would say, they don't cry so much, they don't scream, everything is silent, more or less. But, if they begin crying out loud, so it happens [shrugs]. The wife sometimes cries out, "Why didn't I take care of him?" or "Why are you leaving me?" "What shall I do without you?" There are laments, but not always. You see, it depends.

[What about memorials after the funeral?] Sometimes people, husbands, wives, relatives, they visit as often as they can. They bring flowers, stand for a while. They clean the grave, the monument.

[About gravestones.] The state has monument factories, it's legal, official. They're not all alike, they're different. Some are alike, of course. They haven't too many models, but, if you pay money, you can get engraving, gold leaf, whatever you want. Everybody can't afford it. How big are they? So! [indicating a large object, well over his head, perhaps ten feet high] and the grave [he paces a plot about six feet long and four or five feet across] surrounded in many cases by an iron fence with a lock. On the stone, names, dates, war service in gilt lettering, sometimes a saying: "We'll always remember you" or "Always in our hearts". Sometimes pictures [of the deceased] are set in the stone. Most popular is the Red Star. It is put on top of the grave. A pyramid of stones is heaped up and the Red Star is on top.

Some couples try to make the plot quite large when the first one is buried so that there'll be room for the second. So husband and wife can be together, side by side. This is semilegal.

The grave is dug by two or three workers with shovels. They get good pay but it's a terrible job. They use ropes to lower the casket in the grave. When the coffin is put on the ropes, only then is it finally closed and nailed shut. The noise of the hammering rings through the cemetery. Then the gravediggers fill in the grave and they go away. They're drunks, you know, because it's the work. No, no, there is no superstition. I don't think anyone believes in superstitions.

The secularized funeral of Russian Jews described above differs in a number of details from that celebrated by non-Jewish Russians following the new secular rite. Developed expressly in the 1960s as one means of combating the spread of religious intrusions, the ritual has penetrated some layers of society, mainly in heavily urbanized settings. A professional ritual specialist employed by the state assists at such funerals. The ritual specialist is not engaged in this full time, but usually has another job or profession. For the specialist this is an opportunity to make additional money, but for some it is also an ideological matter. They are assisting atheism in the holy war on religion. The word "holy" is, of course, intentional. According to Chrystel Lane, the word is used in just such contexts in the Soviet Union, and she quotes one example: "Revolutionary traditions are our 'holy of holies' . . . a living spring from which we may draw life-giving strength and emotional health."

Like the ritual already described, the "orthodox" funeral takes place in two recognizable segments, one either at home or in a reception area at the cemetery, the other at graveside. In the first part, the coffin is in a central place, often on a dais, with an honor guard of friends wearing red-on-black mourning armbands. A picture of the deceased is displayed along with any honors received. An orchestra plays mournful music. Individuals in the crowd, relatives and friends, speak of the dead, emphasizing his or her contributions to society. The ritual specialist gives a speech, which is supposed to indicate personal knowledge of the deceased. Usually the coffin has been open to this point. It is now closed and taken to the grave, where candles are lit and one last person speaks. The coffin is lowered, and everyone who wishes to throws a handful of dirt on it. A mourning song may be sung as the grave is filled in, and it is said that the gravestone is set directly in place. Presumably, after this, most of the company returns to the apartment from which they set out, now to take refreshments and hard drink.

Although the Soviet Union and China continue to regard each other warily, at best, a rapprochement would not be surprising. Many features of contemporary Chinese society have been borrowed directly from the Soviet Union. With the years since the rift opened between them (already conspicuous in 1960), some of the direct sociological imports, like the Russian style buildings in Peking, have either fallen into slight disrepair or have undergone a bit of Chinese remodeling.

This is the case with the Chinese system of retirement from positions in industry. Most of the major provisions of the original code, promulgated in 1951 and amended in 1953, are overtly Soviet-inspired. The retirement ages are the same, except that women in China can retire at 50 rather than 55. Even the provisions for workers in hazardous industries are the same, again with the exception of lower age for women's retirement. A further revision of the code, in 1970, introduced no significant changes.

We hear relatively little about actualities of the retirement system in the People's Republic of China. In part that could be attributed to the fact that many of the economists who have been attracted to the system as it was until very recently were impressed by its most radical features. They gravitated towards the heavy use it made of moral incentives as opposed to material rewards. Few of them bother with the pension system.

On the other hand, failure to deal with the Chinese system of retirement can be excused, until now, on the ground that there were very few withdrawals because of age from China's growing industrial labor force.

As of 1955, Chinese statistics reveal that only 7.2% of the labor force in industrial and public sector employment were over 45 years of age; about 75 percent was below 35. In fact, Chinese did not yet feel pressure from retirements or pension payments. While the Cultural Revolution, remarkably, by-passed most of China's industrial plants, it did have something of a disruptive effect, especially on the continuity of work records. When it all gets sorted out, China may find itself moving quickly to the point where pension load will become a serious economic problem, but that problem is probably still a few years away.

At any rate, as indicated, the basic provisions of industrial pensions reflect closely those of the Soviet Union, or are a bit more generous, in the Chinese case. This means that retirees can expect to have to live on roughly 60 percent of the salaries they earned during their last years of continuous employment. Even to a greater degree than the Russians, the Chinese tend to live in somewhat extended families if they have the economic means of doing so. Indeed, not only is grandmother an available, reliable baby and child tender, but so is grandfather. The services of these old people ease the situation of the Chinese woman worker to a great extent.

In the countryside, things are not much different. Parish and Whyte note that the legal requirements for retirement are somewhat hazy, but they report that in practice the women usually move out of the active labor force by 50 or 55, men at about 60. Even earlier retirements for women may occur with their return to child care, taking over the care of their grandchildren so that the children's mother can work. While benefits may be paid to such retirees, they invariably fall well below urban industrial expectations, and vary very much from rich to poor working units.

Although old age is not a universal passport to high status in China (and, of course, never was), it does bring respect, other things being equal. There is an age at which a man can begin to grow a beard; though it varies in different places, it is rarely before fifty and usually at sixty. (The old men of the small city of Ch'u, where Mort lived in 1947–48, watched him grow a beard with mixed feelings. It was regarded as unseemly for a 24-year-old boy to have a beard; on the other hand, when it finally was out enough to be regarded as a true beard, he was asked when and where the banquet would be—the banquet customarily given by an old man to celebrate the beard he has grown to mark his age.) Not uncommonly, the birthday party reappears at age 50 or 60. It is a dinner at which the main guests are the old man (old women now have them too) and his contemporaries, entertained at a small banquet, with a good supply of the drink Chinese call "wine"—a beverage made of either fermented or distilled grain, the latter clear as water but more powerful than bonded bourbon. These celebrations are not annual affairs, but occur every ten years. Parish and Whyte do not have systematic data on this custom, but they believe it may be vanishing in some villages.

It is in funerals that China has seen perhaps the most revolutionary change. You will recall from Chapter Five the kinds of spectacular funerals that can still be seen in Taiwan. That sort of thing is gone from China—well, perhaps not entirely gone. During the Cultural Revolution, when a great many small newspapers were cranked out to circulate the complaints and charges of the Red Guards who were storming about the country, one of the most common complaints was about funerals. Many such papers alleged that officials, some of them very high, still indulged in long procession funerals, with graves all decked out and, worst of all, with extremely lavish postfuneral banquets. It was charged that Liu Shao-ch'i, the highest-ranking of all fallen Party members, had had planes fly in with catered delicacies after his father-in-law's funeral.

During a month of travel in China in 1977, we saw not one single funeral in city or countryside. We do, however, have some second-hand data. We are told that cremation has become popular in some cities, Peking among them. Attempts to encourage cremation in the countryside have been resisted. This is interesting, because certain sects of Buddhists have long traditions of cremation. Most Chinese, however, prefer burial. On a long drive from the beautiful Li River, in Kweichou (Gueizhov), to the provincial capital, Kweilin (Gueilin), we passed mile upon mile of fields and lightly forested land covered with thousands of gravemounds, some of them seemingly fresh. We were surprised, since many of those mounds appeared in areas that might have been suitable for agriculture. It was also a revelation to us that the gravemound would still be countenanced anywhere in China, as it consumes much more space than an ordinary grave—often a circumference of about ten feet at the base and, until it erodes, perhaps seven or eight feet high.

Like the Russians, the Chinese prefer to die at home. Until recently, there was little option to die elsewhere, except in accidents or in other undesirable conditions. But now there are hospitals and clinics. Still, if it is at all possible, the dying patient will be removed to his home to die. If he is a farmer who lives in an old-fashioned house, he will be put in the central room and, if he lives in a house cluster that contains a former lineage shrine—as many still do in Kwangtung—he will be placed there, although the images and the tablets have long since disappeared (probably buried, they may yet reappear).

Cremation is urged in the villages, but Parish and Whyte say that their sample revealed but few uses of the method—those usually associated with a special political status (an official trying to set an example).

As soon as a person dies, funeral incantations are begun, usually sung by old relatives or friends. We are told that Taoist priests were available into the sixties, but cannot say if any still may be found. Parish and Whyte say that the ceremony of ritual buying of water for washing the body seems to continue. What is more, in 25 of the 63 villages in their sample, mourning dress of the kind described in the funerals of Taiwan (see pages 173–174) is still worn, and, in only slightly fewer of the villages, it is said that geomancers covertly seek out places for burial that are most auspicious for the family. Musicians blowing the horn and beating the cymbals are still found at the head of rural funeral processions. More surprising, ghost money is still used and incense still burned to appease and disperse wandering ghosts. The order of the procession closely resembles that described by De Groot almost a century ago. At the grave, there is more incense burning, and firecrackers are set off. Gravediggers complete the entombment as the funeral party returns home by a different way than it came, in order to avoid homeless ghosts. Back home, there is a funeral banquet. People apparently bring small gifts when they attend such a funeral. In other areas, in former times, money would have been the gift. It is not clear if the change to small objects instead of cash is a recent adaptation, or the extension of a local custom. Parish and Whyte, however, did compute that funeral expenditures are somewhat reduced, particularly when compared to expenditures on marriages.

Postfuneral memorials are variable. Some families celebrate key rituals as prescribed in Buddhist or Taoist belief. Others, however, confine memorials only to *Ch'ing-ming,* the Spring day devoted to ancestors, and *Ch'ung-yang,* the ninth day of the ninth lunar month, more variable throughout China, but also widely known as a day devoted to other-world activities. Indeed, on the previously mentioned *Ch'ing-ming* occasions, it is apparently still common for people to visit family graves, tidying them up and laying out sacrifices. It was precisely such activities that stirred up so much trouble for people during the Cultural Revolution. Apparently the belief system has endured, while the radical opponents of the old religion have not. If things continue on their present path, it is not unlikely that China, in the rural areas first and then in the cities, will see a revival of the folk religion. Ancestor tablets may reappear, rural temples may yet be seen again, and a revival may generally be expected to take place regarding the treatment of the dead.

CHAPTER SEVEN

Transitions in Transition

WHEN the Manchu dynasts were finally toppled in 1911, it is said that a party of workmen was sent to the Great Gate on the Yangtze River side of Nanking's city wall. Following their orders, the workers took down the tall, broad, wooden tablets, adorned in gold leaf and red and black lacquer, that proclaimed the city the southern capital of the Ch'ing state. When the massive signs were gathered, one of the workers went for a torch for starting the blaze that would consume them forever. The leader of the group stopped him. "Do we have any idea how long this so-called republic will last?" he is said to have asked. No one could answer. "Then we should not act rashly! Let us take these things to the gate tower where they can be hidden in some straw. If they are not needed again, it will not matter. If they are, our heads won't roll." So, with much toil, they moved all the boards to the lofty top of the gate. There, sure enough, they found a pile of straw, and they began to gather it up. As they removed the straw, they found, to their amazement, another set of imperial signboards. These were the remains of Ming signs that had been removed in 1644.

Rituals are the signboards of life. We have seen something of their variety in a number of cultures of varying scale and degree of technological complexity. Except in the simplest societies, homogeneity of transition rituals is broken by differences of status or by the ethnic heterogeneity of the population. Nonetheless,

256

rituals of recognizable form take place to mark at least some, if not all, of the significant points in the life cycle distinguished in the culture. At times, particularly in politically sophisticated societies, a regime decides that rituals once performed are now to be abandoned, but among the people are those who choose instead to put them aside for possible later retrieval.

One of Arthur Miller's earliest published short stories is about an American Jew in Italy during World War II. The Jewish soldier is with a buddy of Italian descent who is reveling in this return to a homeland never directly experienced. They meet an Italian cloth peddler in a restaurant, who is buying a large round loaf of bread. The Jewish soldier, moved by an exciting sense of familiarity in a previously alien place, tries to detain the Italian, for he believes that the man is Jewish. But the man is Catholic; really a peasant. For him, Jews are people in the Bible. The American tries to keep a conversation going through Vinnie, the Italian-American buddy, but the man will not be delayed. He says he must get home by sundown, with the bread, that is all. It is Friday night.

Many products of culture are as real as anything else in the real world and in the same way. They have a physical structure, and can be touched and handled for good, for evil, or to no particular end. Rituals are something else. To be sure, they have their physical side or apparatus. In the Miller story, it is the *shabes challa,* the sabbath bread, that is being carried home for a simple Friday night supper. Perhaps nothing else remains of the ancient ritual, except that the man should arrive home before sundown. The rest is likely forgotten. The man does not know that what he is doing is part of an ancient Hebrew ceremony, nor does he know that the American believes him to be Jewish. Miller is too good a storyteller to break the spell of ambiguity.

Rituals may be in neat harmony with other aspects of a culture, but they may also show disjuncture. It is likely that all cultures are perpetually in change, but some alter at rates so infinitesimal that they seem unchanging. In others, the rate of change is so fast that people coming to rituals may not know how to behave. There is an irony in this, because one of the functions of ritual is to codify behavior and sanctify it, and thereby make it more probable that people will know how to act.

Under ordinary circumstances, people in simple and peasant

societies have no reason to question that their behavior, including their ritual life, has remained unchanged since time beyond remembrance. Under such circumstances, there is little motivation or opportunity for change. The situation may change rapidly in response to a variety of factors. A series of internal changes in productivity, whereby food or other supplies of great significance mount or dwindle, may produce pressures for changes elsewhere in the system. Among the alterations sparked by such a chain of events may be some in the definition of life's critical transition points, and the appropriate means of dealing with them. Because the pristine transitions whereby societies became horticultural, pastoral, or some combination of these, occurred perhaps eight to ten thousand years ago, or even earlier, there has never been direct observation of such a transformation. There has been observation of the transformation of hunting-gathering peoples to mixed farming and animal breeding through interaction with another culture. The !Kung are an excellent case in point—even as this is being written, it is likely that some of the remnants of the nomadic hunter-gatherer !Kung are moving to villages from their shifting encampments, and that in their new locales they will become sedentary, probably hiring out as day laborers to farmers, perhaps of Herero or other ethnic identity. As they do this, they do not reinvent animal husbandry or cultivation of plants. Nor do they invent new forms of ideology compatible with their new productive economy. Instead, they hold elements of their old ways while taking over a number of things from the new people among whom they now live and whom they wish to emulate. Along with changes in residence patterns, in housing, in the kinds of tools they use, blatant changes in other aspects of their lives also occur: they marry differently (in fact, polygyny begins to increase), and with different ceremonies (often patterned on the ways of people among whom they are living), and there are whole ranges of subtle and not so subtle changes in other areas of life—for example, in the treatment of children, particularly as the number of children being born to one woman is increasing. The transformation of adolescence is related to the change in requirements for marriage. Once these people have moved seriously into sedentary living styles, hunting may be pursued, at best, as a sport and sometime source of windfall protein, all the more appreciated because it is relatively unexpected. But it will lack the regularity once required for it to be the basis on which a young man becomes eligible for marriage.

It should not be concluded from these remarks that the !Kung treatment of transitions in the life cycle were very narrowly determined by their particular technological response to their environment. As attractive (or repellent!) as the notion of technological and environmental determination may be, the actual relations appear to be more complex. Those who are attracted to causal theories of culture based on the interaction of a specific technology with a particular environment must take note of the ranges of variation that may be found between cultures that occupy similar habitats and exploit them with similar means. Their demographic profiles will certainly be similar; tens of square miles or more per person, relatively low fertility, small completed families. Yet their ideologies may be similar only in the broadest outline. More to the point, their ways of marking transitions may show very little resemblance.

That is what is seen when one compares the San peoples of Africa with the so-called Bushmen of Australia. (We regret the use of that term, with its strong suggestion of feral humanity, but there is no substitute in general usage). To be sure, in both areas the same critical transitions of the life career are recognized. But from that point on, there are more differences than similarities. Here are but a few.

The native Australian populations most like the San are those who live in the central regions where water is scarce. Although the flora and fauna are totally dissimilar, they are alike in providing a meager living for a small and relatively stable population. Desert conditions prevail over much of the area, but there are exceptions. Unless an artificial food supply, or an alien one, such as imported grain, is available, ecologists tell us that the carrying capacity of this land is sufficient to support only one person for every hundred square kilometers. So, general conditions of life are similar for the San and the central Australians. What about their delineation and treatment of life transitions?

Behind gross similarites there is a fine tissue of differences. The Bushman have a few items not known to the San, such as the throwing stick or boomerang, the bark beater, and the long wooden carrying bowl. The San have bows and arrows and poison, as well as some less significant equipment, and their hunting methods are quite comparable; so, for that matter, are their general ways of securing food. In both cultures, despite the celebration of the male role in hunting, the basic daily foods are vegetables, small animals, and insects, mainly gathered by the women. Yet the status of women among the San people seems superior to that reported for aboriginal Australian women. For example, men beating women—husbands beating wives—seems much more common among the Australians than among the !Kung; while the latter do some wife-beating, they also have an incidence, however small, of husband-beating by wives.

When it comes to their ritual life, the two cultures are quite distinct, not merely with regard to the details of what they do, but to the broadest outlines. For the !Kung, as we have seen, birth has minimal specifically spiritual quality. This may be seen by the contrast between the simple and direct !Kung notions of birth and those of the Arunta, one of the populations of central Australia. The Arunta share the widespread Australian belief that there are places within their territorial range that are inhabited by spirits. These spirits may or may not be human souls, they can become animals, and, under certain conditions, they can enter the fetus. The matter is much too complex to summarize here. It also involves conceptions of the relations between humans and animals in the ideological form of totemism which, in the Australian case, matches people and foods, often making it forbidden to consume the food with which one has a kin relation. There is nothing remotely like this in San culture. It should also be noted that where the San treat each birth as essentially a new human being, subject only to the notion that people bearing the same name may resemble each other in behavior, if not in looks, the Arunta regard each new birth as recycling of a spirit. The ramifications of this and contingent beliefs are evident in the analysis of the conceptions of another population in the vast reaches of central Australia, the Walbiri. In their cosmology, there is the mundane world of reality and another world that may be translated as "dreamtime." The central Australian view, on inspection, is much more complex than anything reported for the San; their approach to rituals of the life cycle is thus also much more complex than anything reported among the San.

In the treatment of puberty there are certain parallels. But the usual central Australian treatment of initiation has only slight echoes among the !Kung, who do not practice genital mutilation. This is most obvious in the elaborate rites of subincision, the slitting of the underside of the penis deep enough to penetrate the urethra. Details of the procedure aside, this ceremony, like so many others among the Arunta or other central Australians, requires the collection of a supply of food and water sufficient for a fairly large gathering. The content of the rituals is also much more lavish than anything reported for the !Kung.

Differences extend beyond the immediate ritual sphere into the largest patterns of social organization. Little binds the dispersed camps of !Kung together beyond the possibility that some former member of one camp group will also have lived with another. Customs of mutual feasting, ceremony, and entertainment are not well developed among the hunter-gatherer San. To the contrary, the central Australians have richly intertwined social relations between the scattered residential groups. The main armature about which more complex arrangements are formed is the marriage system, which is much too elaborate to be described here in more than sketchy terms. Suffice it to say, the central Australian system is one in which any female encountered can be assigned to one of eight categories. One of these categories is that of "mother," and one's own mother is found in that category as well as all of her sisters and many more women (including some younger than the person using the term), all of whom are addressed as "mother," and who are treated with the respect due one's mother. Another category is for "grandmother—mother's mother," yet another for "grandmother—father's mother." In addition to several categories too numerous to mention, there is one of particular interest. That is "wife." (In each of these categories, the males are appropriately designated "husband," "father," or "grandfather," as the case may be. This means that central Australians integrated the sparse population of their habitat through an elaborate system of kinship. This is *not* a feature of !Kung or any other San society.

It follows from such contrasts that the extent to which the ritual observances associated with life cycle transitions are determined by environmental factors, or the precise character of the mode of production, is only partial. It appears that there is latitude within which other factors and accidents of history may combine to produce a substantial range of variation. If such variations exist among simple cultures, whose simplicity lies in the small number of cultural traits they possess, it is a logical conclusion that even greater variation may be expected in more complex cultures. It must be noted that the simple, logical conclusion is not necessarily a correct one. As in many such statements, there is a suppressed term: *ceteris paribus,* "other things constant." But other things are *not* equal or constant. Complex cultures also have additional means of communication and efficient ways of compelling behavior (government), hence, under quite ordinary circumstances, they are capable of deliberately reducing variant or deviant behaviors. It is possible, then, for a political entity such as the Soviet Union to suppress variations, and to give an impression of a movement toward homogeneity rather than toward greater heterogeneity. Indeed, that seems to be happening in the People's Republic of China in the present state of political and economic liberalization. Yet we are still much too close to the phenomenon to see its entire trajectory, and the same may be said of the USSR.

Each society mentioned in this book, including those chosen to represent the socialist nations, marks some of the transition points we have selected for study. Not every one is celebrated with equal weight in each culture. Nor do certain transitions invariably receive great attention. Others receive consistently less. None is handled "naturally," which is to say in the way it is presented by its biology or physiology. Instead, its treatment is cultural and, consequently, the transition itself becomes transformed. It is often separated from the physical phenomena that characterize it, and the symbolic transition becomes more important than the "real" one. Let us explain.

Birth provides an excellent illustration of the difference between nature and culture. As we saw in Chapter Two, the !Kung provide a period of three days during which the parents, particularly the mother of a newly born infant, might dispose of the infant without penalty, either social or sacred. For three days the child remains without a name and with only a tenuous hold on life. Then its name is bestowed and it becomes a member of the group to the same extent as anyone else, and it will be cared for, fed, and protected. In a sense, then, its birth takes place three days after delivery when it is admitted into the society.

The time of jeopardy was even more protracted in China and Taiwan until quite recently. Until the newborn was received into the kinship unit of its father, it lived in danger and could die of neglect or by forceful means. Validation of the birth took place as much as a month after the actual delivery. If the infant had died during that time, or been put to death, or been exposed and neglected, it would not have been considered a true human being, but an evil spirit whose infiltration had been successfully frustrated. Again, the ceremonial moment of birth, quite different from the biological one, was also of infinitely greater importance.

We have already seen in Chapter Three that puberty is a period marked by wide variation in its onset and duration. To some extent these differences are based on variations in physiological functioning, sometimes related to climatic and dietetic factors. Still, within populations that share a common environment and eat the same foods in roughly equivalent amounts, puberty may be recognized as varying in time of beginning and extent. Thus, dealing with American youngsters at the turn of the century, G. Stanley Hall, who first popularized the term "adolescence," thought it ran from age fourteen to twenty-four. Today, we have tended to drop the beginning of adolescence by a year or two, while remaining very uncertain about its termination. On one hand, the reality of parents' helping to prolong the period of dependence continues, reinforced in certain parts of the population by the indefinite extension of education. On the other hand, state legislators readily vote lower ages of sexual consent (but raise the age at which people can purchase alcoholic beverages).

Lest we jump to the conclusion that uncertainty about puberty or adolescence is a problem solely of modern bourgeois society, we may recollect that Rome, both in republican and imperial days, had a shifting scale of ages for maturity, depending on the activity concerned. For that matter, we note indications of parental interference with maturation in some of the socialist countries, the USSR in particular, although not to the extent noted in the United States.

It is significant that the great bulk of the many theories of adolescence treat the period as a collective disease. Anna Freud entitled one of her papers "Adolescence as a developmental disturbance," and concluded it by remarking that the important thing was to discover which of the many types of "adolescent upheaval is more apt than others to lead to a satisfactory form of adult life." Yet, just as it is difficult to deny that adolescence in the United States is individually difficult and collectively problematic, so it is equally obvious, even from the materials covered earlier in this book, that such difficulties and problems are not universal.

The perception of adolescence in our society as *angst-*ridden is in step with the theories of adolescence generated in this country or in Europe, where the culture is quite similar. Some of the theories are heavily biological, and impute the problems of adolescence to the changes of puberty, whether crudely hormonal or reflecting social psychological conditioning. Either way, the heightened sexuality of the adolescent is seen to clash with cultural repressions. Freudian theory rests heavily upon such assumptions, attributing much adolescent breakdown to the unfortunate concatenation of social demands and biological stress. Beyond this point, the psychoanalytical schools, however many and divergent, tend to see human beings caught in certain relational dilemmas highly productive of conflict and even of breakdown. One major theme is the oedipus/electra one, an inevitable contest between a man and his son for the wife/mother and between a woman and her daughter for the husband/father. Indeed, ignoring cultures that play down or do not provide for the paternal role, some have attributed to this conflict the bulk of adolescent rituals and all contingent surgical manipulation of the initiate's genitalia. Such ritual is seen both as productive of anxiety and as a means of allaying it. So effective is the latter thought to be that societies without profound rituals of adolescence are sometimes regarded as asking for trouble—our ritualless selves providing a major case in point. Yet, again, even the small sample of cultures in this book shows that this simple association of absence of ritual and presence of social problems, such as high rates of delinquency or suicide, is not justified by cross-cultural facts.

If we move now directly to the transition marked by death, we encounter, at last, a transition whose biological circumstances seem too great for cultural manipulation. Yet, even here some room for maneuver has been defined in some cultures. We may begin, however, by admitting that all cultures have gone to great lengths to defeat the decay of death, even if unable to conquer death itself. Mummification and embalming are only two of the many techniques used to maintain the body after life has departed. Nor is such practice to be associated only with archaic cultures. The shrine of Lenin in Moscow and of Mao in Peking perform much the same function and do so, we are interested to note, in societies dominated by state atheism. Obviously, the maintenance of transitions and their rituals need not be coupled with religious beliefs.

It is in the transformation into cultural elements of what otherwise would be only so many biological phenomena that transitions become open to manipulation. The fact that something is cultural, however, does not mean that it is free of constraints. The cultural realm has its own system of necessities. The point of view taken here regards the universe as divided into things at differing levels of integration, where a level of integration comprises that set of phenomena that can be explained in terms of a consistent set of principles and generalizations. It is convenient to recognize three primary levels of integration. The simplest is the realm of matter, space, and time. We and our cultures exist in that realm, and are subject to all its laws. But they are remote from our special subject matter—life's transitions. Much closer is the realm of the biological, composed of living organisms and their processes. The laws that apply here have to do with systems of replication and reproduction, of energy use through such means as photosynthesis or heterotrophy—the eating of other living things that either have converted the energy of the sun (photosynthesis) or have eaten other organisms that had consumed the simpler, photosynthetic ones.

The biological realm ranges over a tremendously wide variety of creatures, from blue green algae, sponges, and protists, to plants and animals. The primary laws affecting developments in this realm are those of evolution, covered by modern revisions of the Darwinian paradigm (natural selection and descent with modification), plus the knowledge of modern genetics and mathematical probability (affecting possibilities of drift and genetic combinations). Yet, if this were all there is, we would have no book. The variations of marking human transitions defy explanation by the application of biological models, including those propounded in the latest biological fad, sociobiology. No sociobiologist can help us to understand why the !Kung lack the matrilineal and patrilineal divisions in their society so strongly present among the central Australians. Or why the Tlingit formerly were organized into matrilineal clans while, not far away, other Northwest Coast people had patrilineal clans. Or why others were bilateral and lacked clans.

Those who would better understand these phenomena and others governing the distribution of different forms of transition rites, must look beyond the biological. To some, this seems as if science is turning over a major subject matter—human behavior—to nonscientific forms of investigation. Such a charge makes no more sense than one attacking astronomers for not using microscopes, or microbiologists for not using telescopes. But the prejudices directed some years ago at the methods used in the social sciences, which differed considerably from those used in the natural sciences, have abated, at least to some extent. So, in regarding a series of cultural phenomena, one does not necessarily expect to utilize methods drawn from the natural or biological sciences.

Conversely, because a phenomenon is associated with a human population and is subject to symbolic transformations does not mean that it is uncaused. What would it mean, practically, to be uncaused? Simply that any society might be able to assemble a repertory of behaviors just on the basis of their appeal to its members. In other words, it would mean that a culture could be formed consciously by its carriers. In a modern setting, that might mean that it was possible for a culture, acting through its leadership, through individuals who occupied positions of respect and authority in its political system, its economy, and its communications system, to make a shopping tour through the supermarket of culture, taking an item or two from this shelf (culture A), and other things from that shelf (culture B). In such a case, the only constraints would be those of a real supermarket—the state of the stock of goods, and the ability of the cartpusher to pay, in one way or another, for what has been taken.

It would be quite simple if things worked that way in cultural development, or if they didn't. The trouble is that they do and they don't. In the contact of cultures at every level of complexity, there are feedbacks and exchanges. These need not be balanced, and indeed almost never are. The technologically dominant culture, which usually wins the privilege of exploiting another, less technologically developed culture, frequently imposes many of its elements on the dominated group. On the other hand, there are examples to the contrary. The technologically less advanced peoples of northern and central Asia periodically burst in upon the Chinese state and seized political control; still, the cultural exchanges usually saw the greater flow from Chinese to "barbarian." Yet in other circumstances there has been a heavy flow of cultural elements from the despised lowly conquered group to the conqueror. Thus, many of the basic crops, such as corn, beans, and squash, of European-settled America were adopted from the Native Americans. Closer to the interest of this book is the history of the word "corroboree," not often heard in American English, but more familiar in Australia and England. It means a big party or dance, and derives from a Native Australian term that originally applied to occasions of celebration, including the initiation rites that were among the most important of Australian ceremonies.

It is not merely a word here and there that may be borrowed. While it seems unlikely that any people picked up the notion of treating one or more of the basic life transitions through diffusion, it is easily demonstrable that this process of transmission of cultural elements has been involved very heavily in the specific content of particular transition rites. Taking one illustration from those in this book, we have seen how current Tlingit marriage ceremonies are composed almost entirely of elements drawn from Euro-American culture. Yet we quickly realize that many aspects of wedding ritual in so-called Western cultures have substantial basis in procedures known much earlier in the Near East. It was the spread of religions in that area that carried these elements around the world. The process did not begin with the rise of

Judaism, Christianity, or Islam. Actually, the process of diffusion is integral to culture and unavoidable, making the concept of a "pure" culture even more ludicrous than the concept of a "pure" race.

Lest it be given less importance than it deserves, we note again that no population ever visited by ethnographers, or known in any detail to history, has ever lacked some observance of the four transitions discussed in this book. But just as certainly, no culture, even those known for extraordinary development of their ceremonial sectors, has given equal attention to all their transition ceremonies. Chinese culture of the past was committed to a ceremonial regime that may have had peers, but yielded to none. That is a somewhat grotesque way of putting it, and probably reveals more the competitive essence of our culture than the place of ceremonial in a comparative sample of world cultures. Yet there are some cultures whose rituals are few and simple, such as the Semai of Malaysia or the Shoshone of the United States Great Basin. But the world's supply of cultures with extensive ritual, and particularly with elaborate transition rituals, would make a long list.

It is possible, then, for cultures to survive with relatively small attention to ritual and also with extraordinarily rich preoccupation with ritual, including life transition ceremonies. We cannot say for sure that a culture cannot exist unless it has a bare minimum of such rituals. It is undoubtably significant that we know of none up to the present time, which suggests that either there never has been such a culture or that it did not survive. And that in turn suggests that ritual plays an important adaptive role in the process of cultural evolution.

Does that mean that we can predict that ritual will always be part of culture? This is a more complex question than it may seem when first broached. It requires much greater attention to the definition of ritual than we have yet attempted, and we will raise only part of the question—the problem of secular as opposed to sacred rituals.

At least as important to this discussion is the weighty problem of the nature of cultural evolution as a process. We have mentioned the significanct fact that no culture, extant or extinct, is known to have lacked all transition rituals. On the other hand, we know that more complex human societies may include individuals who go through life without personally participating in such rituals, either as their object or as a participant. One can readily imagine someone going through life in our own culture without ever being directly touched by transition rituals. Imagine a child deserted at birth and removed to an institution. Remaining single through life, such a person would not have undergone the marriage ceremony and might never have been invited to one. Hypothetically, this hapless soul passes away a lonely pauper and is buried without ritual in some potter's field. Note, however, that one transition ritual has been omitted—that of puberty. Curiously, though this is probably the weakest of the life transition rituals in our society, it is unlikely to be missed even by an institutionalized child. This is a consequence of the widespread linkage of charitable functions and religious structures. In the event such a child is given for adoption or placed in foster care, that the child will not experience a clear pubertal transition rite is probable.

It is important to establish the possibility of numbers of people making their way through life in the total absence of transition marking rituals to indicate that the locus of such institutions is not at the level of the individual, but of the society. We can say more than that. As we noted in Chapter One, there are societies that exist in the absence of culture—societies of insects such as bees, ants, or termites, or the societies of animals such as rhesus monkeys or baboons. Since none of those societies display anything like the rituals of transition described in this book, we can conclude that these rituals are not essential to society as such, but may be a requirement of *cultural* society. A major problem confronting us at this juncture concerns the precise fit between the emergence of culture and the appearance of rituals marking group membership, of which life transition rituals are a major category. We have identified the earliest known rituals of transition with that population of human beings known as the Neandertals, and dated the flower-strewn remains (indicating rituals of death) at roughly 40,-000 years b.c. That falls far short of taking us to the beginnings of culture. Defined by archaeologists, culture is manifested in the shaping of tools to a set and standard pattern, and objects meeting this criterion have been found in East Africa at geochronological levels dated to more than 2,000,000 B.C. Is it possible that culture has involved life transition rituals for only two percent of its duration?

Regrettably, there is no firm answer to this question. We can speculate that such rituals existed before the earliest time of which we currently have direct evidence. After all, it was only thirty years ago that we believed our biological genus, *Homo,* to be no more than half a million years old, a view subsequently exploded by discoveries of new troves of fossil evidence. The archaeological validation of a theory linking culture and ritual is much more difficult. We know that ritual can be carried out with a total absence of physical equipment; the indispensable component of ritual is the symbol, often no more substantial than the puff of air escaping one's lips in speech. Still, there may be some faint clues to the nature of culture as a system of mutual support within sharing populations. One relic of *Homo erectus,* the species that preceeded our own, from which we are probably directly descended, is a thighbone on which is a large bony tumor. As we mentioned in Chapter One, this diseased condition likely interfered with the victim's mobility, but he or she obviously lived on while the tumor grew. Presumably fed by others, this creature's survival leads us to believe that even lower paleolithic cultures may have had coherent ideologies in which some sorts of ritual may have figured.

At the other end of the process of cultural development stretches the future. Can we conceive of cultural society without transition rituals? We have already argued that such rituals are not necessary to the survival of individuals, but function adaptively at the social level. In such adaptation, the content of such rituals is likely to be of little or no importance; what counts is simply its presence or absence. This conclusion is supported by the evidence of the previous chapters. Even though the sample of cultures was quite limited, the range—from the !Kung to the Soviet Union— was great.

It should be obvious, for example, that it does not matter to the survival of society whether the rituals be sacred or secular. While it is true that none of the socialist countries has succeeded in obliterating religious activities among its citizens, it is also apparent that such concerns have been greatly reduced despite continuing fluctuations. Each life transition may be associated with rituals that are rooted either in religious belief or in completely secular ideologies. Both may exist and flourish in the same society, as we believe is the case in our own. What seems to be indispensable for human societies as we know them in their full range, from simple hunter-gatherers to the most complex industrial giants, is their presence. Why should this be?

Like Emile Durkheim and a host of other social scientists, we believe that such rituals enhance social solidarity, and thereby provide an adaptive advantage. Societies lacking such rituals were less well integrated than those that developed or borrowed them. Over the long course of cultural evolution, during two or more million years, societies having such institutions could maintain and expand their populations at the expense of the less coherent societies that lacked them. This is a logical consequence of two specific functions of such rituals: the regulation of group membership and of social roles.

As we have seen, the transition rituals of birth provide socially recognized membership in the group. Birth itself does not do this, particularly under conditions that encourage infanticide. Even where infanticide is negligible or totally absent, the positive value of ritual as symbol of the inclusion of the new baby in the large society is manifest. Curiously, one of the clearest illustrations of this comes from the Soviet Union. Although we did not mention it in our earlier treatment, the completion of the birth certificate of the newborn is providing something of a problem. The category of birth out of wedlock is supposed not to exist in the USSR, but it does in fact have significance. Once again, it is not a matter of individual reaction, but of a collective or, in this case, a cumulative response to a situation. It appears that a majority of unwed women becoming mothers in the Soviet Union prefer to name the father of their child. Soviet law provides the opportunity to do so and restricts the grounds on which such identification may be challenged. Though it may come as a surprise, the Socialist state stands up as the protector of what seems to some merely a bourgeois conceit. Instead, the social identity of the infant member of society continues to be associated with the parental as well as larger social ties. Putting this another way, each of the socialist societies discussed in these pages has come to accept the family as a basic unit of society rather than a disposable relic of the past.

In addition to functioning as an effective means of defining group membership, rituals of transition help structure the division of labor. Rituals of puberty often mark the shift from few or no demands placed on the youngster to a heavier involvement in labor. This generalization must be taken with caution. In many societies, including our own as it was in the nineteenth century, children of seven or eight were found in factories and mines. On the other hand, !Kung children are essentially free of labor until they reach puberty, at which time they begin a gradual entrance into regular work. As a matter of fact, as we have seen, among the !Kung entrance into marriage may precede entrance into regular labor, and this is as likely to be viewed as an anomaly by the !Kung as by us, since so many of their youthful marriages end in separations followed by marriage to other parties. We also note that it is primarily females who are subject to this contradiction of statuses; males are less likely to be in such situations because they must pass the ritual requirement of the first kill before marriage.

Indeed, it reverses some of our stereotypes, but in fact, the erosion of childhood through the early introduction of adult responsibilities seems more likely to be associated with more complex rather than with simpler cultures. In our sample, the heaviest burdens of required labor are found placed on children in Taiwan and in the socialist countries. In the latter instances, the labor involvement is not merely practical but ideological. The labor requirement is carried out in the context of schooling. Elsewhere, the labor required of the young is often a function of social class, running from total engagement in the wage system to the exclusion of schooling, to the indefinite extension of childhood and dependency in higher class levels of capitalist society. The same societies, however, also display an absence of work function in the lowest class levels owing to recurrent crises of their economies; there are simply not enough jobs to go around. However, it is by no means clear that socialist societies have escaped this dilemma. The Chinese tried to deal with it, as we have seen, by sending surplus youths from the cities to the countryside, while the USSR has problems of juvenile crime and delinquency.

Whether taking a full role in the work of a society precedes or follows marriage, there is no question that the two things are strongly related. We realize, of course, that even the simplest of known societies may include individuals who work but do not marry, but there is less opportunity, particularly in small- scale societies, for an individual to marry but not work. Actually, the weight of ethnographic evidence points to the normalness, in a purely statistical sense, of the combination of the assumption of a full adult work load and the responsibilities of marriage. The transition rituals of marriage, then, mark many things. Some pertain to the realm of kinship and the further assignment of individuals to groups. This has reference not only to the defining of such extended kinship structures as clans and lineages, but also to the smallest nuclear units. In both the United States and the Soviet Union, marriage defines the formation of a new family unit. This is true although, particularly in the Soviet Union, many such newly created families must take shelter for an indefinite period with the parents of one spouse or the other. We are also aware that a large number of Soviet women, and a growing number of women in our own society, establish one-parent families. Despite the often shouted demise of the family, the overwhelming majority of adults and children in both societies continue to live in nuclear families in which both husband and wife are included (though both are probably employed out of the house, and one may not be the natural parent of one or more of the children).

Finally, there is the persistence of rituals of death, sometimes in the face of conscious opposition. Curiously, the simplest rituals of the transition as described in this book are those of the simplest culture included. The nomadic !Kung cannot afford prolonged emotional attachment to their dead, nor do they have the physical means to provide elaborate resting places. On the other hand, we have seen that such socialist societies as the USSR and the People's Republic of China continue to see great importance given the disposal of the dead. This extends not only to the ways in which ordinary citizens treat the remains of their relatives but to the way in which the state disposes of its dead leaders who died while still in great favor as far as the Party was concerned. There is a magnificent tomb to hold the mummy of the original leader. Lesser successors achieve smaller immortalities, but the least of these is accorded a public funeral.

Perhaps the remote future will see human societies emerging

that resemble the ritualless insect societies more and the societies of past and present less. Indeed, such similes are often used to arouse fears and antipathies in the members of one society in real or imagined confrontation with another. The bourgeois theoretician points with alarm to the subversion of childhood, youth, and marriage in socialist countries. Even before there were any socialist countries, Marx and Engels ridiculed the capitalist world for its comparable institutions, pointing out various shortcomings and hypocrisies. The refrain continues on both sides. So do the phenomena that are supposed to be vanishing. The rituals of life transition show no tendency to disappear. There is only a transition of the transitions.

Notes

Full titles of works referred to will be found in the Bibliography.

Chapter One

Page 19, line 34   Claeson and Onakomaiya, 1973:21

Chapter Two

Page 29, line 14   Schapera, 1930
Page 30, line 34   Harpending, 1976:156
Page 31, line 11   Marshall, 1976a:368
Page 31, line 34 to
Page 32, line 2   Draper, 1976:199–217; Draper, 1975:89–93;
                                  Konner, 1976:218–245; Shostak, 1976:246–
                                  277
Page 38, line 38   Smith, 1964:145–146
Page 40, line 31   Nadvi, 1974:49
Page 41, line 5   de Laguna, 1972:776–777
Page 42, line 10   Ibid:501
Page 46, line 8   Firth, 1967:36
Page 47, line 3   Ibid:41
Page 49, line 18   Ibid:63
Page 50, line 37   Larson, 1966:ii–5
Page 51, line 18 to end   The Chinese portion of this chapter was pri-

marily based on our field observations and interviews. In addition, however, we relied on the following works: Barnett, 1970; Gallin, 1966; Gould-Martin, 1976; Pillsbury, 1976; Porkert, 1976; Margery Wolf, 1972. For information on breast-feeding, we shall cite only one of the books and a few of the many articles we read: Bari-Kolata, 1974:-932–934; Brown, 1973:556–562; Filer, 1978:-87–95; Frisch, 1978:22–30; Jain, Hsu, Freedman and Chang, 1970: Jelliffe and Jelliffe, 1977:912–915; Knodel, 1977:1111 –1115; Raphael, 1973; Winikoff, 1978:895–902

Chapter Three

Page 59, line 28	Coleman et al., 1973:93
Page 59, line 30	Ibid:94
Page 61, line 20	Aries, 1962
Page 62, line 13	Firth, 1963:378–379
Page 64, line 25	Ibid:401–402
Page 65, line 6	Ibid:402
Page 67, line 33	Larson, 1966:115
Page 74, line 10	Smith, 1965:150
Page 74, line 29	Marshall, 1965:264
Page 75, line 10	Ibid:265
Page 75, line 20	Lee, 1979:239
Page 75, line 28	Truswell and Hansen, 1976:180
Page 76, line 1	Marshall, 1965:265
Page 77, line 3	Ibid:265–266
Page 77, line 9	Levy, 1967:40
Page 77, line 28	Diamond, 1975:3–45
Page 77, line 31	Parish and Whyte, 1978
Page 79, line 3	Kung, 1976:54
Page 79, line 10	Ibid:55
Page 79, line 34	Yang, 1976:134–149
Page 81, line 26	Fried, 1976:45–73
Page 81, line 32	Smith, 1974:337
Page 82, line 23	Snow, 1939:114
Page 82, line 28	T'ang, 1976:243
Page 82, line 39	Wolf, 1970:43
Page 84, line 3	Schak, 1974:138

Page 89, line 15   Krause, 1956:17–18
Page 89, line 30   de Laguna, 1972:181
Page 89, line 32   Krause, 1956:108
Page 90, line 12   Molinari, 1976:3
Page 90, line 24   Rogers, 1960:239
Page 90, line 29   Fried, 1952:391–412
Page 90, line 38   Rogers, 1960:240
Page 91, line 6   Knight, 1978:30
Page 91, line 36   Barnes, 1977:573 citing NIAA, 1975; Akers, 1968; Bacon and Jones, 1968; Straus and Bacon, 1953

Chapter Four

Page 95, line 7   Biesele, 1976:314–316
Page 97, line 18   Harpending, 1976:161–162
Page 98, line 19   Marshall, 1976b:254
Page 98, line 35   Ibid:260
Page 99, line 18   Shostak, 1976:400 citing Marshall, 1959
Page 100, line 1   Ibid:263–264
Page 100, line 6   Ibid:272
Page 100, line 15   Ibid:273
Page 103, line 1   Firth, 1963:442
Page 103, line 7   Larson, 1966:74
Page 105, line 14   Firth, 1963:447
Page 105, line 37   Ibid:450
Page 106, line 24   Ibid:452
Page 107, line 18   Ibid:456
Page 108, line 14   Ibid:119
Page 108, line 21   Ibid:120
Page 109, line 30   Larson, 1966:75
Page 111, line 10   de Laguna, 1972:490
Page 111, line 32   Ibid:526
Page 112, line 25   Krause, 1956:155
Page 115, line 6   Klein, 1979:102
Page 125, line 26   Imokhai, 1979 (unpublished dissertation), citing Hillman, 1975:94
Page 125, line 30   Ibid, citing Kisembo, Laurenti and Aylward, 1977:64–65
Page 126, line 3   Pillsbury, 1973:107–112
Page 127, line 5   Wolf, 1972:135
Page 128, line 23   Ibid:138

Page 129, line 14   Cohen, 1976:188–190
Page 130, line 33   Schak, 1974:135
Page 130, line 35   Ibid:134, citing Grichting, 1971:219–220
Page 131, line 3   Marsh and O'Hara, 1961:1–8
Page 131, line 8   Schak, 1974:149
Page 132, line 3   Wolf, 1972:136
Page 133, line 3   Ibid:132–133
Page 134, line 35   Ibid:119–120
Page 134, line 38   Cohen, 1976:172
Page 135, line 2   Barnett, 1970:440
Page 135, line 17   Wolf, 1972:107
Page 135, line 20   Levy, 1974:80
Page 136, line 4   Ibid: 143–144
Page 136, line 12   Schak, 1974:176
Page 139, line 33   Gallin, 1966:163–166; Barnett, 1970:260–270
Page 140, line 33   Topley, 1975:67–88
Page 141, line 1   Ch'ü, 1972:37–41; Dull, 1978:23–74
Page 141, line 8   Tai, 1978:75–106
Page 142, line 9   Liu, 1973:186–197
Page 142, line 32   Taiwan Statistical Abstract, No. 29, 1970:
                        table 8:32
Page 142, line 33   *New York Times,* April 5, 1979:C7
Page 143, line 11   Arthur Wolf, 1975:105
Page 143, line 20   Ibid:107
Page 143, line 21   Diamond, 1973; 1975
Page 143, line 37   Diamond, 1975:17
Page 144, line 13   Ibid:5

Chapter Five

Page 145, line 3   Firth, 1963:159
Page 145, line 10   Firth, 1967:21
Page 145, line 15   Ibid:21
Page 145, line 18   Firth, 1963:163
Page 145, line 19   Ibid:163
Page 146, line 8   Ibid:169
Page 146, line 12   Ibid:171
Page 146, line 26   Firth, 1959:46
Page 147, line 13   Firth, 1963:164–165
Page 147, line 36   Firth, 1967:343
Page 148, line 4   Firth, 1970:361
Page 148, line 9   Ibid:359

Page 148, line 12   Firth, 1967:19–20
Page 148; line 18   Ibid:99
Page 148, line 27   Ibid:342
Page 149, line 27   Larson, 1966:90
Page 150, line 38   Naomani, 1964:38
Page 151, line 7   Ibid:65
Page 154, line 17   Katz, 1976:281–301
Page 154, line 26   Biesele and Howell, in press
Page 154, line 32   Truswell and Hansen, 1976:171
Page 155, line 12   Biesele and Howell, in press
Page 155, line 13 to
Page 156, line 30   The entire description of a !Kung funeral is based on the field notes of Richard B. Lee
Page 157, line 11   Krause, 1956:157
Page 157, line 15   de Laguna, 1972:532
Page 159, line 23   Ibid:771
Page 162, line 20   De Groot, 1964 Vol. I:150–151
Page 166, line 13   Ibid:178–179
Page 166, line 22   Barnett; 1970:441
Page 172, line 36   Arthur Wolf, 1974:151
Page 173, line 9   Arthur Wolf, 1970:189
Page 173, line 10   De Groot, 1964 Vol II:601

Chapter Six

Page 175, line 6   Lisitsin and Batygin, 1978:130
Page 175, line 16   Mace and Mace, 1963:246
Page 175, line 22   Alt and Alt, 1959:147
Page 176, line 8   Mace and Mace, 1963:247, citing Miller, 1956:54
Page 176, line 17   St. George, 1973:173
Page 176, line 28   Lamaze, 1970:11
Page 176, line 38   Ibid:35
Page 177, line 2   Ibid:16
Page 177, line 30   Ulitskii, 1977:40–43
Page 180, line 3   Kaiser, 1976:25–26
Page 180, line 11   Druzhnikov, 1979:C13
Page 180, line 29   Gorer, 1949:155–166; Mead, 1954:395–409
Page 181, line 39   Smith, 1976:435; Kaiser, 1976:82–85
Page 182, line 9   Mandel, 1975:6
Page 182, line 15   Batygin, 1978:224
Page 183, line 8   Dunn and Dunn, 1977:29

Page 183, line 33	Smith, 1976:145
Page 184, line 23	Lyutova, 1979:12
Page 184, line 33	Bronfenbrenner, 1973:7
Page 185, line 18	*Doshkol'noe vospitanie,* 1973:61
Page 185, line 21	Ibid:62
Page 185, line 25	Ibid:62
Page 186, line 2	Ibid:62
Page 186, line 12	Levinova, 1974:38
Page 186, line 30	Ibid:42
Page 187, line 37	Grant, 1972:62
Page 188, line 9	Ibid:67
Page 188, line 29	Ibid:64
Page 190, line 11	Kessen, 1975:22
Page 190, line 38	Revolutionary Health Committee of Hunan Province, 1977
Page 191, line 7	Wray, 1975:545
Page 191, line 11	Parish & Whyte, 1978:252
Page 191, line 21	Ibid:252–253
Page 192, line 31	Chadwick, 1975:91
Page 192, line 36	Wald, 1978:127
Page 194, line 5	Venger & Mukhina, 1974:90
Page 194, line 11	Wald, 1978:128
Page 194, line 23	Ibid:159
Page 194, line 30	Ibid:159
Page 194, line 38	Ibid:281
Page 195, line 34	Bernstein, 1977:199
Page 196, line 22	Sidel, 1973:83
Page 196, line 36	Kessen, 1975:59
Page 197, line 16	Sidel, 1973:93
Page 198, line 2	Parish & Whyte, 1978:222–223
Page 198, line 8	Ibid:81
Page 198, line 18	Ibid:223
Page 198, line 21	Kessen, 1975:66–68
Page 198, line 33	Sidel, 1973:121; Kessen, 1975:98–99
Page 199, line 14	*New York Times,* August 13, 1979:A4
Page 199, line 18	Ibid
Page 200, line 28	*New York Times,* August 14, 1979:A17
Page 201, line 15	Ryabukin, 1979:3
Page 201, line 28	Smith, 1976:156
Page 201, line 34	Ibid:157
Page 202, line 11	Grant, 1972:53
Page 202, line 32	Prelovskaya, 1976:5

Page 202, line 37   Ibid
Page 203, line 10   Chkhikivishvili, 1979:3
Page 203, line 24   Ibid
Page 204, line 5   Smith, 1976:167
Page 205, line 5   Kaiser, 1975:34
Page 205, line 17   Hechinger, 1967:120
Page 205, line 37   Kaiser, 1976:445–446
Page 206, line 4   Grant, 1972:83–84
Page 206, line 13   Hechinger, 1967:99
Page 206, line 27   Jacoby, 1974:103
Page 206, line 31   Dobson, 1977:274
Page 207, line 2   Ibid
Page 207, line 13   Grant, 1972:83
Page 207, line 33   Rasulova & Tikhonova, 1977:4
Page 208, line 5   *Literaturnaya gazeta,* 1977:12
Page 208, line 26   Sergiyenko, 1977:41–45
Page 209, line 16   Makarov, 1975:2
Page 209, line 23   Ibid
Page 210, line 3   Yudin, 1978:32–37
Page 210, line 24   Mesa-Lago, 1971:ix
Page 211, line 13   Wald, 1978:346
Page 211, line 25   Cohen, 1978:5
Page 211, line 34   Ward, 1978:107
Page 212, line 10   Ibid:103
Page 212, line 13   Ibid
Page 212, line 22   Mesa-Lago, 1971:102
Page 212, line 29   Ibid
Page 212, line 35   Ward, 1978:372
Page 213, line 11   Benglesdorf and Hageman, 1974:6
Page 213, line 35   San Martin and Bonachea, 1977:405
Page 214, line 6   Castro, 1974:21
Page 214, line 15   Ibid
Page 215, line 24   Mao, 1966:290–291
Page 218, line 37   Bernstein, 1977
Page 219, line 35   Ling, 1972
Page 220, line 34   Bestuzhev-Lada, 1976:208–221
Page 223, line 32   Kharchev, 1964:31–41
Page 226, line 36   Lapidus, 1978:249, n32
Page 227, line 14   Dunn and Dunn, 1977:49
Page 228, line 18 to
Page 230, line 17   Fisher, 1976 citing Rudnev, 1971:136–138
Page 230, line 29   Mandel, 1975:244

Page 232, line 2	Kaiser, 1976:95
Page 232, line 21	Mace and Mace, 1963:213; cf. Curtis, 1967:-157
Page 232, line 28	Lapidus, 1978:251, table 30
Page 233, line 2	Levin and Levin, 1978:12
Page 233, line 17	Mandel, 1975:248
Page 233, line 23	Ryurikov, 1974:13
Page 234, line 21	Witke, 1977:251–252
Page 234, line 30	Ibid:253
Page 235, line 13	Legge, 1872, Vol. 4:561
Page 236, line 16	Chen, 1973
Page 237, line 9	Parish and Whyte, 1978:180
Page 239, line 19	Cuban Family Code, 1975:1
Page 240, line 5	Ibid:5–6
Page 240, line 36	Ibid:8
Page 241, line 23	Subor, 1975:13
Page 242, line 2	Ibid:13
Page 243, line 24	Batygin, 1978:150
Page 243, line 37	Litvinov, 1979:11
Page 246, line 1	Kaiser, 1976:98
Page 246, line 11	Batygin, 1978:196
Page 246, line 29	Kaiser, 1976:100–102
Page 251, line 4	Lane, 1979:256 citing Kulagin, 1974:17–18
Page 251, line 22	Lane, 1979:259
Page 252, line 14	Hoffman, 1974:32, table 2.2
Page 254, line 27	Parish and Whyte, 1978:261

Chapter Seven

Page 263, line 26	Hall, 1904
Page 264, line 9	Freud, 1975:250

Bibliography

Ahern, Emily M.
  1975.   "The Power and Pollution of Chinese Women." In *Women in Chinese Society,* edited by Margery Wolf and Roxane Witke. Stanford: Stanford University Press, pp. 193–214.

Alt, Herschel and Edith
  1959.   *Russia's Children.* New York: Bookman Associates.

Ariès, Philippe
  1962.   *Centuries of Childhood: A Social History of Family Life.* New York: Vintage Books.

Bari-Kolata, Gina
  1974.   "!Kung Hunter-Gatherers: Feminism, Diet and Birth Control." *Science* 185:932–934.

Barnes, Grace M.
  1977.   "The Development of Adolescent Drinking Behavior: An Evaluative Review of the Impact of the Socialization Process Within the Family." *Adolescence* vol. 12, no. 48:571–591.

Barnett, William Kester
  1970.   *An Ethnographic Description of Sanlei Ts'un, Taiwan, With Emphasis on Women's Roles Overcoming Research Problems Caused by the Presence of a Great Tradition.* Ann Arbor: University Microfilms. A Xerox Company.

Batygin, Konstantin and Lisitsin, Yuri
  1978.   *The USSR: Public Health and Social Security.* Moscow: Progress Publishers.

Benglesdorf, Carollee and Hageman, Alice
    1974. "Women and Work." *Cuba Review* 4:3–12.

Bernstein, Thomas
    1977. *Up to the Mountains and Down to the Villages: The Transfer of Youth from Urban to Rural China.* New Haven: Yale University Press.

Bestuzhev-Lada, I. V.
    1978. "Social Problems of the Soviet Way of Life." *Soviet Review* vol. 19, no. 3, (1978):30. "Sotsial'nye problemy sovetskogo obraza zhini." *Novy mir* (1976) no. 7, pp. 208–221.

Biesele, Megan
    1976. "Aspects of !Kung Folklore." In *Kalahari Hunter-Gatherers: Studies of the !Kung San and Their Neighbors,* edited by Richard B. Lee and Irven DeVore. Cambridge, Mass. and London: Harvard University Press, pp. 302–324.

Biesele, Megan and Howell, Nancy
    1980. "The Old People Give You Life: Aging Among !Kung Hunter-Gatherers." In *Other Ways of Growing Old,* edited by Pamela T. Amoss and Stevan Harrell. Stanford: Stanford University Press. In press.

Bronfenbrenner, Urie
    1973. *Two Worlds of Childhood: US and USSR.* New York: Pocket Books.

Brown, Roy E.
    1973. "Breast Feeding in Modern Times." *The American Journal of Clinical Nutrition* 26:556–562.

Buxbaum, David C.
    1978. Editor, *Chinese Family Law and Social Change.* Seattle: University of Washington Press.

Castro, Fidel
    1974. Speech at Closing Session of 2nd Congress of the Federation of Cuban Women, *Cuba Review* 8:4, pp. 17–23.

Chadwick, Lee
    1975. *Cuba Today.* Westport: Lawrence Hill.

Chen, Jack
    1973. *A Year in Upper Felicity.* New York: Macmillan.

Chesterton, Ada Elizabeth
    1942. *Salute to the Soviet.* London: Chapman and Hall.

Chkhikivishvili, D.
    1979. "Real Knowledge or Deadweight?" *Pravda* 6 March 1979, p. 3. *CDSP* vol. 31, no. 10 (1979):4.

Ch'ü, T'ung-tsu
   1972. *Han Social Structure.* Seattle: University of Washington Press.

Claeson, C. F. and Onakomaiya, S. O.
   1973. "The Spatio-ethnic structures of Northern Nigerian Population." *The Nigerian Geographical Journal* vol. 16, no. 1:19–38.

Cohen, Myron L.
   1976. *House United, House Divided: The Chinese Family in Taiwan.* New
   York and London: Columbia University Press.

Cohen, Robert
   1978. "Cuba's New Generation: Coming of Age." *Cuba Review* 8:2,
   pp. 3–12.

Coleman, James S. et al.
   1973. *Youth: Transition to Adulthood.* Report of the Panel on Youth of
   the President's Science Advisory Committee, Office of Science and
   Technology, Executive Office of the President.

Crapanzano, Vincent
   1978. "Rite of Return: Circumcision in Morocco." Unpublished
   paper.

Cuban Family Code
   1975. *Center for Cuban Studies Newsletter* vol. 2, no. 4, New York (official Cuban translation).

Cunningham, Allan S.
   1977. "Morbidity in Breast-fed and Artificially Fed Infants." *The
   Journal of Pediatrics* vol. 90, no. 5:726–729.

Curtis, Charlotte
   1967. "The Way People Live." In *The Soviet Union: The Fifty Years,*
   edited by Harrison E. Salisbury. New York: Harcourt, Brace & World.

De Groot, J. J. M.
   1964. *The Religious System of China.* Taipei: Literature House.

de Laguna, Frederica
   1972. *Under Mount Saint Elias: The History and Culture of the Yakutat
   Tlingit.* Smithsonian Contributions to Anthropology vol. 7. Washington: Smithsonian Institution.

Demos, John and Virginia
   1969. "Adolescence in Historical Perspective." *Journal of Marriage and
   the Family,* pp. 632–638.

DeVore, Irven
   1976. Co-editor, *Kalahari Hunter-Gatherers: Studies of the !Kung San and
   Their Neighbors.* Cambridge, Mass. and London: Harvard University
   Press.

Diamond, Norma

1973. "The Status of Women in Taiwan." In *Women in China,* edited by Marilyn Young. Ann Arbor: University of Michigan, Center for Chinese Studies, pp. 211–242.

1975. "Women Under Kuomintang Rule: Variations on the Feminine Mystique." *Modern China* vol. 1, no. 1:3–45.

Dillingham, Beth W. and Isaac, Barry L.

1975. "Defining Marriage Cross-Culturally." In *Being Female: Reproduction, Power, and Change,* edited by Dana Raphael. The Hague, Paris: Mouton Publishers. Distributed in the USA and Canada by Aldine, Chicago, pp. 55–63.

Dobson, Richard B.

1977. "Educational Policies and Attainment." In *Women in Russia,* edited by Dorothy Atkinson, Alexander Dallin, and Gail Warshowsky Lapidus. Stanford: Stanford University Press, pp. 267–292.

Dorovini-Zis, Katerina and Dolman, Clarisse L.

1978. "Gestational Development of Brain." *Obstetrical and Gynecological Survey* vol. 33, no. 1:14–17.

Doshkol'noe vospitanie

1973. "Brief Guidelines on the 'Preschool Education Program.'" *Soviet Education* vol. 16, no. 8, June 1974, pp. 54–77.

Draper, Patricia

1975. "!Kung Women: Contrasts in Sexual Egalitarianism in Foraging and Sedentary Contexts." In *Toward an Anthropology of Women,* edited by Rayna R. Reiter. New York and London: Monthly Review Press, pp. 77–109.

1976. "Social and Economic Constraints on Child Life Among the !Kung." In *Kalahari Hunter-Gatherers: Studies of the !Kung and Their Neighbors,* edited by Richard B. Lee and Irven DeVore. Cambridge, Mass. and London: Harvard University Press, pp. 199–217.

Drobotov, V.

1979. "An Apartment for the Newlyweds." *Sovestskaya Rossia,* 14 February 1979, p. 3. *CDSP* vol. 31, no. 8 (1979):13.

Druzhnikov, Yuri

1979. "Gas lines botherin' ya, bubbie?" *Bergen Record,* 26 July 1979:C-13.

Dull, Jack L.

1978. "Marriage and Divorce in Han China: a Glimpse at 'Pre-Confucian' Society." In Buxbaum, 1978:23–74.

Dunn, Stephen P. and Ethel

1977. *The Study of the Soviet Family in the USSR and in the West.* Slavic

Studies Working Paper #1. Columbus, Ohio: American Association for the Advancement of Slavic Studies.

Erikson, Erik H.
1963. *Childhood and Society.* New York: W. W. Norton & Company.

Fan, Kuang-Yu
1976. "A Study on the Nutritional Status and Growth and Development of Infants and Children in Taichung City, Taiwan." *Proceedings of the National Science Council* no. 9, part 2:155–169.

Filer, Lloyd J. Jr.
1978. "Early Nutrition: Its Long-term Role." *Hospital Practice,* pp. 87–95.

Firth, Raymond
1959. *Social Change in Tikopia.* New York: Macmillan.
1963. *We, The Tikopia.* Boston: Beacon Press.
1967. *Tikopia Ritual and Belief.* Boston: Beacon Press.
1970. *Rank and Religion in Tikopia.* Boston: Beacon Press.

Fisher, Wesley A.
1976. "The Soviet marriage market: marriage patterns in the U.S.S.R. since World War II." New York: Columbia University. Unpublished dissertation.

Fomon, Samuel J.
1975. "What are infants fed in the United States?" *Pediatrics* vol. 56, no. 3:350–354.

Freedman, Maurice
1970. Editor, *Family and Kinship in Chinese Society.* Stanford: Stanford University Press.

Freud, Anna
1975. "Adolescence as a Developmental Disturbance." As reprinted in *Human Life Cycle,* edited by William C. Sze. New York: Jason Aronson, pp. 245–250.

Fried, Morton H.
1952. "Land Tenure, Geography and Ecology in the Contact of Cultures." *American Journal of Economics and Sociology* vol 11:4, pp. 391–412.
1976. "Chinese Culture, Society and Personality in Transition." In *Responses to Change,* edited by George DeVos. New York/Cincinnati/Toronto/London/Melbourne: D. Van Nostrand, pp. 45–73.

Friedman, Ruth
1975. "The Vicissitudes of Adolescent Development and What It Activates in Adults." *Adolescence* vol. 10, no. 40:520–526.

Frisch, Rose E.
    1978. "Population, Food Intake, and Fertility." *Science* vol. 199:-
    22–30.

Gallin, Bernard
    1966. *Hsin Hsing, Taiwan: A Chinese Village in Change.* Berkeley and Los
    Angeles: University of California Press.

Gibbs, James L. Jr.
    1965. Editor, *Peoples of Africa.* New York: Holt, Rinehart & Win-
    ston.

Golod, S. I.
    1970. "Sociological problems of sexual morality." *Soviet Review* vol.
    11:2 (1970):127–147. Dissertation abstract (1968), Leningrad State
    University.

Gorer, Geoffrey
    1949. "Some aspects of the psychology of the people of Great
    Russia." *American Slavic and East European Review* 8:155–166.

Gould-Martin, Katherine
    1976. *Women Asking Women: An Ethnography of Health Care in Rural
    Taiwan.* New Brunswick, New Jersey: Rutgers University. Unpub-
    lished dissertation.

Grant, Nigel
    1972. *Soviet Education.* Baltimore: Pelican.

Greenberg, Joseph
    1946. *The Influence of Islam on a Sudanese Religion.* New York: J. J. Augus-
    tin.

Grichting, Wolfgang L.
    1971. *The Value System in Taiwan, 1970: A preliminary report.* Taipei.
    Published by the author.

Hall, G. Stanley
    1904. *Adolescence: Its Psychology and Its Relations to Physiology, Anthropology,
    Sociology, Sex, Crime, Religion and Education.* New York and London: D.
    Appleton.

Hambraeus, Leif
    1977. "Proprietary milk versus human breast milk in infant feed-
    ing. A critical appraisal from the nutritional point of view." *Pediatric
    Clinics of North America* vol. 24, no. 1:17–33.

Harpending, Henry
    1976. "Regional variation in !Kung populations." In Lee and
    DeVore, 1976:152–165.

Hechinger, Fred
    1967. "Education: the preschool child." In *The Soviet Union: The Fifty*

Years, edited by Harrison E. Salisbury. New York: Harcourt, Brace & World.

Hill, Polly
1972. *Rural Hausa.* Cambridge and New York: Cambridge University Press.

Hillman, Eugene
1975. *Polygamy Reconsidered: African Plural Marriage and the Christian Churches.* New York: Orbis.

Hoffman, Charles
1974. *The Chinese Worker.* Albany: State University of New York Press.

Holinger, Paul C.
1978. "Adolescent suicide: an epidemiological study of recent trends." *American Journal of Psychiatry* 135:6, pp. 754–756.

Horowitz, Irving Louis
1977. Editor, *Cuban Communism.* New Brunswick: Transaction Books.

Imokhai, Charles Anwame
1979. "The missionization of Uzairue: a study of missionary impact on traditional marriages." New York: Columbia University. Unpublished dissertation.

Ishihara, Akira and Levy, Howard S.
1968. *The Tao of Sex: An Annotated Translation of the Twenty-eighth Section of the Essence of Medical Prescriptions.* Yokohama, Japan.

Jacoby, Susan
1974. *Inside Soviet Schools.* New York: Schocken.

Jain, Anrudh, Hsu, T. C., Freedman, Ronald, and Chang, M. C.
1970. "Demographic aspects of lactation and postpartum amenorrhea." *Demography* vol. 7, no. 2.

Jelliffe, Derrick B. and Jelliffe, E. F. Patrice
1977. "Breast is Best: Modern Meanings." *The New England Journal of Medicine* vol. 297, no. 17:912–915.

Kaiser, Robert G.
1976. *Russia: The People and the Power.* New York: Atheneum.

Katz, Richard
1976. "Education for transcendence: !Kia-healing with the Kalanari !Kung." In Lee and DeVore, 1976:281–301.

Kessen, William
1975. *Childhood in China.* New Haven: Yale University Press.

Kharchev, A. G.
1964. "On Some Results of a Study of the Motives for Marriage."

Soviet Review vol. 5, no. 2 (1964):3–13. *Nauchnye doklady vysshei shkoly, filosofskie nauki* (1963), no. 4.

Kisembo, Benezeri, Laurenti, Magesa, and Aylward, Shorter
1977. *African Christian Marriage.* London: Geoffrey Chapman.

Klein, Laura F.
1980. "Contending with Colonization: Tlingit Men and Women in Change." In *Women and Colonization: Anthropological Perspectives,* edited by Mona Etienne and Eleanor Burke Leacock. New York: Praeger/J. F. Bergin, pp. 88–108.

Knight, Rolf
1978. *Indians at Work.* Vancouver: New Star Books.

Knodel, John
1977. "Breast-feeding and population growth." *Science* vol. 198:-1111–1115.

Kolbanovskii, V. N.
1964. "The Sex Upbringing of the Rising Generation." *Soviet Review* vol. 5, no. 3 (1964):51–62. *Sovetskaya pedagogika* (1964) no. 3.

Konner, Melvin
1976. "Maternal care, infant behavior and development among the !Kung." In Lee and DeVore, 1976:218–245.

Krause, Aurel
1956. *The Tlingit Indians,* translated by Erna Gunther. Seattle: University of Washington Press.

Kung, Lydia
1976. "Factory work and women in Taiwan: Changes in self-image and status." *Signs, Journal of Women in Culture and Society* vol 2, no. 1:35–58.

La Fontaine, J. S.
1972. Editor, *The Interpretation of Ritual.* London: Tavistock Publications.

Lamaze, Fernand
1970. *Painless Childbirth.* Chicago: Contemporary Books.

Lane, Chrystel
1979. "Ritual and ceremony in contemporary Soviet society." *The Sociological Review* vol. 27, no. 2:253–278.

Lapidus, Gail Warshowsky
1978. *Women in Soviet Society: Equality, Development and Social Change.* Berkeley: University of California Press.

Larson, Eric H.
1966. *Nukufero: A Tikopian Colony in the Russell Islands.* Eugene: Department of Anthropology, University of Oregon.

Lee, Richard B.

1968. "What hunters do for a living, or, how to make out on scarce resources." In *Man the Hunter,* edited by Richard B. Lee and Irven DeVore. Chicago: Aldine Atherton.

1974. "Male-female residence arrangements and political power in human hunter-gatherers." *Archives of Sexual Behavior* vol 3, no. 2:-167–173.

1976. Editor, *Kalahari Hunter-Gatherers: Studies of the !Kung San and Their Neighbors.* Cambridge, Mass. and London: Harvard University Press.

1979. *The !Kung San: Men Women and Work in a Foraging Society.* Cambridge and New York: Cambridge University Press.

Legge, James

1872. *The Chinese Classics, Vol. 4. The She King.*

Levin, B. and Levin, M.

1978. "Women's Drinking." *Literaturnaya gazeta* 20 December 1978, p. 12. *CDSP* vol. 31, no. 3 (1979):5–6.

Levinova, L.

1973. "Labor Training in the Family." *Doshkol'noe vospitanie,* no. 9 *Soviet Education,* 1974:38–53.

Levy, Howard S.

1967. *Chinese Footbinding, the History of a Curious Erotic Custom.* New York: Bell.

1974. *Chinese Sex Jokes in Traditional Times.* The Chinese Association for Folklore, Asian Folklore and Social Life Monograph vol. 58. Taipei: The Orient Cultural Service.

Lin, Tsung-yi

1958. "Tai-pau and Liu-mang: Two types of delinquent youths in Chinese society." *British Journal of Delinquency* vol. 8, no. 4:244–256.

Ling, Ken (pseud.)

1972. *The Revenge of Heaven: journal of a young Chinese.* New York: Putnam.

Lisitsin, Yuri and Batygin, Konstantin

1978. *The USSR: Public Health and Social Security.* Moscow: Progress Publishers.

Literaturnaya gazeta

1977. "Difficult Youngsters Discuss Themselves." 28 December 1977, p. 12. *CDSP* vol. 30, no. 1 (1978):12.

Litvinov, I.

1979. "How Can a Retiree Work?" *Nedelya* no. 15, 9–15 April 1979, p. 11. *CDSP* vol. 31, no. 21 (1979):10.

Liu, Chu-chih
    1973. "Divorce System of Republic of China," *Lawasia* 4:2: 186–197. Sydney, Australia.

Lord, Edith Elizabeth
    1975. "Changing Roles of Women in Two African Muslim Cultures." In *Being Female: Reproduction, Power, and Change,* edited by Dana Raphael. The Hague; Paris: Chicago: Mouton Publishers. Distributed by Aldine. pp. 249–253.

Lurie, Nancy Oestreich
    1971. "The contemporary American Indian scene." In *North American Indians in Historical Perspective,* edited by Eleanor Burke Leacock and Nancy Oestreich Lurie. New York: Random House.

Lyutova, T.
    1978. "The Youngster and Kindergarten." *Trud* 11 November 1978, p. 4. *CDSP* vol. 31, no. 1 (1979):12.

Mace, David and Vera
    1963. *The Soviet Family.* Garden City: Doubleday.

Makarov, S.
    1975. "Heavy Fur." *Komsomolskaya Pravda* 10 January 1975, p. 2. *CDSP* vol. 27, no. 4 (1975):4.

Mandel, William M.
    1975. *Soviet Women.* Garden City: Anchor Books.

Mao, Tse-tung
    1966. *Quotations from Chairman Mao Tse-tung.* Peking: Foreign Languages Press, pp. 290–291. Original from "A youth shock brigade of the No. 9 Agricultural Producers' co-operative in Hsinping Township, Chungshan County," 1955.

Marsh, Robert M. and O'Hara, Albert R.
    1961. "Attitudes toward marriage and the family in Taiwan," *American Journal of Sociology* vol. 67, no. 1:1–8.

Marshall, Lorna
    1965. "The !Kung bushmen of the Kalahari Desert." In *Peoples of Africa,* edited by James L. Gibbs, Jr. New York: Holt, Rinehart & Winston, pp. 241–278.
    1976a. "Sharing, talking, and giving: relief of social tensions among the *!Kung.*" In Lee and DeVore (1976), pp. 349–371.
    1976b. *The !Kung of Nyae Nyae.* Cambridge: Harvard University Press.

Mead, Margaret
    1954. "The Swaddling Hypothesis: Its Reception." *American Anthropologist* 56:395–409.

Mesa-Lago, Carmelo
  1971. Editor, *Revolutionary Change in Cuba*. Pittsburgh: University of
  Pittsburgh Press.

Miller, Arthur
  1969. "Monte Sant' Angelo." As reprinted in *I Don't Need You Any
  More*. Penguin Books in association with Secker & Warburg. pp.
  57–72.

Miller, Maurice S.
  1956. *Window on Russia*. London: Lawrence & Wishart.

Molinari, Carol
  1976. "Alcoholism: Alaska's number 1 health problem," *Alcohol
  Health and Research World*. Summer, pp. 2–6.

Mushkina, Yelina
  1978. "Great Expectations." *Zhurnalist* no. 12, December 1978, pp.
  49–51. *CDSP* vol. 31, no. 8 (1979):12–13.

Nadvi, S. Sacman
  1974. "Islamic approach to abortion." In *The Great Debate: Abortion in
  the South African Context*, edited by G. C. Oosthuizen, G. Abbott and
  M. Notelovitz. Human Sciences Research Council, Publication Series
  No. 47. Cape Town: Howard Timmins, pp. 48–49.

Naomani, M. Manzoor
  1964. *What Islam Is?* Translated by Asif Kidwai, Academy of Islamic
  Research and Publications Nadwatul Ulema, Lucknow: Chowdhry
  Press.

Newton, Niles
  1975. "Birth rituals in cross-cultural perspective: some practical
  applications." In *Being Female: Reproduction, Power, and Change*, edited by
  Dana Raphael, pp. 37–41.

New York Times
  13 August 1979:A4.

New York Times
  14 August 1979:A17.

Oberg, Kalervo
  1973. *The Social Economy of the Tlingit Indians*. Seattle: University of
  Washington Press.

Oosthuizen, G. C., Abbott, G., and Notelovitz, M.
  1974. Editors, *The Great Debate: Abortion in the South African Context*.
  Cape Town: Howard Timmins.

Parish, William L. and Whyte, Martin King
  1978. *Village and Family in Contemporary China*. Chicago and London:
  The University of Chicago Press.

Pillsbury, Barbara L. K.

    1973. *Cohesion and Cleavage in a Chinese Muslim Community.* Doctoral Thesis in Anthropology, Columbia University.

    1976. "Doing the Month: Confinement and convalescence of Chinese women after childbirth." Unpublished paper, presented at the American Anthropological Association 75th Annual Meeting.

Porkert, Manfred

    1976. "The intellectual and social impulses behind the evolution of traditional Chinese medicine." In *Asian Medical Systems,* edited by Charles Leslie. Berkeley, Los Angeles, London: University of California Press, pp. 63–76.

Prelovskaya, I.

    1976. "Institute Helps Secondary School Pupil." *Izvestia* 3 June 1976, p. 5. *CDSP* vol. 27, no. 22 (1976):22.

Raphael, Dana

    1973. *The Tender Gift: Breastfeeding,* Englewood Cliffs: Prentice-Hall.

    1975. Editor, *Being Female: Reproduction, Power, and Change.* The Hague, Paris, Chicago: Mouton Publishers. Distributed by Aldine.

Rasulova, N. and Tikhonova, G.

    1977. "On Pedagogical Themes: Schoolchild's Appearance." *Turmenskaya Iskra* 13 December 1977, p. 4. *CDSP* vol. 31, no. 1 (1978):13.

Revolutionary Health Committee of Hunan Province

    1977. (Orig. 1970.) *A Barefoot Doctor's Manual,* translated by Titus Yu, Lam Wah Bong, and Kwok Chiu. Mayne Isle: Cloudburst Press.

Read, Grantly Dick

    1953. *Childbirth Without Fear.* New York: Harper & Brothers.

Rogers, George W.

    1960. *Alaska in Transition.* Baltimore: The Johns Hopkins Press.

    1970. Editor, *Change in Alaska.* University of Alaska Press.

Rosenkrantz, Arthur L.

    1978. "A note on adolescent suicide: incidence, dynamics and some suggestions for treatment," *Adolescence* vol. 13: no. 50:209–214.

Rossi, Alice S.

    1975. "Transition to parenthood." In Sze, 1975.

Ryabukin, A.

    1979. "This must not be tolerated." *Izvestia* 27 March 1979, p. 3. *CDSP* vol. 31, no. 13 (1979):16.

Ryurikov, Yury

    1974. "Love Alone?" *Literaturnaya gazeta* 17 July 1974, p. 13. *CDSP* vol. 27, no. 1 (1975):1–2.

San Martin, Marta and Bonachea, Ramon L.
> 1977. "The military dimension of the Cuban revolution." In *Cuban Communism,* edited by Irving Louis Horowitz. New Brunswick: Transaction Books, pp. 389–420.

Schak, David C.
> 1974. *Dating and Mate Selection in Modern Taiwan.* Asian Folklore and Social Life Monographs, vol 55. Taipei: The Orient Cultural Service.

Schapera, I.
> 1930. *The Khoisan Peoples of South Africa: Bushmen and Hottentots.* London: Routledge and Kegan Paul.

Sergiyenko, Ye.
> 1977. "We Shall Remain Faithful," *Nauka i religia* 10 October 1977: 41–45. *CDSP,* vol. 30 no. 4 (1978):19.

Shliapentokh, V.
> 1971. "Acquaintanceships and Weddings: A Sociological Analysis of the Data of a Discussion." *Soviet Review* vol. 13, no. 1 (1972):83–93. *Literaturnaya gazeta* 9 June 1971, p. 12.

Sidel, Ruth
> 1973. *Women and Child Care in China: A firsthand report.* Baltimore: Penguin.

Shostak, Marjorie
> 1976. "A !Kung woman's memories of childhood." In Lee & DeVore, 1976:246–277.

Smith, Hedrick
> 1976. *The Russians.* New York: Quadrangle.

Smith, Mary
> 1964. *Baba of Karo.* New York: Praeger.

Smith, M. G.
> 1965. "The Hausa of Northern Nigeria." In Gibbs, 1965:119–155.

Smith, Robert J.
> 1974. "Afterword." In *Religion and Ritual in Chinese Society,* edited by Arthur P. Wolf. Stanford: Stanford University Press, pp. 337–348.

Snow, Edgar
> 1939. *Red Star Over China.* Garden City: Garden City Press.

St. George, George
> 1973. *Our Soviet Sister.* Washington: Robert B. Luce, Inc.

Subor, Mary Lou
> 1975. "Growing with the Family Code." *Cuba Review* 5:4 pp. 12–15.

Sze, William
> 1975. Editor, *Human Life Cycle.* New York: Jason Aronson, Inc.

Tai, Yen -hui
　　1978. "Divorce in Chinese Traditional Law." In Buxbaum, 1978:-
　　75–106.

Tang, M. C.
　　1976. "Parental Authority and Family Size: a Chinese Case."
　　In *Youth in a Changing World,* edited by Estelle Fuchs. The Hague:
　　Chicago: Mouton Publishers. Distributed by Aldine, pp. 239–
　　252.

Topley, Marjorie
　　1975. "Marriage resistance in rural Kwangtung." In *Women in Chi-
　　nese Society,* edited by Margery Wolf and Roxane Witke. Stanford:
　　Stanford University Press, pp. 67–88.

Tozzer, Alfred Marston
　　1925. *Social Origins and Social Continuities.* New York: Macmillan.

Truswell, A. Stewart and Hansen, John D. L.
　　1976. "Medical research among the !Kung." In Lee and DeVore,
　　1976, pp. 166–194.

Turner, Victor
　　1967. *The Forest of Symbols: Aspects of Ndembu Ritual.* Ithaca: Cornell
　　University Press.

Ulitskii, S.
　　1977. "Sanctions for performing illegal abortions." *Sotsialisticheskaia
　　zakonnost* no. 7. *Soviet Law and Government,* 17:1 (1978):40–43.

van Gennep, Arnold
　　1960. *The Rites of Passage.* Chicago: The University of Chicago Press.

Venger, L. and Mukhina, V.
　　1973. "The development of motivated behavior and the formation
　　of self-awareness in the child." *Doshkol'noe vospitanie* no. 8, *Soviet Educa-
　　tion,* May 1974:88–101.

Wald, Karen
　　1978. *Children of Che: Childcare and Education in Cuba.* Palo Alto: Ram-
　　parts Press.

Ward, Fred
　　1978. *Inside Cuba Today.* New York: Crown Publishers.

Whitney, Craig
　　1979. *New York Times,* 26 August 1979, 1:12.

Winikoff, Beverly
　　1978. "Nutrition, population, and health: some implications for
　　policy." *Science* vol. 200:895–902.

Witke, Roxane
　　1977. *Comrade Chiang Ch'ing.* Boston: Little Brown.

Wolf, Arthur P.
    1970. "Chinese Kinship and Mourning Dress." In *Family and Kinship in Chinese Society,* edited by Maurice Freedman. Stanford: Stanford University Press, pp. 189–207.
    1974. Editor, *Religion and Ritual in Chinese Society.* Stanford: Stanford University Press.
    1974. "Gods, Ghosts and Ancestors." In Wolf, 1974:131–182.
    1975. "The Women of Hai-shan." In Wolf and Witke, pp. 89–110.
Wolf, Margery
    1970. "Child Training and the Chinese Family." In Freedman, 1970, pp. 37–62.
    1972. *Women and the Family in Rural Taiwan.* Stanford: Stanford University Press.
    1975. Editor, *Women in Chinese Society.* Stanford: Stanford University Press.
Wray, Joe D.
    1975. "Child Care in the People's Republic of China." *Pediatrics* 55, no. 4:539–550.
Wright, Erna
    1966. *The New Childbirth.* New York: Hart Publishing Company.
Yang, Ch'ing-Ch'u
    1976. *Selected Stories.* Translated and with an introduction by Thomas B. Gold. Kaohsiung, Taiwan: Tur-li Publishing Company.
Yglesias, Jose
    1970. *Down There.* New York: World.
Yudin, N.
    1978. "The Dialectics of Rural Life." *Nauka i religia,* 11 November 1978, pp. 32–37. *CDSP* vol. 31, no. 5 (1979):17.
Zenin, I.
    1975. "Completely Free." *Komsomolskaya Pravda,* 18 January 1975, p. 2. *CDSP* vol. 27, no. 4 (1975):2–4.

Index

Adolescence, *see* Puberty/adolescence; names of countries and cultures
Alaska, University of, 90
Alaskan Indians
General Allotment Act, 90
see also the Tlingit
American Delegation on Early Childhood Education, 196–98
Analects (Confucius), 22
Angel dust, 209
Ariés, Philippe, 61
Ariki Kafika, 49
Aristotle, 60
Arunta, 260, 261
Ashley-Montagu, M. F., 69 *n*

Barnett, William Kester, 134–35, 166
Batygin, Konstantin, 182, 243
Benet, Sula, 243
Bernstein, Thomas, 218
Bestuzhev-Lada, Dr. I. V., 221, 222
Biafra, 19
Biafran war, 70
Biesele, Megan, 93
Birth
rituals of, 24

see also names of countries and cultures
Book of Odes, (Shih Ching), 235
Bound feet (lotus feet), 77
British Solomon Islands Protectorate, 50
Bronfenbrenner, Urie, 183–84
Bryk, Felix, 69 *n*
Buddhism, 23, 140, 171, 254, 255
Bushmen, (Australia), 17 *n*, 259–60
Bykov, 176
Byzantine Empire, 61

Camilo Cienfuegos Schools, 213
Cannibalism, in New Guinea, 15
Castro, Fidel, 210–14
Catholicism, 61
Censorius, 60
Center for Alcohol and Addiction Studies (University of Alaska), 90
Chad, Lake, 19
Chen, Jack, 236
Chen Muhua, 199
Chesterton, Ada Elizabeth, 175
Chiang Ch'ing, *see* Jiang Qing (Chiang Ch'ing)

Chiang Kai-shek, 55
Child abuse (Western cultures), 58
China, *see* People's Republic of China;
    Taiwan
Chinese Nationalists, 22
Ch'ing Dynasty, 21
Chkhikvshvili, Professor D., 203
Chou, Duke of, 135
Christian Hausa, 19
Christianity, 268
Cohen, Myron L., 134
Committee for the Defense of the Rev-
    olution (CDR), 213
Communist Youth League (People's
    Republic of China), 219
Confucianism, 23
Confucius, 22, 219
"Con las Mujeres Cubanas" (film), 241
Corroboree, 267
Couvade, 45
Crapanzano, Vincent, 69 *n*
Cuba, 17, 22
    birth, 189–90
        pregnancy, 190
    childhood
        child care, 192–93, 194
        education, 192
        youth organizations, 194
    homosexuality, 220
    marriage, 239–42
        divorce and, 242
        the Family Code, 239–41, 242
        wedding ceremony, 242
    puberty/adolescence
        education, 210–12
        Isle of Youth experiment, 210–12
        military service, 213–14
        school dropouts, 212
    reduction of illiteracy, 192
    women, status of, 213–14
Cuban Revolution, 210
Culture, major characteristic of, 17–18

Darwinism, 266
Death
    rituals of, 24–25

see also names of countries and cul-
    tures
De Groot, J.J.M., 255
Delegation of Applied Linguists, 200
Diamond, Norma, 143–44
Dobson, Richard B., 206
Dorjahn, Vernon R., 125
Dorticos, Oswaldo, 239
Druzhnikov, Yuri, 180
Dunn, Ethel, 182–83
Dunn, Steven J., 182–83
Durkheim, Emile, 23, 271

Endocannibalism, 15
Engels, Friedrich, 274
Equal Rights Amendment (ERA), 144
Escuela Secondaria Basica, 194
Etruscans, 60

Fisher, Wesley, 205, 230
Firth, Sir Raymond, 20–21, 45, 48, 50,
    67, 102–105, 108, 146, 147
Fore people (New Guinea), 15
Freud, Anna, 264
Freudian theory, 264
Fukien province (China), 21
Fulani, (Nigeria), 20, 35
Fulfulde (language), 35 *n*

Gang of Four, 199, 216
General Allotment Act (1887), 90
Glacier National Park, 20
Grant, Nigel, 187, 206
Great Leap Forward (1958), 198, 216
Great Proletarian Cultural Revolution,
    214–17, 218
Great Soviet Encyclopedia, 175, 180

Hakka, (Taiwan), 21, 77
Hall, G. Stanley, 263
Harpending, Henry, 97
Hausa, Muslim (Nigeria), 17, 18, 19
    birth, 33–40
        abortion, 40
        adoption by relatives, 38, 39–40
        midwives for, 33, 34, 37

Hausa, Muslim *(continued)*
  naming day ceremony, 36–37
  pregnancy, 33–35, 39
  kinship in, 70, 73–74
  language of, 19
  marriage, 26, 40, 117–25
    divorce and, 40, 121–25
    engagement, 118
    extra-marital sex, 123
    impotent husbands, 123–24
    parental arrangements for, 117–18
    polygyny, 33, 125
    remarriage, 121–22
    ritual dressing for newlyweds, 119–20, 121
    wedding ceremony, 118–19
  mothers
    nursing of children, 38, 39
    ritual bathing of, 37–38
  old age and death
    burial, 152
    funeral services, 152–54
    parental respect, 149–50
  puberty/adolescence, 67–74
    bond-friendships, 73–74
    circumcision ritual, 67–69
    females, 71–74
    males, 67–71
    menarche, 59
    menstruation, 71–73
    sexual interests, 71
  ritual practices of, 150–51
  Westernization of, 20
  women
    changing status of, 122
    spinsters, 122
Hechinger, Fred, 205
Hillman, Eugene, 125
Hinduism, 23
Homo erectus, 14–15, 270
Homo sapiens, 14
Homosexuality in Socialist countries, 220, 222
Hong Kong, women's vegetarian halls in, 140–41

Ibo, (Nigeria), 19
  secessionism, 70
Islam, 268
Isle of Youth (Isle of Pines), 210–11

Jacoby, Susan, 206
Jiang Qing (Chiang Ch'ing), 137, 199, 216, 234–35
Joking relationships, 76
Judaism, 268

Kaiser, Robert, 179–82, 204, 205, 208, 231, 246
Kalahari desert, 18, 28, 33, 74
KGB, 205
Kharchev A. G., 223, 226
Klein, Laura, 114
Komsomol (Young Communists League), 200, 205, 207, 209
Koran, 36, 40, 73, 149, 150
Krause, Aurel, 89, 156
Kuan-yin (Buddhist goddess), 51
!Kung, (Kalahari desert—Africa), 17, 266
  the Arunta and, 260, 261
  birth, 28–33, 263
    mothers and babies, 30–31
    pregnancy, 28, 29–30
  Bushmen and, 259–60
  celebration limitations of, 24
  changing life-styles of, 18–19, 258–59
  childhood, 31–32
    ritual haircuts, 31
  distribution rights of, 96–97
  fear of menstrual blood, 76
  food, 18–19
  habitat, 18
  incest taboos, 98
  language, 17 *n*
  marriage, 25, 26, 29, 51, 95–102
    commitments for, 95–96, 97
    divorce and, 100
    extra-marital sex, 101–102
    myths of, 93–95
    neolocality pattern of, 97

!Kung, *(continued)*
    plural marriage, 101
    remarriage, 100–101
    sexual relations, 99–100
    wedding ceremony, 98–99
  old age and death, 154–56, 273
    funeral services, 155
    parental respect, 154–55
  puberty/adolescence, 74–77, 272
    Eland Dance, 76
    females, 75–77
    males, 74
    menstruation, 75–76, 96
    Rite of the First Kill, 75
    relationship between men and women, 28–29
  social organization, 32
Kung, Lydia, 76, 77
Kuomintang, 136
Kwangtung province (China), 21

Lamaze, Dr. Fernand, 176–77
Lane, Chrystel, 250–51
La Perouse, Commodore Jean Françoise de, 89
Lapidus, Gail Warshowsky, 226
Larson, Eric H., 50, 67, 149
Lee, Richard B., 155
Lenin, V. I., 188, 265
Lenin Vocational School, 211–12
Levers Pacific Plantations, 50
Levy, Howard S., 135
Liber de Die Natale (Censorius), 60
Ling, Ken, 219
Lissner, Zoya, 183
Litvinov, L., 243–44
Liu Shao-ch'i, 253
Louis XVI, 89
LSD, 209

Makarov, S., 209
Mandel, William, 182, 230, 233
Mao Tse-tung, 82, 137, 170, 189, 192, 215, 218, 234, 235, 265
Mariana Grajales Platoon, 213–14

Marriage
  divorce and, 25
  rituals of, 25–26
  see also names of countries and cultures
Marriage Law of 1950, (P.R.C.), 234, 235, 236
Marshall, Lorna, 98
Marx, Karl, 274
Melanesia, 20
Miller, Arthur, 257
Miller, Dr. Maurice S., 176
Ming Dynasty, 21
Moiety, 111 *n*
Molinari, Carol, 90
Moscow State Institute for International Relations, 205
Moscow State University, 204
Muhammad, 40
Muslim Hausa, *see* Hausa, Muslim

National Peking University, 216–17
National Taiwan University, 82
National Taiwan University Hospital, 166
Neandertal man, 15, 269
Nekipelov, Victor, 200
Neolocality, 97
New Guinea, cannibalism in, 15
New Hebrides Island, 44
Nicolaiev, 176
Nigeria, 19, 70
  abortion laws in, 40
  mortality rate in, 35
  petroleum in, 19
Northwest Coast culture, 20
Nukufero colony (Russell Islands), 50–51, 67, 102, 109, 149

Obligatory Military Service (SMO) draft cards, 213
Octobrists (youth group), 188, 199
Old age, *see* names of countries and cultures
OPEC bloc, 19

Pagan Hausa, 19
Palaces of Weddings, 228, 229
Parish, Wm. J., 197–98, 237, 252, 253,
    254
Pavlov, Ivan, 176
People's Republic of China, 17, 22, 262
    birth, 189–91
    methods of, 190–91
    pregnancy, 190
    childhood
    child care, 193, 196–99
    education, 192, 195, 198–99
    group organizations, 199–200
    Great Leap Forward, 198, 216
    Great Proletarian Cultural Revolu-
        tion, 214–17, 218
    homosexuality in, 220
    marriage, 25, 26, 234–39
    divorce and, 141, 238–39
    old age and death, 26, 251–55
    funeral services, 170, 253–55
    parental respect, 253
    postfuneral memorials, 255
    retirement system, 251–53
    puberty/adolescence
    education, 216–18, 220
    juvenile delinquency, 220
    sexual activities, 220–21
    work in the countryside, 218–19,
        272
    youth organizations, 219–20
    women, changing status of, 77
Pioneers (youth group), 188–89, 200,
    207
Popov, V. D., 206
Post, Emily, 228
Puberty/adolescence
    age range of, 263–64
    in ancient Greece, 60
    in ancient Rome, 60–61, 263
    menarche, 59
    menstruation, 59
    reproductive capacities and, 58–59
    rituals of, 25
    in U.S. males and females, 59
    in Western society, 61–62, 264–65

see also names of countries and cul-
    tures

Ramadan, 73, 150
Red Guards, 199–200, 217, 219, 253
Rites de Passage, Les (van Gennep), 16
Rogers, George W., 90
Rostov Teacher Training Institute, 184
Russell Islands, 21, 50
Ryabukhin, A., 201

San language, 17 *n*
Shostak, Marjorie, 99–100
Sidel, Ruth, 196–97, 198
Sinanthropus, 15
Smith, Hedrick, 181, 182, 183, 201,
    203–204
Smith, M. G., 74
Smith, Mary, 38
Snow, Edgar, 82
Socialist Education Movement, 216
Solecki, Ralph, 15
Solomon Islands, 21, 51
Soviet Etiquette, 228, 229, 230
Soviet Union, *see* Union of Soviet So-
    cialist Republics
Spillius, James, 48
Stalin, Josef, 227, 233
Subor, Mary Lou, 241
Suñol, Eddy, 213–14

Taiwan, 17, 21–22
    birth, 51–57, 263
    the *man yueh* ceremony, 55
    mothers and babies, 53–56
    pregnancy, 51–53
    toilet training, 56
    birth control, 55
    childhood, 56
    education in, 79–81, 83–84
    importance of kin groups, 56–57
    marriage, 26, 51, 125–44
    the bride price, 134–35
    divorce and, 141–43
    irregular types, 138–39
    pre-marital sex, 132

Taiwan *(continued)*
  remarriage, 143
  rituals and customs of, 130–36
  wedding ceremony, 126–30
  old age and death, 161–74
    burial plots, 168–69
    funeral services, 161–66
    grave types, 170
    mourning rituals, 173–74
    sacrifices to the dead, 170–72
  prehistory of, 21
  puberty/adolescence, 77–85
    change in parental relationships, 82–83
    females, 77–81
    juvenile delinquency, 84–85
    schooling and, 79–81
    sexual repression, 79–81
    violence and, 84–85
  sexual life, 135–38
  women
    changing status of, 77–80
    female infanticide, 51
    prostitution, 77
Tai Yen-hui, 141
T'ang Mei-chun, 82
Taoism, 138, 254, 255
Teng Hsiao-p'ing, 198, 218
Tikopia, 17, 20–21
  birth, 44–51
    illegitimacy, 44
    naming of child, 48
    pregnancy, 44–48
  childhood, 47–50
    boys, ceremonies for, 50
    girls, ceremonies for, 48–50
  Christianity in, 47, 51
  colony on island of Nukufero, 50–51, 67, 102, 109, 149
  double standard for the sexes, 102, 108
  familial closeness in, 145–46
  food of, 21
  the kava ceremony, 49
  marriage, 26, 102–10
    by capture, 102–106

    divorce and, 109
    exchange of food and gifts, 107–108
    feasting, 106–107
    to outsiders, 109–10
    "oven of joining" ceremony, 105–106
    polygyny, 108
  old age and death
    burial customs, 147, 148–49
    funeral rituals, 148
    suicide, 147
  puberty/adolescence, 62–67
    females, 62, 67
    males, 62–67
    superincision of penis ritual, 63–67, 69
  women
    subordinate position of, 109, 110
    unwed mother's plight, 102
Tlingit, 17, 20, 266
  alcoholism and, 89–92, 115–16
  birth, 40–44
    midwives, 41–42
    mothers and babies, 42–43
    naming of child, 42
    pregnancy, 41–42, 44
  celebration limitations of, 24
  childhood
    magical practices for growth, 42–43
    weaning, 44
  concept of Heaven, 158–60
  fear of menstrual blood, 76
  hostility toward whites, 90–91
  marriage, 26, 110–16
    divorce and, 116
    exchange of gifts, 111–12
    parental arrangements for, 110–11
    polygyny, 112, 116
    present-day changes in, 112–14
    unfaithfulness, 112
    wedding ceremony, 111, 267
    wife-beating, 115–16
  old age and death, 156–61
    funeral services, 156–58, 160–61

Tlingit *(continued)*
  grave houses, 158
  the potlatch, 158
  puberty/adolescence, 85–92
    boredom with present-day life,
      88–89
    females, 86–87, 92
    illegitimacy and, 87
    juvenile delinquency, 87–89
    males, 85–86, 92
    menstruation, 86–87
    ritual hunting expedition, 85–86
  reincarnation beliefs, 41, 160,
    161
  sexual division of labor, 114–15
  women, 92
    secondary status of, 111
Topley, Marjorie, 140

Union of Pioneers of Cuba (youth
  group), 194
Union of Soviet Socialist Republics, 17,
  22, 262
  birth, 175–89, 271
    abortions, 177–78
    baptism, 181–82
    maternal and infant mortality
      rates, 175, 180
    medical attention assisting,
      179–81
    methods of, 175–76
    midwives, 180–81
    pregnancy, 178–80
  childhood
    child care, 182–87, 193–94
    education, 187
    group organizations, 187–89
  homosexuality in, 220, 222
  marriage, 26, 221–34, 273
    difficulties in couples meeting,
      222–24
    divorce and, 226–27, 231–33
    housing shortage and, 231
    Palaces of Weddings, 228, 229
    pre-marital sex, 221–22
    reasons given for, 225–26
  unwed motherhood, 222
  wedding ceremonies, 228–230
  old age and death, 26, 243–51, 273
    funeral services, 246–50
    old-age homes, 245–46
    the "orthodox" funeral, 251
    pensioners' problems, 243–45
  puberty/adolescence
    clothing and accessories, 207–208
    drinking and drugs, 208–209
    education, 202–207
    juvenile delinquency ("hooligan-
      ism"), 200–201, 206, 208–209,
      272
    work and, 206–207
    youth organizations, 205
  ritual ceremonies in, 22–23
USSR Academy of Pedagogical
  Sciences, 184, 185
USSR State Committee on Labor and
  Social Questions, 244

Vanderbilt, Amy, 228
Van Gennep, Arnold, 16

Walbiri, (Australia), 260–61
Wald, Karen, 192, 211
Ward, Fred, 211, 212
Whitney, Craig, 227 *n*
Whyte, Martin King, 197–98, 237, 252,
  253, 254, 255
Witke, Roxanne, 234
Wittoto, 45
Wolf, Arthur, 139, 142–43, 172, 173
Wolf, Margery, 82, 131, 135
Women
  Cuba, 213–14
  Hausa, Muslim
    changing status of, 122
    spinsters, 122
  Hong Kong
    unmarried clubs, 140–41
  People's Republic of China, changing
    status of, 77
  Taiwan
    changing status of, 77–80

Women *(continued)*
  female infanticide, 51
  prostitution, 77
 Tikopia
  subordinate position of, 109, 110
  unwed mother's plight, 102
 Tlingit, 92
  secondary status of, 111

Yakutat Alcoholism Program, 91, 114
Yakutat Community Health Center, 91

Yang and yin, 137, 171
*Yellow Emperor's Classic of Internal Medicine,
  The,* 137
Yglesias, Jose, 220
Young Communists League, 200, 205,
  207, 209
Young Pioneers (youth organization),
  219

ZAGS (civil registry office), 228, 232